The Novel from Sterne to James:

Essays on the Relation of Literature to Life

By

Juliet and Rowland McMaster

M

First published 1981 by
THE MACMILLAN PRESS LTD
London and Basingstoke
Companies and representatives throughout the world

ISBN 0 333 27658 2

Printed in Hong Kong

THE NOVEL FROM STERNE TO JAMES

Also by Juliet McMaster

THACKERAY: THE MAJOR NOVELS
JANE AUSTEN ON LOVE
TROLLOPE'S PALLISER NOVELS:
  THEME AND PATTERN
JANE AUSTEN'S ACHIEVEMENT (*Editor*)

Also by R. D. McMaster

GREAT EXPECTATIONS (*Editor*)
LITTLE DORRIT (*Editor*)

Contents

List of Illustrations

Preface

"Life imitates Art far more than Art imitates Life", insisted Oscar Wilde. "This results not merely from Life's imitative instinct, but from the fact that the self-conscious aim of Life is to find expression, and that Art offers it certain beautiful forms through which it may realize that energy." What was a critical paradox for Wilde's contemporaries is in our day of structuralist criticism closer to being received truth. The dogma of realism, which novelists so eagerly adopted as peculiarly their own, needs some radical revision if it is to accommodate to Wilde's doctrine. If it is not art that holds the mirror up to nature, but nature that mirrors art, then the more real realism is to imitate life imitating novels. But the novelists in fact didn't need Wilde to teach them so much. Don Quixote, who set out on a quest to live a romance, is a patron saint for novelists and for their characters. His story is already a prime example of the conscious aim of life to find expression through the forms of art.

This concern of the novel is a connecting thread in the following essays. They have been written by two authors over a number of years, and we had at the outset no premeditated design of their forming together a continuous work. They remain essentially individual studies; but we have shared a continuing interest in the novelist's concern with the relation of life to language, experience to expression, thing to word, and our selection and revision have been with a view to illuminating this recurring concern of our novelists as it is articulated in their works.

Richardson, who would seem at first glance to immerse his characters and his readers in the unself-conscious living through of experience, was already exploring in his epistolary mode the possibility that the mere record of experience could by a kind of verbal revolution become its determinant: so Mr B, avidly reading Pamela's letters about himself as fast as he can get his hands on them (and almost as fast as he can get his hands on *her*), pleads that he must have the latest batch, so that he may discover his role and learn how to act it out. "As I have furnished you with the Subject, I have a Title to see the Fruits of your Pen", he urges. "– Besides, said he, there is such a pretty Air of Romance, as you relate them, in your Plots, and my Plots, that I shall be better directed in what manner to wind up the Catastrophe of the pretty Novel."

Our own explorations of the interaction of life with the patterns of literature begin later in the history of the novel. From Sterne, who draws attention to "the unsteady uses of words", and the dangers of "placing a number of tall, opake words, one before another, in a right line, betwixt your own and your reader's conception", to James, who in *The Sacred Fount* created an inquisitive narrator who hovers between detecting relationships and inventing them according to his elaborate artistic preconceptions, novelists have been intensely self-conscious about their medium, intent on the complicated interaction between event and narration of the event, response and verbal articulation of the response. Jane Austen's Emma is an "imaginist", "myself creating what I saw", as she comes to realise – almost usurping her author's function of creation. Thackeray habitually uses his sense of the actual to turn the tables on romance, then turns them back again to show life, which thought itself so singular, fulfilling the eternal patterns of Ecclesiastes. Trollope in *He Knew He Was Right* explores a marriage that is wrecked not by actions or feelings simply, but by the destructive momentum of language. James's governess in *The Turn of the Screw*, like Wilde's example of the lady who felt bound to imitate, step by step, the career of the heroine of a serial novel, feels "compelled to reproduce" her apparitions in life.

The tendency of life to seek the coherence and unity of art operates on two scales, which may be intermingled. Thackeray shows us characters more or less consciously engaged in stylising their everyday lives according to the patterns of romance, while on a larger scale the whole pattern of a book's events is often an implicit questioning or affirmation of coherence in the world. Thackeray's "farrago of old fables" broken up by the rude entrance of butcher and ploughboy at the commencement of *The Newcomes* reminds us both of the eternally recurring designs of Aesop and Ecclesiastes and of the eternally recurring frustrations. We live by creating designs, but novelists, immersed in the process, are often not only self-conscious but suspicious about the process. The enactment of a design, a fable, a romance, may be creative, an affirmation; it may also be entrapment, limitation, possession. In *To the Lighthouse* the aesthetic design of flux and concurrence is also a comment on life, an affirmation: "In the midst of chaos there was shape." "To such a tremulous wisp constantly re-forming itself on the stream," says Pater, "to a single sharp impression, with a sense in it, a relic more or less fleeting, of such moments gone by, what is real in our life fines itself down." One supposes it is such a wisp that Strether is enjoying, "exactly the right thing", when recognition of the rowers in his pastoral idyll, "a sharp fantastic crisis that had popped up as if in a dream", makes him "feel it as quite horrible".

Not all our essays here are centred on this recurring concern. If Dickens, Thackeray and James have particular prominence, it is because they have been our special interests, as well as because of the ways in which they have explored the relation between life and art in their works. Our selection of authors and works is intended to be representative rather than exhaustive. But we have focused primarily on what Wilde articulated most memorably for the nineteenth century, and what Ortega y Gasset, perhaps, has as vividly stated for our own. In his essay on "History as a System", he sees it as man's duty to make himself: "It is too often forgotten that man is impossible without imagination, without the capacity to invent for himself a conception of life, to 'ideate' the character he is going to be. Whether he be original or a plagiarist, man is the novelist of himself." It is such a proposition that our novelists, not without some moral reservations, set out to explore.

1980 JULIET AND ROWLAND MCMASTER

Acknowledgements

Versions of many of these essays have appeared elsewhere, and we are grateful to the original publishers for permission to reprint: Chapter 1 originally appeared in *Modern Language Quarterly*, 32:1 (1971); Chapter 3 in *Dalhousie Review*, 38:1 (1958); Chapter 4 in *Studies in the Novel*, 1 (1969); Chapter 5 as the introduction to the Macmillan College Classics in English edition of *Great Expectations*, edited by R. D. McMaster (Toronto, 1965); Chapter 6 in *The Victorian Experience: The Novelists* edited by Richard A. Levine (Athens: Ohio University Press, 1976); Chapter 9 in *American Literature*, 45:1 (1973), copyright 1973 by Duke University Press; Chapter 7 is © 1975 by the Regents of the University of California; reprinted from *Nineteenth-Century Fiction*, Vol. 29, No. 1, pp. 22–39, by permission of The Regents. Chapter 8 © 1978 by the Regents of the University of California; reprinted from *Nineteenth-Century Fiction*, Vol. 32, No. 4, pp. 399–419, by permission of The Regents.

1 Experience to Expression in *Tristram Shandy*

Tristram Shandy, a novel of which the subject is its own composition, is necessarily concerned with the relation between reality and art, experience and expression, and with the process by which the flesh is transformed into words, and the word is made flesh. Sterne as novelist and Tristram as autobiographer are self-conscious authors *par excellence*, making their presence as artists the very lifeblood of the book, and scrutinizing the means by which experience can be narrated and a piece of narration can itself have the quality of experience, in an attempt, as Henri Fluchère has put it, "to bridge the gap that separates an artistic creation from reality".[1] When Tristram throws off a phrase, "as long as I live or write (which in my case means the same thing)",[2] he reminds us again that this volume, *Tristram Shandy*, is in some sense indeed the *life* as well as the opinions of Tristram Shandy, gentleman. And as Tristram makes the process of ordering chapters, fitting in necessary digressions, manipulating chronology, retaining the reader's attention – in fact, the whole craft of writing – his constant subject matter, so Sterne has deliberately invented incidents and created characters that, besides having a vital life force of their own, are part of his main subject of the relation between experience and expression, the world of things and the world of words. He explores and articulates this relation particularly through the alignments and conflicts between his four major characters, the Shandy brothers Walter and Toby, and the son of one and servant of the other, Tristram and Trim.

"I believe in my soul," declares Tristram solemnly, "the hand of the supreme Maker and first Designer of all things, never made or put a family together (in that period at least of it, which I have sat down to write the story of) – where the characters of it were cast or contrasted with so dramatic a felicity as ours was" (236). Tristram quite characteristically sees God primarily in his role as artist, with a fine eye for drama and felicitous contrast, and as autobiographer he takes satisfaction in the Lord's artistic disposition of the personnel of the Shandy history.

It is plain enough that Walter Shandy, an appropriate parent for a writer, is committed to the world of words. For him significant experience is verbal, and significant action is mental. By his son's testimony he was "born an orator" (52), and was "never at a loss what to say to any man, upon any subject" (395). Robert J. Griffin calls him "a language addict",[3] and John Traugott[4] points out that he commits the Lockean sin of taking words for things.[5]

Sterne's methods of suggesting this mad commitment to words and mental constructs, as opposed to things and the physical world, are ingenious and hilarious. Defined as he is, like the other characters, by his hobbyhorse, Walter is a fanatic believer in all kinds of systems and hypotheses, the most characteristic of his obsessions being his belief in the power of names. The word by which we name a thing or a person is for him a powerful determinant, almost the thing or person itself. "How many CAESARS and POMPEYS, he would say, by mere inspiration of the names, have been render'd worthy of them?" (50). For him the virile appellation of Trismegistus would compensate for the debilitating physical abbreviation of his son's nose.

It is part of the sexual comedy that Walter, for all his anxieties and shortcomings in the act of physical generation, is shown as a most potent generator of theories, definitions, and hypotheses. The semen in his body flows sluggishly, but the words and ideas in his mind copulate and reproduce with copious fecundity. If he is frustrated, as A. R. Towers describes him,[6] he is frustrated not in the desire to get his wife with child but in his attempt to sow the seed of an idea in her mind:

> Cursed luck! said he, biting his lip as he shut the door, – for a man to be master of one of the finest chains of reasoning in nature, – and have a wife at the same time with such a head-piece, that he cannot hang up a single inference within side of it, to save his soul from destruction. (147)

In the reproduction of hypotheses he is forced to act both the male and the female role, since his wife "cannot conceive" (437), in order to produce "as notable and curious a dissertation as ever was engendered in the womb of speculation" (102–3). A generative metaphor is frequently used of mental processes. After declining the auxiliaries of the white bear in all moods and tenses, he says enthusiastically of his educational system: "every word, *Yorick*, by this means, you see, is converted into a thesis or an hypothesis; – every thesis and hypothesis have an offspring of propositions . . ." (409).

There is a similar contrast of Walter's practical incompetence with his verbal virtuosity. "His rhetoric and conduct were at perpetual handy-cuffs", we hear, apropos of his never getting the squeaking doorhinge oiled because he so enjoys his own eloquence in complaining about it (203). It is the same with the bend sinister, accidentally incorporated into the Shandy arms on the family carriage: he would rather grumble at it than have it repainted (314).

Since mental and verbal constructs are his reality, he has evolved a curiously physical way of imagining them, a process by which he makes the abstract concrete. He finds it necessary to endow the various activities of the mind with a local habitation as well as a name: hence his conviction that the soul is seated in the cerebellum, and his fanatical anxiety that his son's head should not be subjected to the 470 pounds' pressure of the mother's contractions during labour. The individual mind has for him a geography of its own; it has location and capacity and contents. It is perhaps a cupboard, like Mrs Shandy's, with a devastating scarcity of pegs to hang inferences on; or wet tinder, like Uncle Toby's (236), impossible to fire with enthusiasm for theories; or a leaky vessel, like Susannah's (287), that spills precious syllables, so that from the rich vintage of Trismegistus only the bitter lees of Tristram remain.

Language is so much Walter's milieu that his body seems little more to him than "a sort of battered kettle at the heel" (in Yeats's phrase), an appendage rather than an incarnation. When Toby accidentally hits him "a desperate blow souse upon his shin-bone" with his crutch, and Walter is able to use the accident as an illustration for his dissertation on chance, the "success of my father's repartees tickled off the pain of his shin at once" (280). On the other hand unpleasant words, like the proverbial sticks and stones, do have the power to hurt him: when Dr Slop interrupts him with an irritating pun about hornworks in the head, we hear that for Walter "to be broke in upon by [a pun], in a serious discourse, was as bad, he would say, as a fillip upon the nose; – he saw no difference" (111). His emotions, like his body, are equally subordinate to his mental and verbal activity. At the death of his son, he embarks on an oration, and "found he got great ease" (353). And when Obadiah allows his favourite mare to be mated by a donkey instead of an Arab stud,

> See here! you rascal, cried my father, pointing to the mule, what you have done! – It was not me, said *Obadiah.* – How do I know that? replied my father.
>
> Triumph swam in my father's eyes, at the repartee – the *Attic* salt brought water into them – and so *Obadiah* heard no more about it. (353)

His own witticism moves him, even to ears.

For the world of things, sensations, actions, and emotions, Walter has substituted a world of words, hypotheses, speculations, intellection. Who needs to encounter a white bear in order to discourse on one? Walter has sufficient experience of his subject merely in having the words and epithets for it, and a command of the auxiliaries:

> If I never have, can, must or shall see a white bear alive; have I ever seen the skin of one? . . . How would the white bear have behaved? Is he wild? Tame? Terrible? Rough? Smooth?
>
> – Is the white bear worth seeing? (407)

So he extends his experience through language as he "danced his white bear backwards and forwards through half a dozen pages" (409).

There is even a sense in which for him a fact becomes so by being stated, and is not so until it has been put into words. The past can become present by being narrated; the future can be lived by putting one's mind to it. His horse Patriot has been sold by his order months previously, yet the sale is apparently not consummated in his mind until it is announced:

> Then take PATRIOT, cried my father, and shut the door – PATRIOT is sold, said *Obadiah* – Here's for you! cried my father, making a pause, and looking in my uncle *Toby's* face, as if the thing had not been a matter of fact. (348–9)

The exchange between Walter and Obadiah at this point illustrates how fully Walter can locate himself, spatially and temporally, within his own mind. Because he is calculating the stages of Bobby's European tour, he is approaching Nevers from Calais rather than within Shandy Hall; and when Obadiah tells him, "But the waters are out", he has to abandon the one journey and shift in time and place because Obadiah's statement has become, through being stated, a reality to him: "This second attack of *Obadiah's*, in opening the door and laying the whole country under water, was too much . . . there was nothing for him to do, but to return back to *Calais*" (349).

It is not surprising that events should turn against so thoroughly unpractical a man. And Walter is dogged by disaster as one project after another is thwarted. Even as an orator he is not a success – during his funeral oration Toby thinks he has gone mad and his wife thinks he has committed adultery – for he has so substituted words for things that they have ceased to be effective tools of communication. And his *Tristrapoedia*, by which he is to educate his son, never keeps up with Tristram's actual growth and development. But his loyalty to theories is greater than his loyalty to persons. "What is the character of a family to an hypothesis? . . . Nay, if you come to that – what is the life of a family" (69). For all Sterne's and Tristram's affection for Walter and delight in his madness, he is explicitly judged for his propensity to "twist and torture every thing in nature to support his hypothesis" (53). At the end of the book, Tristram pronounces: "Never man crucified TRUTH at the rate he did" (644). It is Locke's judgment on those who, by taking names for things, tend to "charm men into notions far remote from the truth of things".[7] But Walter's punishment of being unable to communicate his hypotheses so fits his crime that the offence is expiated, and he retains Tristram's affection and ours.

"My uncle *Toby*, by nature, was not eloquent", Tristram tells us early in our acquaintance (92). As Walter is the champion of words, so Toby is the champion of things. Walter's troubles come from leaving things behind in his speculations and orations; Toby's are a result of his inability to bridge the gap in the other direction. He has experience and ideas to communicate, but he is inhibited in expressing them by "the unsteady uses of words. . . . 'Twas not by ideas, – by heaven! his life was put in jeopardy by words" (86–7). Locke's image for the man who "has complex ideas without particular names for them" is of a bookseller with a warehouse full of unbound and untitled volumes, "which he could therefore make known to others only by showing the loose sheets, and communicate them only by tale [i.e. tally]".[8] It is a succinct image for Sterne's elaborate conception of Toby. For, like the modern critic of the novel, Toby prefers "showing" to "telling" – but he applies the doctrine literally.

Toby is under the same necessity as Walter, Trim, and Tristram to *express* his ideas. When Tristram tells us that Toby's life is put in jeopardy by words, he speaks literally: Toby's health and even his survival depend on his managing to communicate to his visitors exactly how he got his wound in the groin. Walter tells Dr Slop that when moved to swear, "I swear on, till I find myself easy" (169); expression has a similar necessary therapeutic function for Toby, but words will not answer the purpose.

His hobbyhorse therefore becomes a most elaborate scheme to express himself without words – or at least with the minimum of them – and to manage instead with things, like Locke's bookseller. In his own unsophisticated way, he arrives at a solution that Swift's hypersubtle philosophers seek to practise at the Academy of Lagado: these professors concoct "a scheme for entirely abolishing all words whatsoever":

> An Expedient was therefore offered, that since Words are only Names for *Things*, it would be more convenient for all Men to carry about them, such *Things* as were necessary to express the particular Business they are to discourse on.[9]

The exponents of this scheme walk about with sacks of objects on their backs so that they can exchange the time of day with each other on the street. (Sterne includes what is perhaps a reminiscence of Swift when he tells us of Dr Slop's "singular stroke of eloquence" in deciding to produce the forceps themselves out of his bag of instruments, rather than naming them in his discourse.) Because Toby cannot explain verbally about the angle, trajectory, and velocity of the missile in communicating how he got his wound, he resorts to maps, diagrams, models. His means of expression is another attempt to reconstruct reality, but he does it, not verbally as Walter would, but by a physical projection, through his whole layout of fortifications on the bowling green. Through these he becomes articulate; the map of Namur enables him to "form his discourse with passable perspicuity" (88), and by the time he and Trim have excavated the bowling green, with this physical construct to fall back on he can even become garrulous on his own subject. But when what he has to communicate is not of a nature to be physically projected, he is constrained to fall back on whistling "Lillabullero" as "the usual channel thro' which his passions got vent" (69).

When Trim first proposes the scheme for the bowling green, Toby's imagination is fired, but it is noticeable that he prefers the bare minimum of words to create the picture in his mind. *"Trim,"* he repeats, "thou hast said enough. . . . Say no more, *Trim*" (97). But a mental image is not enough for him: as Walter is temperamentally constrained to put his ideas into words, so Toby must "put his design in execution" (93). And when the scheme is perpetrated, we hear how each day he sallies forth with the *Gazette* in his hand, with Trim's help "to execute the contents" (445), to re-enact what most people are content to rehearse in language alone. Toby and Trim are soldiers, men of deeds rather than words. And against Walter's theory of names they define themselves as committed to action and independent of appellations:

> I fought just as well . . . when the regiment called me *Trim*, as when they called me *James Butler* – And for my own part, said my uncle *Toby*, though I should blush to boast of myself, *Trim*, – yet had my name been *Alexander*, I could have done no more at *Namur* than my duty – Bless your honour! cried *Trim*, advancing three steps as he spoke, does a man think of his christian name when he goes upon the attack? – Or

> when he stands in the trench, *Trim*? cried my uncle *Toby*, looking firm – Or when he enters a breach? said *Trim*, pushing in between two chairs – Or forces the lines? cried my uncle, rising up, and pushing his crutch like a pike – Or facing a platoon, cried *Trim*, presenting his stick like a firelock – Or when he marches up the glacis, cried my uncle *Toby*, looking warm and setting his foot upon his stool. (295)

Toby's mental processes are similarly affected by things rather than words: his very modesty he acquired, Tristram says, by "a blow from a stone, broke off by a ball from the parapet of a horn-work at the siege of *Namur*"(67). And before he is sure he is in love, he needs a physical sign: only when the blister on the nethermost part of him breaks without easing him of the other discomfort does he know that his wound is "not a skin-deep-wound – but that it had gone to his heart"(580). Once assured, he is irresistibly tempted to express his beloved's perfections, like the siege of Namur, in diagram form, and sets about drawing up an ordered list of her virtues. His concrete imagination is constantly illustrated by his propensity to take metaphors literally. And when Walter and Yorick talk of the precocious Lipsius, who "composed a work the day he was born", Toby responds: "They should have wiped it up . . . and said no more about it"(411–12).

Toby is not so explicitly judged as Walter: Sterne treats him tenderly for his practical and simple humanitarian views, which allow him to be effectively loving, whereas Walter's theories cut him off from others. When Walter suggests that it is not love itself that is important but the *system* of love, and the definition of which kind of love it is, Toby's simple view of the matter evidently has Sterne's sympathy: "What signifies it, brother *Shandy,* replied my uncle *Toby*, which of the two it is, provided it will but make a man marry, and love his wife, and get a few children"(585–6). Though Walter may prefer verbal generation, Toby is certainly not of the belief "*That talking of love, is making it*" (634). Toby is uniformly and genuinely concerned with what has actually happened and its effects on people: when Walter is arguing to and fro about the results of Tristram's violent circumcision by the window-sash, "But is the child, cried my uncle *Toby*, the worse? – The *Troglodytes* say not, replied my father"(386). Toby's tender sensibility is itself connected, in fact, with his inability to express himself verbally. At Bobby's death Trim declares:

> Now I pity the captain the most of any one in the family .... – Madam will get ease of heart in weeping, – and the Squire in talking about it, – but my poor master will keep it all in silence to himself. – I shall hear him sigh in his bed for a whole month together, as he did for lieutenant *Le Fever*. (365)

Hence his active charity, which is not dispersed in sounding brass and tinkling cymbals.

However, Toby does his share of crucifying the truth. He too is close to madness in substituting his own reconstruction of reality for reality itself and transmuting experience into things. When in pursuit of his scheme, "he would forget himself, his wound, his confinement, his dinner"(88). Tristram tells us it is fortunate that the model firing pieces Trim constructs produce only smoke, because, in his enthusiasm for authenticity, Toby would otherwise have "infallibly shot away all his estate"(449). And as Walter transfers himself in time and place by rhetoric, so Toby does through his reconstruction of the campaigns in Europe:

> We will begin with the outworks ... – then we'll demolish the mole, – next fill up the harbour, – then retire into the citadel, and blow it up into the air; and having done that, corporal, we'll embark for *England*. – We are there, quoth the corporal, recollecting himself – Very true, said my uncle *Toby* – looking at the church. (465)

This tendency to locate reality in his fortifications has its significant effect on the course of his life: when the Widow Wadman asks him where he received his wound, instead of touching the place on his body he sends for a map – with memorable consequences, including lifelong bachelorhood.

Between the two opposed attitudes of Walter and Toby, the two other major characters, Trim and Tristram (the similarity in their names is not accidental), are set to bridge the gap between words and things, to unite narration with action. Trim's task is that of the rhetorician, whose vocation it is to move men to action through eloquence; Tristram's, the more complex, is that of the artist, who must recount experience in a verbal form without losing its immediacy and impact.

Trim is splendidly qualified for his task. On the one hand, he is like Walter: he loves to hear himself talk. "But set his tongue a-going, – you had no hold of him; – he was voluble" (95). Fluchère points out: "Language presents no problems for him . . . . Of all the inhabitants of Shandy Hall, he is even the one for whom words have the most precise and least debatable concrete meaning, the one most able to adapt language to circumstances and to his interlocutor."[10] Trim is not only an orator, but a successful one. While Walter's funeral oration is being misunderstood in the parlour, Trim below stairs, on the same subject, is moving his audience to admiration and tears. Even more than Walter he can be carried away by his own delivery, as when the sermon enrages him for his brother Tom's sufferings in the Inquisition; yet he does have a firm grasp of the difference between what goes on in the mind and what goes on in the world. And where Toby and Walter can converse for hours at continual cross-purposes, without succeeding in conveying an idea or hanging up an inference in each other's minds, Trim can communicate: by a few simple suggestions he can paint a vivid picture on the retina of his interlocutor's fancy (98).

On the other hand, like Toby he is a practical man, and committed to the world of things and actions. While Walter delights in the sheer ingenuity of Rabelais's account of Gymnast's fight with Tripet, Trim is exasperated when he realises that there are more words than realism in the encounter:

> – Good God! cried *Trim*, losing all patience, – one home thrust of a bayonet is worth it all. – I think so too, replied *Yorick*. –
>
> – I am of a contrary opinion, quoth my father. (389)

Not the kind of man to leave a door-hinge squeaking, Trim is a resourceful contriver; he can turn jackboots into mortars and lead weights into cannon, as well as bowling greens into battle sites. If the life of a family were weighed against a hypothesis, he is not in doubt which to prefer. He has a sound practical view of what it means to honour your father and mother: it is allowing them "three half pence a day out of my pay" when they grow old, a definition that Yorick approves of (393). Then, again like Toby, he believes in practical demonstrations and is most ready to be convinced by outward and visible signs. They are mutually concerned about the right uniform for courting; and Trim too discovers he is in love when his body tells him so – when the seductive young nun stimulates him to an erection.

But although Trim shares Toby's enthusiasm for the fortification game and is the one who originally proposed the scheme, he is not carried away by that hobbyhorse. He is the one who firmly reminds Toby they are in England, not Europe; and when, in discussion with Bridget over a map, he is faced with the dual possibilities of "where" Toby received his wound, he is able to deal with both the geographical and the anatomical locations at once:

> And this, said he, is the town of *Namur* – and this the citadel – and there lay the *French* – and here lay his honour and myself – and in this cursed trench, Mrs. *Bridget*, quoth the Corporal, taking her by the hand, did he receive the wound which crush'd him so miserably *here* – In pronouncing which he slightly press'd the back of her hand towards the part he felt for – and let it fall. (639)

Since Sterne is concerned to emphasise Trim's ability to relate words and deeds, mind and body, he shows him as particularly skilled in gesture, the action that has meaning, "the psycho-physical crossroads of life", as McKillop has described it.[11] Gestures and attitudes are described in detail all through the novel, but the gestures of each character are different in kind. Walter's are the textbook rhetorician's gestures,[12] subtle, but to his audience incomprehensible; Toby's are far less conscious, and though eloquent, like the benignant expression on his face as he settles his chin on his crutch to watch Walter, are not intentionally so. Tristram's gestures are characteristically explosive, as when, in a moment of exasperation, "instantly I snatch'd off my wig, and threw it perpendicularly, with all imaginable violence, up to the top of the room" (293); like a cork bursting from a bottle, they ease pressure, but do not convey meaning. Trim's gestures, however, are artistically executed, like Walter's, but they communicate volumes: when he drops his hat in exactly the right manner, his audience is impressed with the essence of mortality; when he strikes across his forefinger with the edge of his other hand, the whole story of Tristram's accidental circumcision is delicately conveyed; and when he flourishes his stick to suggest the freedom of the bachelor, "a thousand of my father's most subtle syllogisms could not have said more for celibacy" (604).

In that project of Sterne's to bridge the gap that separates artistic creation from reality, Tristram, the artist attempting to produce not just an autobiography but a life, is his instrument. And in the structural pattern of contrasts and relationships, it is appropriate that Tristram should have the double heritage from Toby and his father, enabling him, so far as possible, to unite the worlds of things and words, actions and speculations, experience and expression. As a writer he is vividly aware that an account of life must itself have life, that a chronicle of events should be, not a mere "description" (as Walter is content to take Yorick's account of the Inquisition), but in some sense (as Trim takes the same account) a real enactment in itself – a "happening", in the popular idiom. So, on the one hand, Tristram needs Toby's commitment to actions, emotions, historical fact, and authenticity; and he shows his allegiance by his judgment in favour of Toby's kind of modesty, which is "modesty in the truest sense of it; and that is, Madam, not in regard to words, for he was so unhappy as to have very little choice in them, – but to things" (66). Yet, on the other hand, he needs also Walter's faith in the validity of a verbal sequence, his conviction that a structure of words has its own beauty, his own truth, its own reality.

In the course of Tristram's narration, we have constant reminders of his dual heritage. He tells us, "I write as a man of erudition" (85), and words for him are a necessary anodyne for unpleasant occurrences like unexpected expense: "I had nothing else for it, but to say some smart thing upon the occasion, worth the money" (527). Yet, like Toby, he has his moments of distrust of definitions and verbal sequences, and is unwilling to place "a number of tall, opake words, one before another, in a right line, betwixt your own and your reader's conception"; and so he chooses to elucidate his ideas of wit and judgment by reference to a solid object like a cane chair (200). In the moral concern of the book, Tristram emerges as combining a value for both the head and the heart:

> I write a careless kind of a civil, nonsensical, good humoured *Shandean* book, which will do all your hearts good – – And all your heads too, – provided you understand it. (436)

Like his father he ranks genius as the highest attainment (428), but his frequent outbursts of tenderness over his uncle's memory show his practical devotion to the man who would not hurt a fly. Tristram has a decent interest in both their hobbyhorses. His father wishes the whole science of fortification at the devil, but during his travels in France, Tristram is almost ready to become addicted to it himself. Yet he occasionally works out his own Walter-like hypotheses, such as his conviction that he will write more purely the cleaner his body is: "For this cause, when your honours and reverences would know whether I write clean and fit to be read, you will be able to judge full as well by looking into my Laundress's bill, as my book" (617). The theory, like many of Walter's, is disproved by practice, but Tristram does, as Toby would, put it into practice; and it is characteristic that his hypothesis should be an offshoot of his belief in the close relation of mind and body: "the soul and body are joint-sharers in every thing they get: A man cannot dress, but his ideas get cloath'd at the same time" (616). In love too Tristram has inherited from both. Like his father, Tristram has his difficulties in consummating his love, with Jenny, but he is emphatic on Toby's side that talking love is *not* making it: "I would as soon set about making a black-pudding by the same receipt" (634) – an enterprise that would probably have engaged Walter's enthusiasm.

As names and theories are Walter's hobbyhorse, the reality to which he is primarily committed, and models and diagrams and physical reconstructions are Toby's, so Tristram's hobbyhorse is *Tristram Shandy* itself. "For my hobby-horse . . . – 'Tis the sporting little filly-folly which carries you out for the present hour" (584). (It is one he shares with Sterne, who wrote in a letter of 1761, "I am scribbling away at my Tristram. . . . – I shall write as long as I live, 'tis, in fact, my hobby-horse."[13]) Tristram's commitment to his book as his reality makes him, perhaps, as mad as Walter and Toby, but the man's madness is the creator's gift, for he is to make his account *live* for the reader.

There is a constant and deliberate intermixture of Tristram's life with the narration of it. Living and writing are the same thing. While he travelled post across France, he "*wrote galloping*" (482). The reader is reminded to keep the midwife in mind "because when she is wanted, we can no way do without her" (35), for the delivery of Tristram the infant and *Tristram Shandy* the novel are inextricably involved:

> My mother, madam, had been delivered sooner than the green bag infallibly – at least by twenty *knots*. – Sport of small accidents, *Tristram Shandy!* that thou art, and ever will be! . . . but 'tis over, – all but the account of 'em, which cannot be given to the curious till I am got out into the world. (166)

The hurry of events in the narrative actually impedes him in the narration, so that he cannot get on with writing his preface until all his characters are quietly settled and off his hands, nor write a chapter on sleep until they oblingingly drop off. Then, when he finds himself unable to recount how Toby and Walter get off the stairs, he calls in a chairman and a critic and pays them to hoist his characters away (285–7). The action being narrated is partly the progress of the narration itself: "The fifteenth chapter is come at last. . . . For in talking of my digression – I declare before heaven I have made it" (618). And the action of the story is interfused with the stages of recounting it: "The door hastily opening in the next chapter but one – put an end to the affair" (179). Perhaps most memorable is the much-quoted passage in which Tristram realises that in order to keep up with himself "at this rate I should just live 364 times faster than I should write" (286). So he also mingles the time of the events narrated with the time it takes to narrate them. As for Walter a statement becomes a fact, and for Toby a reconstruction of events replaces those events in time and space, so for Tristram, in the process of narrating his life, time past becomes time present. This aspect of the novel has been extensively dealt with. In the most illuminating study, Jean-Jacques Mayoux has shown how Sterne is

> in pursuit of a more authentic reality and a purer time, that of the very book in the process of creation, carrying its movement across the temporal structures that it absorbs. ... The pseudo-reality of the story dwindles while the reality of the writer and the process of writing increases proportionately.[14]

The best illustration of Tristram's ability to experience various periods of time simultaneously by putting his mind to them and recounting them is the passage where, on his way through Auxerre, "I have been getting forwards in two different journies together, and with the same dash of the pen" (515).

All this is more than just literary clowning. The vitality of *Tristram Shandy* as a novel is to a large extent dependent on Tristram's immediate and personal involvement in all he writes about. "My uncle *Toby*'s amours running all the way in my head, they had the same effect upon me as if they had been my own", Tristram tells us (629); and knowing how he experiences what he relates, we are apt to believe him, and we reap the benefit of his participation. And there is an added touch of pathos about his own character in that his narrative is to be in some sense a substitute for the life he is to lose: "I . . . must be cut short in the midst of my days, and taste no more of 'em than what I borrow from my imagination" (495). Then, in talking so readily of the process of writing, and in addressing the reader so constantly and intimately, Tristram, and Sterne too, intricately involve us in the action. The author's necessary sympathy with the characters he creates, and the narrator's love for the relatives he describes, mingled as they are, make a powerful bond between the reader and the characters too, so that even solemn critics are induced to talk familiarly of "my father" and "my Uncle Toby", and Tristram's experience becomes, perhaps more than most fiction, our own.

Besides making a present palpable reality out of the past, Tristram's narrative has a kind of magic in making words animate and things articulate. As gestures, the physical motions that have meaning, are prominent in the drama of the novel, in the confrontation and communication (so far as it happens) between characters, so words and things, and a kind of mixture between them, are important in another direction of confrontation, that between the author and the reader. Concrete objects are constantly used for expression, and have a wild and often perverse animation and articulation: the hot chestnut chastises Phutatorius with a fiendish appropriateness, the knobs on the cane chair better demonstrate Tristram's views on wit and judgment than "tall, opake words", the disposition of the widow's nightgown and corking pin makes it "plain that widow *Wadman* was in love with my uncle *Toby*" (548). One could multiply instances.[15] Not only do things *mean*, but words *do*: they are endowed with an almost physical force in promoting action. The single noun "wife", overheard by Mrs Shandy, "caught hold of her by the weak part of the whole sex: – You shall not mistake me, – I mean her curiosity" (368), and fastens her with her ear to the keyhole for the length of several chapters. "Weakness", reminding Walter of his own doubtful virility, is a "tormenting word! which led his imagination a thorny dance, and, before all was over, play'd the duce and all with him" (42). "*Fouter*" and "*bouger*" are supposed to have an irresistible power to budge a stubborn mule. We are reminded, too, how the written or printed word has actually acquired substance: Tristram's "remarks", in a "large parcel", have a little Odyssey of their own, travelling in the chaise pocket, sold by mistake to the chaise-vamper, and used as curling-papers by the chaise-vamper's wife, who

> took them from her curls, and put them gravely one by one into my hat – one was twisted this way – another twisted that – ay! by my faith; and when they are published, quoth I, –
>
> They will be worse twisted still. (531)

The reader is constantly reminded that he is in a physical relation with this bundle of words, *Tristram Shandy*, and that if the literary magic is working, they are indeed leading his imagination a thorny dance. The physical and even carnal powers of the printed word are bawdily suggested in the prescription for Phutatorius's particular wound: the part is to be wrapped in fresh moist proof-sheets from his chapter "*de re concubinaria*"! We are never told what monstrous birth would result from this act of literary coition, but Yorick is earnest in discouraging it (326). By such means does Sterne remind us of his theme that in the process of literary creation the word is made flesh.

This physical conception of language is characteristic of the genre that Sterne was partly writing in, "the tradition of learned wit", as D. W. Jefferson calls it,[16] or, as Northrop Frye has since defined it, Menippean satire.[17] In *The Battle of the Books*, Swift's action consists of a series of field encounters between volumes of the works of Ancients and Moderns; a chapter of *Ulysses* demonstrates the birth and development of English while it describes the delivery of a child; and in *Tittivulus*, a more recent foray in the genre, certain fiends collect verbiage in sacks, and one of them keeps a paragraph of Henry James in a hutch as a pet, stroking and pampering it and crossing it with a parenthetic clause from Emerson in the hope that they will breed.[18] But Sterne manages to bring his inkhorn fantasies to life, for his lithe and energetic words are complemented by a solidly imagined structure of objects, so that *Tristram Shandy*, like Uncle Toby's fortifications, has almost a geography of its own, a set of relationships in time and space. And although his characters neatly embody mental attitudes, in the manner of Menippean satire, that is by no means the limit of their existence, for they have a vital life force of their own that subsumes their function in the structure of ideas.

Sterne turns the spotlight on the process of creation, not only by his direct comments through Tristram on the subject, but by the pattern of relationships between the characters, which is a kind of allegory of the relation between the physical and the conceptual worlds. Walter, the champion of language and mental action, and Toby, committed to things and physical demonstration, are brothers, and the son of the one and the servant of the other are able to produce articulate structures to express and re-create experience.

NOTES

1. Henri Fluchère, *Laurence Sterne: From Tristram to Yorick*, trans. and abr. Barbara Bray (London, 1965) p. 23.
2. Laurence Sterne, *The Life and Opinions of Tristram Shandy, Gentlemen*, ed. James Aiken Work (New York, 1940) p. 162; all quotations from *Tristram Shandy* are from this edition.
3. Robert J. Griffin, "Tristram Shandy and Language", *College English*, 23 (1961) p. 109.
4. John Traugott, *Tristram Shandy's World: Sterne's Philosophical Rhetoric* (Berkeley, 1954) p. 59.
5. John Locke, *An Essay Concerning Human Understanding*, ed. Alexander Campbell Fraser, vol. II (1894; rpt. New York, 1959) p. 132.
6. See A. R. Towers's study of the sexual comedy of *Tristram Shandy*, "Sterne's Cock and Bull Story", *English Literary History*, 24 (1957) 12–29.
7. John Locke, *Essay*, II, 135.
8. John Locke, *Essay*, II, 143.
9. *Gulliver's Travels*, in Herbert Davis (ed.), *Prose Works of Jonathan Swift*, Vol. XI (Oxford, 1941) p. 169.
10. Henri Fluchère, *Laurence Sterne: From Tristram to Yorick*, p. 303.
11. Alan Dugald McKillop, "The Reinterpretation of Laurence Sterne", *Etudes Anglaises*, 7 (1954) p. 38.
12. A close if not accurate relation of Walter's gestures to those expounded by such authorities as Quintilian is demonstrated by William J. Farrell, "Nature Versus Art as a Comic Pattern in *Tristram Shandy*", *English Literary History*, 30 (1963) 16–35.
13. Lewis Perry Curtis (ed.) *Letters of Laurence Sterne* (Oxford, 1935) p. 143.
14. "Laurence Sterne", trans. John Traugott, in John Traugott (ed.), *Laurence Sterne: A Collection of Critical Essays*, (Englewood Cliffs, 1968) p. 121. I am also indebted to Mayoux's paper, "Variations on the Time-Sense in *Tristram Shandy*", delivered at the Sterne Bicentenary Conference at York in 1968, and subsequently published in *The Winged Skull*, eds Arthur H. Cash and John M. Stedmond (London, 1971) 3–18.
15. E. M. Forster classified *Tristram Shandy* as fantasy because of the tendency of inanimate objects there to become alive: *Aspects of the Novel* (London, 1927) pp. 145–6.
16. D. W. Jefferson, "*Tristram Shandy* and the Tradition of Learned Wit", *Essays in Criticism*, 1 (1951) 225–48.
17. See Northrop Frye, *Anatomy of Criticism* (Princeton, 1957) pp. 308–12.
18. See Michael Ayrton, *Tittivulus* (London, 1953) pp. 112–13.

2 *Pride and Prejudice*: "Acting by Design"

"I meant to be uncommonly clever in taking so decided a dislike to him, without any reason", Elizabeth Bennet admits of Darcy in one of her moments of self-knowledge and confession (225).[1] She meant to be clever. It is a phrase that makes clear a refinement of the theme of *Pride and Prejudice*. Elizabeth is not only a misguided heroine who makes mistakes and learns the error of her ways: but she *wilfully* makes mistakes, almost according to a programme she has laid down for herself. Her meaning to be clever connects her with Trollope's characters, who characteristically "teach themselves to believe" this or that, and with James's Isabel Archer, who consciously forms herself as though she were a work of art. As Eliot puts it in "The Hollow Men",

> Between the idea
> And the reality
> Between the motion
> And the act
> Falls the shadow.

The nineteenth-century novel does not, by and large, deal with hollow men, but it certainly suggests the movement in that direction. Austen and Trollope and James are alike interested in the shadow that falls between the motion and the act: in that moment of choice between impulse and action, the interval wherein the mind takes its decision, I will do or be this and not that, because this becomes the person that I intend to make myself. It is the movement towards not just self-realisation, but self-creation, that fascinates such authors.

Often enough the model for the self-creator is literary. Don Quixote was the most memorable self-creator of all, and he patterned his behaviour on precedents drawn from chivalric romance. The Quixote theme is of course a prominent one in the Jane Austen canon. In *Love and Freindship* she was already producing satire on high-flown sentiments derived from sentimental novels: "Where, Edward in the name of wonder," asks a sensible father of his ranting romantic son, "did you pick up this unmeaning gibberish? You have been studying Novels I suspect" (VI, 81). *Northanger Abbey* is Jane Austen's version of *The Female Quixote*, a prolonged consideration of the trouble one can get into if one tries to live life as though it were a Gothic novel. *Sense and Sensibility*, with its further strictures on the conventional literary constituent in Marianne's emotional excesses, continues to pursue several of the issues more humorously raised in *Love and Freindship*.

Emma, the imaginist, is the most inventive Quixote of all, even though the Quixote theme in the novel is not so clamorously to the fore as it is in *Northanger Abbey*. Emma is not only a self-creator, but she creates roles for the people who surround her too, and does all she can to make them live the roles she has cast them in. We hear less about her literary precedents than we do of Catherine Morland's, but her preconceptions are quite clearly drawn from similar sources. It is from her reading, not her experience, that she has become convinced of certain rules of existence: for instance, that a child of unknown parents must be of noble birth (ergo, that Harriet Smith, Highbury's princess in disguise, is worthy of Mr Elton); that a man who rescues a woman from physical danger must simultaneously fall in love with her and gain her affections (therefore, that Mr Dixon and Jane must be in love, because he once saved her from falling out of a boat); and that love is blind (hence, that Mr Knightley can't be in love with her, because he so evidently sees her faults). With these kinds of preconceptions, Emma sets about her task of marrying off the people around her and making them live happily ever after; and as in *Don Quixote*, much of the comedy of the novel arises from the inconsistency between the benevolent fictions she endeavours to enact and the stubborn stuff of life that resists them – just as the windmills resist the construction the Don seeks to impose on them.

Pride and Prejudice has a place in this pattern. Its heroine is a self-creator, too, who is not always successful in the enactment of her designs. Unlike Emma, but like Isabel Archer, it is her self rather than others that she uses as her primary material, though like Emma she is fortunate in being unsuccessful in the creation of her destiny.

Like many of Jane Austen's novels, *Pride and Prejudice* constitutes a strong qualification of the theme of the novel that preceded it. In *Sense and Sensibility*, for all its internal concessions about the importance of strong feeling, Sense is by and large endorsed at the expense of Sensibility, and the heart is subordinated to the head. Marianne, the heroine of Sensibility, must finally acknowledge the superiority of her sister's "strength of understanding, and coolness of judgment", and learn to control per passion by her reason (*S & S*, 6). In *Pride and Prejudice*, however, the emphasis is not on the excesses of feeling but on the excesses of mental activity. It is the besetting sin of the heroine that she means to be clever, and she is moreover surrounded by other characters who similarly distort reality by subordinating feeling to calculation.

Of all the completed novels,[2] *Pride and Prejudice* is the closest to being what Northrop Frye calls a Menippean satire,[3] a satire on eggheads and diseases of the intellect. It is not ungoverned passions that threaten the happiness of the heroine, but ungoverned opinions, and the society at large is subject to a kind of cancer of the mind whereby ratiocination is in danger of usurping the proper functions of the heart. Lucy Steele, as the heroine's antagonist in *Sense and Sensibility*, is a caricature of what Elinor represents, an appalling example of the triumph of prudence over feeling. But the spirit of Lucy Steele seems to preside over the characters and action of *Pride and Prejudice*, where it is a truth universally acknowledged that eligible young bachelors are the rightful property of the unmarried girls of the district. The feelings of either party are not to be taken into account, any more than they are by Mrs Bennet in that famous opening scene. "You must know that I am thinking of his marrying one of them", she tells her husband, in trying to persuade him to call on Mr Bingley. Her syntax is indicative – the proposition of Bingley's marrying one of her daughters is subordinate to her *thinking* and her husband's *knowing*: feeling doesn't get a look in. "Is that his design in settling here?" her husband asks, parodying her mode of calculation (4). Bingley in fact is innocent of designs, as is Jane, but there are designers enough about them almost to ruin their happiness.

The prudential marriage motive is of course a major issue in this novel,[4] as has often been pointed out. From the opening scene onwards we have constantly before us examples of how money, status, patronage, and "an establishment" figure overwhelmingly in the calculations of who is to marry whom, and love scarcely has a place among the considerations. Marriages are planned, projected in advance, and the behaviour of the principals is adapted to the successful completion of the plan. The issue of the propriety of manifesting feeling, so fully canvassed in *Sense and Sensibility*, is here canvassed again between Charlotte Lucas and Elizabeth. "In nine cases out of ten," argues Charlotte, "a woman had better show *more* affection than she feels" – the better to catch her man by encouragement. "Your plan is a good one", Elizabeth acknowledges, "when nothing is in question but the desire of being well married" (22) – and that is of course the case with Charlotte herself, who marries Mr Collins "from the pure and disinterested desire of an establishment" (122). Likewise Miss Bingley plans to entrap Darcy, who is already marked out from birth by Lady Catherine as the rightful property of his cousin; and Mr Collins, before being snapped up by Charlotte, is ready to marry any one of the five misses Bennet, sight unseen: "This was his plan of amends – of atonement – for inheriting their father's estate; and he thought it an excellent one, full of eligibility and suitableness" (70).

To complement this pattern of prudence and planning in marriage, another manifestation of the domination of head over heart is the repetition of situations where calculation takes the place of spontaneity. Elizabeth's sin of prejudice, the judgment that precedes due process, is not only a manifestation of her "quickness" (5), the cleverness of a "headstrong" girl (110), it is also part of a pattern of prejudgment and premeditation, the mental activity that pre-empts feeling and immediate response. Along with "prejudice", a number of words with the same prefix have a special resonance in this novel: "prepossession", "preference", "premeditation", "precipitance", "previous study". They testify to the same short-circuiting of organic emotional processes. Mr Collins, for instance, not only marries according to plan; he lives and loves (or thinks he does) according to plan, and even pays compliments by the same method. Mr Bennet, drawing him out, asks whether his elegant verbal courtesies "proceed from the impulse of the moment, or are the result of previous study?" Collins has at his fingertips a whole aesthetics of the art of flattery, including the concept of *ars celare artem*:

> They arise chiefly from what is passing at the time, and though I sometimes amuse myself with suggesting and arranging such little elegant compliments as may be adapted to ordinary occasions, I always wish to give them as unstudied an air as possible. (68)

Charlotte, with her theory that a woman should do what she can to secure a man first, as "there will be leisure for falling in love as much as she chuses" afterwards (22), is in many ways a perfect match for him, as she too can work at giving her calculations as unstudied an air as possible: during his brief and successful campaign, when she sees him approach Lucas Lodge, she "instantly set out to meet him accidentally in the lane" (121). In this world where calculation displaces spontaneity, even a cough can be considered as a piece of strategy:

> "Don't keep coughing so, Kitty, for heaven's sake! Have a little compassion on my nerves. You tear them to pieces."
> "Kitty has no discretion in her coughs," said her father; "she times them ill."
> "I do not cough for my own amusement," replied Kitty fretfully. (6)

If in this case we believe her, it's only because we know Kitty hasn't the wit to cough artistically.

We are recurrently shown the tendency of the mind to usurp the functions of the other faculties, the physical as well as the emotional. Miss Bingley, who wants to impress the intellectual Darcy, suggests a reform in the conduct of balls: "It would surely be more rational if conversation instead of dancing made the order of the day." "Much more rational, . . .I dare say," concedes her brother, "but it would not be near so much like a ball" (55–6). For once the rational is to be kept within proper bounds. The character in the novel who is most genuinely spontaneous and impulsive, Bingley, is firmly put in his place. His manner of moving to the district is characteristic: "he was tempted by an accidental recommendation to look at Netherfield House. He did look at it and into it for half an hour, was pleased . . . and took it immediately" (16). But when he intimates that he would leave it as quickly Darcy is severe: "When you told Mrs. Bennet this morning that if you ever resolved on quitting Netherfield you should be gone in five minutes, you meant it to be a sort of panegyric, of compliment of yourself – and yet what is there so very laudable in a precipitance which must leave very necessary business undone . . .?" (49). Bingley's impulsive sensibility must be made to serve Darcy's cooler sense, and it is one of Darcy's faults that he takes advantage of Bingley's "ductility". Elizabeth is partly justified in her impatience at "that want of proper resolution which now made him the slave of his designing friends" (133). Darcy himself becomes subject to a more skilled designer than himself, Mr Bennet, who calculates with satisfaction that he will now not have to pay off his debt on the price of Wickham: "these violent young lovers carry everything their own way. I shall offer to pay him tomorrow; he will rant and storm about his love for you, and there will be an end of the matter" (377).

"Every impulse of feeling should be guided by reason" (32). In *Sense and Sensibility* such a sentiment might have proceeded from the narrator, but in *Pride and Prejudice* it is put into the mouth of Mary Bennet, that specialist in "thread-bare morality" (60). Mary is another of the characters who remind us how the moral climate has changed since the previous novel. Here the danger is not that the impulse of feeling may elude the guidance of reason, but that it may be trampled on and virtually annihilated by reason, or at least by some mental activity that would claim the name. Mary, "who . . . in consequence of being the only plain one in the family, worked hard for knowledge and accomplishments" (25), is a salient example of one who so subordinates her feelings to her mind that the feelings have atrophied, and she is Jane Austen's version of those women that D. H. Lawrence was appalled by, all head and no body. By the time we hear her drawing a "useful lesson" about the irretrievability of female virtue from the moral disgrace of her youngest sister, we, like Elizabeth, have ceased to be amused (289). But although Mary is a caricature, we need to remember that she, like Elizabeth, is clearly her father's daughter.

Mr Bennet is Jane Austen's Walter Shandy, a man with a set of hobby-horses, mental constructs that he has substituted for the reality that surrounds him. His feelings are seldom described, but his mental operations have the force of passions. His attitude is carefully accounted for. We are to suppose that since his emotional life has been a disaster, he has retreated to a cerebral irony, whereby all the troubles and disappointments of life are to be viewed as mere amusements. His "conjugal felicity," by the time we know the Bennets, has been reduced to the kind of satisfaction we see him deriving from his verbal barbs at his wife's expense in the first scene.

> To his wife he was very little otherwise indebted, than as her ignorance and folly had contributed to his amusement. This is not the sort of happiness which a man would in general wish to owe his wife; but where other powers of entertainment are wanting, the true philosopher will derive benefit from such as are given. (236).

Like Walter, another "true philosopher", he can even contemplate the death of a child with equanimity, as long as it gives him the opportunity of a *bon mot*. "Well, my dear," he tells Mrs Bennet when the news comes that Jane is confined at Netherfield after being sent out in the rain to dine with the Bingleys, "if your daughter should have a dangerous fit of illness, if she should die, it would be a comfort to know that it was all in pursuit of Mr. Bingley, and under your orders" (31).

He has deliberately set aside the natural preference of a father for his offspring, in favour of a clinical lack of bias: "If my children are silly I must hope to be always sensible of it", he announces coolly (29). There is a searing quality about his wit and his lack of compassion. In the face of Jane's genuine unhappiness when Bingley abandons her, he can respond only with the critical satisfaction of a spectator at a play: "Next to being married, a girl likes to be crossed in love a little now and then. It is something to think of, and gives her a sort of distinction among her companions" (137–8).

He can successfully separate his personal interest from his

aesthetic appreciation of Wickham's roguery when he considers the matter of the price Wickham sets on himself as a husband for Lydia: "Wickham's a fool, if he takes her with a farthing less than ten thousand pounds. I should be sorry to think so ill of him, in the very beginning of our relationship" (304). For Mr Bennet is a connoisseur, a spectator and critic of the kind dear to Browning and James. If in his cerebral detachment and delight in verbal play he is a descendant of Walter Shandy, in his aesthetic response to the life around him he is an ancestor of Ralph Touchett, the narrator of *The Sacred Fount*, and the Bishop of St Praxed's. "For what do we live, but to make sport for our neighbours, and laugh at them in our turn?" asks Mr Bennet, not expecting an answer (364). Ralph Touchett's rhetorical question about his position has more pathos, but it equally announces his aesthetic stance, the outlook of critically engaged spectator rather than emotionally involved participant. "What's the use of being ill and disabled and restricted to mere spectatorship at the game of life if I really can't see the show when I've paid so much for my ticket?" (*Portrait of a Lady*, Ch. 15) There are in fact answers to the questions that Mr Bennet and Ralph propound, which are argued at large in the novels they inhabit. There isn't and shouldn't be any kind of "use" in Ralph's pathetic disability, and the Bennets of the world are put into it for more purposes than simply to laugh and be laughed at. Mr Bennet's stance of intellectual detachment is sometimes exposed almost as a negation of itself, a moral idiocy. As in *Love and Freindship*, where acute sensibility to the pains of others is finally shown to be an elaborate kind of selfishness, in *Pride and Prejudice* we see Mr Bennet's wit and acuity as a kind of obtuseness. When he tries to share a joke about the rumour of Darcy's courtship with Elizabeth, even she, his disciple, is unable to participate: "It was necessary to laugh, when she would rather have cried. Her father had most cruelly mortified her, . . . and she could do nothing but wonder at his want of penetration" (364).

The judgment on Mr Bennet for neglecting his responsibilities as husband and father is clear enough, but the reader is very ready to forgive him. For it is in large measure the sins of Mr Bennet and his favourite daughter, their overweening intelligence and relish for the absurd, that make *Pride and Prejudice* such delightful reading. He in particular is our onstage spectator and critic, articulating and sometimes creating for us our delight in the people and incidents around him. Mr Collins in himself is a fine creation, but it is Mr Collins as savoured and drawn out by Mr Bennet who becomes immortal. We share in his hopes that Collins may prove the reverse of sensible, and are gratified when he does. Wickham the hypocrite might even be a little sinister but for being taken over, appreciated, and set in a frame by Mr Bennet: "He is a fine a fellow as ever I saw. He simpers, and smirks, and makes love to us all. I am prodigiously proud of him. I defy even Sir William Lucas himself to produce a more valuable son-in-law" (330). It is Mr Bennet, and that part of him inherited and carried on in Elizabeth, that go far towards making *Pride and Prejudice* the light, bright and sparkling novel it is: their aesthetic appreciation, though accessible for our moral judgment, is the catalyst of our own aesthetic delight.

Elizabeth, to her lasting glory, has style, and much of her style is an inheritance from her father. "She had a lively, playful disposition", we hear at the outset, "which delighted in any thing ridiculous" (12). In fact, so far as she is one of the Quixotes in Jane Austen's novels, she behaves not so much according to the model of romance as according to the model set by her father. It is because she wants to live up to her position as his favourite daughter that she means to be clever. After she has read and absorbed Darcy's letter, and so come to know herself, she is able to recognise the exact nature of her failing.

> I meant to be uncommonly clever in taking so decided dislike to him, without any reason. It is such a spur to one's genius, such an opening for wit to have a dislike of that kind. (225–6)

Spurs to one's genius and openings for wit are likely to be items coveted by a devoted daughter of Mr Bennet. And as the process of Catherine Morland's and Emma's education involves their discarding romantic models of experience, so Elizabeth learns by gradually sloughing off the influence of her father's aesthetic detachment.

At the outset it is strong. She comes on as delighting in the ridiculous, she accepts the title of "a studier of character" (42), and announces "Follies and nonsense, whims and inconsistencies *do* divert me, I own, and I laugh at them whenever I can" (57). Like her father, she is a vehicle for much of the reader's appreciation in taking on the examinatión and elucidation of character, as she does of Bingley's and Darcy's during her stay at Netherfield. She also becomes the critic and exponent of her own character (not always a reliable one), and the traits she chooses to emphasise bear perhaps more relation to a model derived from her father than to the truth. "Compliments always take *you* by surprise, and *me* never" (14), she tells Jane, with more style than accuracy. (When Darcy pays her the great compliment of proposing, she is astounded.) "I always delight in overthrowing . . . schemes, and cheating a person of their premeditated contempt", she tells Darcy when she expects him to despise her taste (52). It is the same delight manifested by Mr Bennet when he refuses to call on Bingley, and subsequently visits him on the sly. To be whimsical and unpredictable is his mode also. And in her as in her father we see that interpenetration of emotional with intellectual response, so that mental operations have the force of strong feeling. "You take delight in vexing me", Mrs Bennet accuses her husband, with unusual perspicacity (5). Similarly Elizabeth is glad to be "restored . . . to the enjoyment of all her original dislike" towards the Bingley sisters (35). By a characteristic process, her emotion becomes subordinate to the consciousness of the emotion.

Elizabeth takes pains to live up to her father and share his attitudes. Their exchange on Collins's letter – "Can he be a sensible man, sir?" "No, my dear; I think not. I have great hopes of finding him quite the reverse" (64) – neatly demonstrates their roles, as Elizabeth faithfully serves her father with cues for his witticisms. When Mr Bennet is joking about Jane's being jilted, Elizabeth enters into the spirit of his irony: at his suggestion that Wickham "would jilt you creditably", she replies, "Thank you, Sir, but a less agreeable man would satisfy me. We must not all expect Jane's good fortune" (138). She takes up his proposition in her letter to her aunt, in which she humorously announces that Wickham *has* jilted her; but here she is able to make a sensible qualification:

I am now convinced, my dear aunt, that I have never been

> much in love; for had I really experienced that pure and elevating passion, I should at present detest his very name, and wish him all manner of evil. But my feelings are not only cordial towards *him*; they are even impartial towards Miss King .... There can be no love in all this. My watchfulness has been effectual; and though I should certainly be a more interesting object to all my acquaintance, were I distractedly in love with him, I cannot say that I regret my comparative insignificance. Importance may sometimes be purchased too dearly. (150)

The passage shows her propensity to snatch up an emotional subject and cunningly encase it in an intellectual web. She had been enough in love with Wickham, at one time, to have "her head full of him" (not her heart, we notice). But such emotion as she has felt is successfully analysed and dissected, and proves to have been little more than an idea, a mere opinion. Now like her father she can mock love by her parodic terminology – "that pure and elevating passion", "distractedly in love" – and presently her desertion by Wickham is imagined as a spectacle for others, wherein she is to figure as the "interesting object". However, her mental health is such that she will not be seduced by this attraction, and she sensibly concludes "Importance may sometimes be purchased too dearly." Though she was ready to participate in her father's savouring of the aesthetic pleasure in the spectacle of the jilted lady, she will not surrender her happiness in order to have the satisfaction of providing the spectacle. This is comedy, after all, and a light, bright and sparkling one at that. It remained for James to pursue the tragic implications of that self-creating impulse in *The Portrait of a Lady.*

Elizabeth's misjudgment of the relative merits of Darcy and Wickham is in large measure a result of her aesthetic stance. Darcy offends her by saying she is not handsome enough to tempt him; Wickham wins her allegiance by telling her a story. His version of his youth and blighted prospects has the verbal embellishment of romantic fiction:

> His estate there is a noble one .... I verily believe I could forgive him any thing and every thing, rather than his disappointing the hopes and disgracing the memory of his

> father. . . . I have been a disappointed man, and my spirits will not bear solitude. (77–9)

The satisfying fiction, along with Wickham's professional delivery, charms Elizabeth, and she believes it because she wants to. As her father takes life to be a spectacle, Elizabeth will accept a fiction as life. She leaves Wickham with her head full of him, and insists "there was truth in his looks"(86). Subsequently she is to elaborate on his story, and construct from it her own version of the fable of the virtuous and idle apprentices.

After Darcy's letter Elizabeth cannot be in concert with her father. The education about the errors of prejudice and first impressions goes with a discarding of attitudes she had imbibed from him. Now she urges the unsuitability of Lydia's going to Brighton, and is exasperated by Mr Bennet's irresponsible detachment. Though she had "never been blind to the impropriety of her father's behaviour as a husband", we hear, it is only now that her judgment overcomes her partiality and loyalty: "she had never felt so strongly as now, the disadvantages which must attend the children of so unsuitable a marriage, nor ever been so fully aware of the evils arising from so ill-judged a direction of talents"(236–7). The failure in sympathy between father and daughter persists until the final fortunate culmination. He becomes the painful reminder of her own follies by continuing to assume her "pointed dislike" of Darcy, and by his revival of her prejudice: "We all know him to be a proud, unpleasant sort of man", he says of the man she proposes to marry (376).

Of course it is not only Mr Bennet who is to blame for his daughter's misguided following in his footsteps. Elizabeth is responsible, and very clearly elects her own path. There is an emphasis not just on her mistakes, but on her wilful choice of them. If she goes astray, she does so very consciously, even though she is unaware of the full extent of her wandering. In discussing Jane's behaviour with Charlotte, Elizabeth insists that Jane, unlike the husband-hunting girl that Charlotte posits, has no "plan", "she is not acting by design"(22). It is one more of the points of contrast between the sisters by which Jane Austen defines Elizabeth's character; for Elizabeth by contrast *is* acting by design, though to an extent she does not herself recognise. "Design" is another word that recurs in the novel with pointed frequency, and is often connected with the pattern of planned matches. Mr Bennet asks if marrying one of the Bennet girls is Bingley's "design in settling here"(4). Wickham pursues Georgiana Darcy to Ramsgate, "undoubtedly by design" (202). Mr Collins admits during his proposal that he came to Hertfordshire "with the design of selecting a wife"(105), and congratulates himself after his marriage that he and his wife "seem to have been designed for each other"(216). Except in the case of Jane, Elizabeth is prone to attribute "design" to others – she sees through Miss Bingley's "designs" on Darcy (170), and considers Bingley the slave of his "designing friends" (133). Less clear-sightedly, she angrily accuses Darcy of proposing to her "with so evident a design of offending and insulting me" (190). But she often accuses others of faults she does not recognise in herself.

If Elizabeth acts by "design", the word connotes not just a preconceived plan of action, but an aesthetic structure. Her style is I think in some senses a design, a deliberately adopted set of responses by which she projects herself among her acquaintance. Her wit and vivacity are no doubt innate, but the manifestation of them again shows that discontinuity between stimulus and reaction that signals a chosen image. Her style, delightful though it is, is in some senses *other* than herself, and it is the artificially adopted part of her style that she has ultimately to recognise as extraneous and to discard. When she discovers the extent to which she has been "blind, partial, prejudiced, absurd", she connects the discovery with the self-image she has created: "I, who have prided myself on my discernment! – I, who have valued myself on my abilities! who have often disdained the the generous candour of my sister, and gratified my vanity, in useless or blameable distrust" (208). We judge her, and she judges herself, not only for her "prepossession and ignorance", but because, as she says, she has *courted* prepossession and ignorance (208), as she has *encouraged* prejudices (226), and been *determined* to hate Darcy (90).

It is Darcy, in fact, who is most clear-sighted about the artificial aspect of Elizabeth's style. In the playful discussion between them at Netherfield when they spar on the subject of each other's characters, Darcy develops within the comic context a theory of the fatal flaw, a kind of comic hamartia that is this novel's version of Hamlet's "vicious mole of nature":

> "There is, I believe, in every disposition a tendency to some particular evil, a natural defect, which not even the best education can overcome."
> "And *your* defect is a propensity to hate everybody."
> "And yours," he replied with a smile, "is wilfully to misunderstand them." (58)

Darcy has hit off her flaw quite accurately, and shows himself in this case to be a more effective studier of character than Elizabeth the specialist. It is the wilful elements in Elizabeth's misunderstandings that are most clearly judged, morally speaking – as they are most enjoyably savoured, aesthetically speaking. Darcy is appreciative of her style, and attracted by it, even while recognising some of its manifestations as mere verbal play that by no means conveys reality. When Elizabeth hears his final self-reproaches, and offers the confident advice, "You must learn some of my philosophy. Think only of the past as its remembrance gives you pleasure", Darcy again recognises a front and staunchly argues, "I cannot give you credit for any philosophy of the kind" (369). He is right, of course – that philosophy is being preached by one who not long before was taking a solitary walk in order to "indulge in all the delight of unpleasant recollections" (212). He again shows his perspicacity about her adopted style at Rosings, where he tells her, "I have had the pleasure of your acquaintance long enough to know, that you find great enjoyment in occasionally professing opinions which in fact are not your own" (174).

In context we hear that "Elizabeth laughed heartily at this picture of herself"; but in fact her "opinions", the strength of which is part of her attraction, take a hard beating in the course of the novel. When Lady Catherine portentously comments, in the face of Elizabeth's spirited defence of the early "coming out" of younger sisters, "Upon my word . . . you give your opinion very decidedly for so young a person" (165–6), we are inclined to side with Elizabeth; but not long after we see her strenuously urging her father to restrain Lydia, whom she is sorry to see "Vain, ignorant, idle, and absolutely uncontrouled!" (231). Her opinions, as an appropriate nemesis, come back to haunt her after she has, as she thinks, safely buried them. After her engagement, when Jane reminds her how she dislikes Darcy, Elizabeth breezily dismisses the proposition; "*That* is all to be forgot. Perhaps I did not always love him so well as I do now. But in such cases as these, a good memory is unpardonable. This is the last time I shall ever remember it myself" (373). But her father reminds her, when she asks for his consent to the marriage, that she had "always hated him". "How earnestly did she then wish that her former opinions had been more reasonable, her expressions more moderate!" (376). She at last wryly admits to Darcy "we have both reason to think my opinions not entirely unalterable" (368).

It is part of the pattern of the novel that Elizabeth, the studier of character, the clever girl who prides herself on her discernment, should constantly and surprisingly emerge as less astute than the relative dullards who surround her. Such is her wit and charm that the reader nearly always takes her side against others; but we are to recognise too that she is guilty of the faults of which she accuses them. At the Netherfield ball, particularly, when she is championing the cause of Wickham, she strides about clad in complete confidence in the rectitude of her own judgment and the erring ways of everybody else. She is impatient of Bingley's "blind partiality" to his friend, of Miss Bingley's "wilful ignorance" about Wickham, of Mr Collins's "determined air of following his own inclination" (90, 95, 97) – all besetting sins of her own. When Jane hesitatingly suggests "one does not know what to think" about Wickham's wrongs at Darcy's hand, Elizabeth patronisingly contradicts her, "I beg your pardon; – one knows exactly what to think" (86). Such confidence is Elizabeth's comic hubris, as her tendency wilfully to misunderstand is her comic hamartia. Recurrently, the fools and clowns who surround her show up the failings she thought fell to their share alone. Mr Collins is absurd when he asserts that young ladies always refuse a proposal at the first asking, but in the event Elizabeth is what she assures him she is not – "one of those young ladies (if such young ladies there are) who are so daring as to risk their happiness on the chance of being asked a second time" (107). Her sharp prejudice against Darcy and decided preference for Wickham, attitudes she takes such pride in as spurs to her genius, are enlarged and parodied in the collective attitudes of that least astute of communities, Meryton, whose gossipy views go through just such an evolution as Elizabeth's: after Wickham's elopement with Lydia, "All Meryton seemed striving to blacken the man, who, but three months before, had been almost an angel of light" (294). Gossip is to Meryton what the more elaborate fictions she chooses to believe in are to Elizabeth. Even Mrs Bennet, the mother whom Elizabeth and most other people would least like to resemble, is recognisable not as a contrast to but as a caricature of Elizabeth. The reformed Elizabeth is pained that her mother keeps calling the man she loves "that disagreeable Mr Darcy" (her own epithet), and she is faintly ashamed of Mrs Bennet's *volte face* after his proposal: "Such a charming man! – so handsome! so tall! – Oh, my dear Lizzy! pray apologise for my having disliked him so much before. I hope he will overlook it" (378). Both the dislike and its reversal are expressed in terms characteristic of Mrs Bennet, but their substance is reminiscent of the reversal of Elizabeth's own feelings. We may even see in Mrs Bennet's propensity to "fanc[y] herself nervous" (5) an exercise of the fictive imagination that is parallel to Elizabeth's meaning to be clever.

We are recurrently shown that, while the best-laid plans of such people as Elizabeth and Darcy are apt to go agley, they may be rescued from the dilemmas that their designs land them in by random or ill-intentioned actions of others. It is Lydia's thoughtless letting slip the fact of Darcy's presence at her wedding that leads to Elizabeth's finding out Darcy's part in the transaction, and so her determination to thank him, and so his proposal. It is Lady Catherine's ill-judged expedition to frighten Elizabeth out of marrying Darcy that extracts her avowal that she wouldn't refuse him, and hence Darcy's renewed hope, and hence his renewed offer. The two of them, conscious of dangers overcome, quests achieved, and an approaching ending that will allow them to live happily ever after, playfully discuss this matter of the outcome's moral consonance with the action:

> "I wonder when you *would* have spoken, if I had not asked you! [Elizabeth speculates.] My resolution of thanking you

for your kindness to Lydia had certainly great effect. *Too much*, I am afraid; for what becomes of the moral, if our comfort springs from a breach of promise . . .? This will never do."

"You need not distress yourself. The moral will be perfectly fair. Lady Catherine's unjustifiable endeavours to separate us, were the means of removing all my doubts . . .. I was not in a humour to wait for any opening of your's. My aunt's intelligence had given me hope, and I was determined at once to know every thing." (381)

In the last chapter of *Northanger Abbey* the narrator draws attention to "the tell-tale compression of the pages", the signal "that we are all hastening together to perfect felicity", and speculates about the moral, "whether the tendency of this work be altogether to recommend parental tyranny, or reward filial disobediance" (*NA*, 250, 252). But in *Pride and Prejudice* it is appropriately the central characters themselves who playfully discourse on their own experience as a story with a moral, an aesthetic structure.

The outcome of the story is fortunate, sparkling, and if Elizabeth has had to abandon some of her stylish fictions, she has yet been allowed to retain much of her style. But in her undoubted successor in the next novel, Mary Crawford in *Mansfield Park*, we are shown in more sombre terms the consequences of the disjunction of style from principle. Elizabeth is triumphant, but we have seen her come close to disaster because of her tendency to interfere in her own responses, to subordinate feeling and the due process of judgment to a smart stylishness, and to project an image of herself that is distinct from the real self. Although her style is what attracts us and Darcy, it is also clear that in acting by design she almost comes to grief.

NOTES

1. I use R. W. Chapman (ed.), The Oxford Illustrated Jane Austen, 3rd ed., 5 vols (London, 1933), and the *Minor Works* in the same series (London, 1954). *Pride and Prejudice* is vol. III in this series. Subsequent references will be in the text.
2. The fragment *Sanditon* is likewise a satire of mental attitudes and

projectors. See B. C. Southam, "*Sanditon*: the Seventh Novel", in Juliet McMaster (ed.) *Jane Austen's Achievement*, (London, 1976) 1–26.

3. See Northrop Frye, *The Anatomy of Criticisim* (Princeton, 1957) pp. 309ff.
4. See especially Mark Schorer, "Pride Unprejudiced", *Kenyon Review* 18 (Winter, 1956) pp. 85ff.

3 Dickens and the Horrific

Charles Dickens, "a great reader of good fiction at an unusually early age",[1] was also a reader of uncommonly bad literature at an early age. Most discussions of his early reading, however, dwell on the "good fiction", young Copperfield's library, and neglect his taste for grisly sensationalism.[2] Dickens said of his reading at Wellington House Academy:

> I used, when I was at school, to take in the *Terrific Register*, making myself unspeakably miserable, and frightening my very wits out of my head, for the small charge of a penny weekly; which considering that there was an illustration to every number, in which there was always a pool of blood, and at least one body, was cheap.[3]

If we refuse to be intimidated, we find that this sanguinary journal merits examination for several reasons: first, of course, because more than with other authors it is useful to know the nature of what Dickens read as a child – as George Gissing observed, "Those which he read first were practically the only books which influenced Dickens as an author";[4] secondly, because material in the *Terrific Register* turns up in his novels; and thirdly, because we get an unusual view of what the Victorians might read as children – the *Terrific Register* should be particularly interesting to those who hark back to the good old days before crime and horror comics, and violence on TV, when children read wholesome, improving literature. This periodical, in its gross vulgarity, exemplifies a type of popular press which, exploiting sensationalism for commercial profit, had a vast public throughout Dickens's career. As we shall see, he competed with this press on its own grounds.

The horrific, however, is more than a surface attraction in his novels: it constitutes, especially in his later works such as

Our Mutual Friend, the very fibre of the web he weaves. His obsession with ghastliness is so constant, indeed, and so profound, that one hestitates to accept Edmund Wilson's view that it resulted from one emotional experience, even so devastating a one as he suffered at Warren's blacking warehouse. If Dickens's stories about his childhood are to be believed, as Edgar Johnson assumes, then his education in ghastliness commenced much earlier, when his nurse, Mary Weller, cultivated his infant fancy with nightly stories "of bloody vengeance and supernatural hauntings".[5] She "had a fiendish enjoyment of my terrors," says Dickens, "and used to begin, I remember – as a sort of introductory overture – by clawing the air with both hands, and uttering a long low hollow groan" (*UT*, 153). Her histrionics met with an already appreciative, though terrified, audience and were an excellent introduction to the more extensive and peculiar survey of brutality and strange vice that he pursued in the pages of the *Terrific Register*.

The Terrific Register; or, Record of Crimes, Judgements, Providences, And Calamities [London, 1824–5] was as loathsome a periodical as one could wish. What it lacked in graphic illustration (a grisly plate did, indeed, grace each week's instalment) it made up for in detailed and bloodcurdling verbal description. The stories, varying in length from half a page to three pages, purport to be true and even to have a moral purpose, which is to show "God's revenge against murder". They do not, however, restrict themselves to the prosaic monotony of murder but range into torture, incest, the devouring of decayed human bodies, physical details of various horrible methods of execution, and a variety of other such pleasant and profitable subjects.

One sample, "The Monster of Scotland",[6] so comprehensively incorporates the attractions to be found in the *Terrific Register* that it typifies the magazine's general tone and content superbly: it should adequately account for the deep impression made on young Dickens's mind. The story tells how an "idle and vicious hedger" and an "idle and profligate" young woman, from their seaside cave, maraud the countryside with ghoulish economy and ghastly self-reliance, concealing their robberies by murdering the victims, and feeding themselves by devouring the bodies:

> they carried them to their den, quartered them, salted and pickled the members, and dried them for food. In this manner they lived, carrying on their depredations and murder, until they had eight sons and six daughters, eighteen grand-sons and fourteen grand-daughters, all the offspring of incest.

When prosperity brings a "superabundance of provisions", they cast dehydrated limbs into the sea, "to the great consternation and dismay of all the surrounding inhabitants". Eventually the inhabitants of a terrified and considerably depopulated countryside obtain the king's aid and, discovering the cave, are shocked to behold

> a sight unequalled in Scotland .... Legs, arms, thighs, hands and feet, of men, women, and children, were suspended in rows like dried beef. Some limbs and other members were soaked in pickle; while a great mass of money, both of gold and silver, watches, rings, pistols, cloths, both woollen and linen, with an inconceivable quantity of other articles, were thrown together in heaps, or suspended on the sides of the cave.

The conclusion of this story, by dwelling upon the brutality of the culprits' execution, the severity of which is improvised to match the enormity of their crimes, throws into the shade the comic-book convention of bringing the criminal to justice.

Along with such delights as these, which have no direct relation to Dickens's novels, one finds other profitable matter in the *Terrific Register*, including some passages that may, in their grisly fashion, have stuck in the author's memory. From the history of the French Revolution the magazine plundered many a bloodthirsty tale, among them the execution of Louis XVI, descriptions of the citizens' courts and the prisons, and the hanging of Foulon, which Dickens makes far more terrible by his depiction of mob passion and violence. The *Terrific Register*'s first story, accompanied by an illustration, describes how Damiens, who tried to assassinate Louis XV, was tortured to death: in *A Tale of Two Cities* Dickens tells the same story with the same details. Here is the periodical version:

1 "The Monster of Scotland", from the *Terrific Register*

> He was then laid on the scaffold, to which he was instantly tied, and soon afterwards fastened by two iron gyves, or fetters, one placed over his breast below his arms, and the other over his belly, just above his thighs. Then the executioner burnt his right hand (with which the villainous stab had been given) in flames of brimstone [the accompanying illustration shows the knife in Damiens' hand as in Dickens's account]; during which operation Damiens gave a very loud and continued cry, which was heard at a great distance from the place of execution, after which, Damiens raising his head as well as he could, looked for some time at the burnt hand, with great earnestness and composure. The executioner then proceeded to pinch him in the arms, thighs, and breast with redhot pinchers; and Damiens, at every pinch, shrieked in the same manner as he had done when his hand was scorched with the brimstone; and viewed and gazed at every one of the wounds, and ceased crying as soon as the executioner gave over the pinching. Then boiling oil, melted wax and rosin, and melted lead, were poured into all the wounds, and except those on the breast: which made him give as loud shrieks and cries, as he had done before when his hand was burnt with sulphur, and his breast, arms, and thighs, torn with hot pinchers.

The description proceeds to his dismemberment by four horses, the duration of his tortures to near nightfall, and the burning of his body. As Squeers said of the meals at Dotheboys Hall, "here's richness!" Dickens uses this story in *A Tale of Two Cities* to intensify one of the main threads of his narrative: the cruelty of Monseigneur and his class, and the vengeance which that cruelty inspires, a vengeance that will lead to the death sentence for Charles Darnay. When the father whose child Monseigneur ran down with his coach has killed Monseigneur and been captured, the townsmen speculate about his fate. The roadmender is talking to Defarge and the three Jaques:

> "they whisper at the fountain," resumed the countryman, "that he is brought down into our country to be executed on the spot, and that he will very certainly be executed. They even whisper that because he has slain Monseigneur, and

> because Monseigneur was the father of his tenants – serfs – what you will – he will be executed as a parricide. One old man says at the fountain, that his right hand, armed with the knife, will be burnt off before his face; that, into the wounds which will be made in his arms, his breast, and his legs, there will be poured boiling oil, melted lead, hot resin, wax, and sulphur; finally, that he will be torn limb from limb by four strong horses. That old man says, all this was actually done to a prisoner who made an attempt on the life of the late King, Louis Fifteen. But how do I know if he lies? I am not a scholar.
>
> "Listen once again then, Jaques!" said the man with the restless hand and the craving air. "The name of that prisoner was Damiens, and it was all done in open day, in the open streets of this city of Paris; and nothing was more noticed in the vast concourse that saw it done, than the crowd of ladies of quality and fashion, who were full of eager attention to the last – to the last, Jaques, prolonged until nightfall, when he had lost two legs and an arm, and still breathed!" (*TTC*, 162–3)

In retelling this story Dickens does two things: he associates it with the Evremonds, thus preparing for Darnay's death sentence; and, while losing none of the original brutality, he shifts his emphasis to the bloodthirsty ladies of fashion, aristocratic counterparts of Madame Defarge's furies. The one incident serves, therefore, in precipitating both the personal and the historical tragedies.

Another article in the *Terrific Register*, one which tells of alcoholics who died by spontaneous combustion, may well have been the original inspiration for a very famous incident in Dickens, the death of Krook in *Bleak House*. Krook, "short, cadaverous, and withered; with his head sunk sideways between his shoulders, and the breath issuing in visible smoke from his mouth, as if he were on fire within" (*BH*, 50), absorbs gin steadily, copiously, and at length, until at last he does catch fire within; and that is the end of him. To observe how Dickens fleshes out the perfunctory grisliness of the original story is quite amusing. Here is the *Terrific Register*'s version:

> At the distance of about four feet from the bed was a heap of

> ashes, in which could be distinguished the legs and arms untouched. ... The furniture and tapestry were covered with a moist kind of soot of the colour of ashes, which had penetrated into the drawers, and dirtied the linen. This soot having been conveyed to a neighbouring kitchen, adhered to the walls and utensils. A piece of bread in the cupboard was covered with it, and no dog would touch it. The infectious odour had been communicated to other apartments.[7]

The odour, the soot, and the animal's reaction – one after another Dickens elaborates them in a climactic pattern. The pervasive odour provokes a grim little comedy between Snagsby and Weevle as they meet outside Krook's rag and bottle shop:

> "Don't you observe," says Mr. Snagsby, pausing to sniff and taste the air a little; "don't you observe, Mr. Weevle, that you're – not to put too fine a point upon it – that you're rather greasy here, sir?"
>
> "Why, I have noticed myself that there is a queer kind of flavour in the place tonight," Mr. Weevle rejoins. "I suppose it's chops at the Sol's Arms."
>
> "Chops, do you think? Oh! – Chops, eh?" Mr. Snagsby sniffs and tastes again. "Well, sir, I suppose it is. But I should say their cook at the Sol wanted a little looking after. She has been burning 'em, sir! And I don't think;" Mr. Snagsby sniffs and tastes again, and then spits and wipes his mouth; "I don't think – not to put too fine a point upon it – that they were quite fresh, when they were shown the gridiron."
>
> "That's very likely. It's a tainting sort of weather."
>
> "It *is* a tainting sort of weather," says Mr. Snagsby, "and I find it sinking to the spirits."
>
> "By George! *I* find it gives me the horrors," returns Mr. Weevle. (*BH*, 445)

And now the soot: inside Krook's house young Mr Guppy no sooner brushes the foul soot from his sleeves than he gets his hand in a thick, yellow liquor:

> look here – and look here! When he brings the candle, here, from the corner of the window-sill, it slowly drips, and creeps away down the bricks; here, lies in a little thick nauseous pool. (*BH*, 454)

Animal terror is kept for the final shock:

> They go down, more dead than alive, and holding one another, push open the door of the back shop. The cat has retreated close to it, and stands snarling – not at them; at something on the ground, before the fire. . . . Here is a small burnt patch of flooring; here is the tinder from a little bundle of burnt paper, but not so light as usual, seeming to be steeped in something; and here is – is it the cinder of a small charred and broken log of wood sprinkled with white ashes, or is it coal? (*BH*, 455)

The passage on spontaneous combustion which I have quoted from the *Terrific Register* describes the death of the Countess Cesenate, the identical incident of which Dickens writes in the Preface to *Bleak House*: "The appearances beyond all rational doubt observed in that case, are the appearances observed in Mr. Krook's case." As further evidence of the possibility of spontaneous combustion, he mentions a story from Le Cat's memoirs, and that story also forms a part of the *Terrific Register*'s article. We may reasonably assume, therefore, that although Dickens, as we know from one of his letters, acquired information on this nasty process from his friend, Dr Elliotson,[8] and "took pains to investigate the subject" as he says, the subject itself may have occurred to him originally from his reading of the *Terrific Register*. That he was familiar with the idea of spontaneous combustion much earlier than the fifties is shown by a passage he deleted from "The Prisoners' Van" when revising it for *Sketches by Boz*. "The Prisoners' Van" appeared first in *Bell's Life in London*, November 29, 1835. He writes:

> We revel in a crowd of any kind – a street "row" is our delight – even a woman in a fit is by no means to be despised, especially in a fourth-rate street, where all the female inhabitants run out of their houses, and discharge

> large jugs of cold water over the patient, as if she were dying of spontaneous combustion, and wanted putting out.

A better known passage, from *A Christmas Carol* (1943), records Scrooge's alarm at finding himself the centre of a blaze of ruddy light as he awaits the coming of the second spirit: he "was sometimes apprehensive that he might be at that very moment an interesting case of spontaneous combustion, without having the consolation of knowing it" (*CB*, 38).

Hot and hasty exit that it is, spontaneous combustion seems at best an eccentric way to die. Did it not seem so to Dickens's readers? It certainly did to those whose objections he answers in his preface. But a little searching shows that he was not the only author of note to use the idea. A case occurs in Marryat's *Jacob Faithful* (Ch. 1); and in Gogol's *Dead Souls* (I, Ch. 3). Nastasya Petrovna's intemperate blacksmith catches fire and dies "wrapped in a blue flame", an event which prompts Chichikov to observe, "There is no denying the wisdom of God."[9] How might the ReverendMr Stiggins have capitalised on the idea when addressing the Dorking Branch of the United Grand Junction Ebeneezer Temperance Association! At any rate De Quincey tells how it frightened him:

> Nervous irritation forced me, at times, upon frightful excesses [of opium]; but terror from anomalous symptoms sooner or later forced me back. This terror was strengthened by the vague hypothesis current at that period about spontaneous combustion. Might I not myself take leave of the literary world in that fashion? According to the popular fancy, there were two modes of this spontaneity, and really very little to choose between them. Upon one variety of this explosion, a man blew up in the dark, without match or candle near him, leaving nothing behind him but some bones, of no use to anybody, and which were supposed to be *his* only because nobody else ever applied for them. It was fancied that some volcanic agency – an unknown deposition – accumulated from some vast redundancy of brandy, furnished the self-exploding principle. But this startled the faith of most people; and a more plausible scheme suggested itself, which depended upon

> the concurrence of a lucifer-match. . . . Opium, however, it will occur to the reader, is not alcohol. That is true. But it might, for anything that was known experimentally, be ultimately worse.[10]

When Dickens decided to incinerate Krook, not only was he exploiting a popular taste for grisliness, he was also playing upon the general uneasiness attaching to a popular superstition.[11]

One naturally asks at this point how direct the *Terrific Register*'s influence was upon Dickens. To consider only the texts discussed: between 1824, when he read the periodical, and 1852, when *Bleak House* appeared, twenty-eight years had passed; between 1824 and the appearance of *A Tale of Two Cities* thirty-five years had passed. This makes a direct influence unlikely. On the other hand, as Gissing and others have noted, Dickens's memory of his early reading was extremely retentive. And however little the *Terrific Register* merited such recollection, he did in fact remember the magazine well enough to write Forster about it "in his later years".[12] It is possible, therefore, that these memories directed his attention to the subjects, if not to the particular texts, we have just examined. However that may be, it is reasonable to assume that the periodical encouraged an already active interest in the gruesome, an interest that continued and is reflected throughout his works. The kinship between the sensationalism of the popular press and the ghastliness and brutality in his novels is quite clear.

For sheer ghoulishness the *Terrific Register* is, of course, in a class by itself, but macabre penny journals sold extensively throughout Dickens's lifetime and competed with his novels for popular favour. One of his chief rivals, as George Ford has noted, was G. W. M. Reynolds, "the Mickey Spillane of the Victorian Age",[13] whose work a Manchester news agent described thus:

> [It] draws scenes of profligacy as strongly as it is possible for any writer to do, and the feelings are excited to a very high pich by it, [but] it is not in reality an indecent publication, because I do not believe that any words appear that are vulgar . . . . A great many females buy the 'Court of Lon-

> don,' and young men; a sort of spreeing young men; young men who go to taverns, and put cigars in their mouths in a flourishing way.[14]

An article in *The Times* that Ford quotes commends Dickens for the contribution he made to popular education by writing stories sensational enough to capture Reynolds' public but with literary merit enough to please "the better class of reader".[15] The most interesting aspect of this rivalry, however, is the degree to which Dickens took over Reynolds's type of material. Jerry Cruncher, the "resurrection man" (body snatcher) in *A Tale of Two Cities*, has his counterpart in one of Reynolds' principal characters in the *Mysteries of London*, the Resurrection Man, whom with his friends, the Cracksman and the Buffer, Reynolds painstakingly describes pursuing his dismal vocation.[16] Reynolds's Resurrection Man also dabbles in piracy on the Thames in an atmosphere of squalid vice reminiscent of the river scenes in *Our Mutual Friend*, in the first chapter of which we find Hexam scavenging the river for drowned bodies to plunder.

The kinship between much of Dickens's material and that of periodicals like the *Terrific Register* and the *Mysteries of London* suggests one cause of his popularity; it also reflects a quality of his vision. As Carlyle wrote to Forster, beneath Dickens's "sparkling, clear, and sunny utterance" are "deeper than all, if one has the eye to see deep enough, dark fateful silent elements, tragical to look upon, and hiding amid dazzling radiances as of the sun, the elements of death itself".[17] Carlyle's insight is a sound one, backed up by modern biography and psychological criticism which tend to suggest that Dickens "was possibly not himself fully conscious of what he was putting into his books".[18] A careful examination shows, however, that Dickens frequently manipulates the morbid and terrible detail of his novels with such skilful and conscious artistry that it can hardly be regarded as merely a haphazard expression of gloomy depths in his unconscious. This detail has, in fact, both moral and aesthetic significance. Its moral significance is apparent not only in his penetrating studies of guilt and moral degeneration in individuals, but also in his symbolic representations of decay in the whole social body; its aesthetic significance is apparent not only in the exciting variety of tone and incident it affords, but also in its provision of symbols contributing to structural unity and ironic richness.

The grisly death of Krook in *Bleak House*, who is nicknamed the Lord Chancellor and whose shop is called the Court of Chancery, is an effective but relatively simple example of Dickens's craftsmanship in making gruesomeness further the artistic and ethical integration of his material. Krook's end and the manner of it are emblematic of the impending disintegration of both the actual court system and the corrupt society that tolerates such a system:[19] "The Lord Chancellor of that Court, true to his title in his last act, had died the death of all Lord Chancellors in all Courts, and of all authorities in all places under all names soever, where false pretences are made, and where injustice is done" (*BH*, 455–6). In *A Tale of Two Cities*, which is based throughout on the theme of resurrection, the technique is more sophisticated. Mr Lorry, on his way to France to bring back Manette (*TTC*, 12) dreams recurrently that he is "on his way to dig some one out of a grave" (Dickens had thought of calling the book *Buried Alive*);[20] Darnay, acquitted of the charge of spying, is, in Jerry Cruncher's view, "Recalled to Life" (*TTC*, 73), and is recalled a second time when Carton changes places with him in prison; the theme is reiterated in Carton's moral regeneration: he goes to the guillotine saying, "I am the Resurrection and the Life, saith the Lord" (*TTC*, 357). With these things in mind, we can hardly regard the ghoulish occupation of Jerry Cruncher, the resurrection man, as a fortuitous element in the novel. His body snatching is nothing less than a grimly comic parody of the main theme.

Macabre symbols, recurring at every level, suggesting basic similarities in diverse characters and events, evoking a sinister moral atmosphere, welding all into a consistent, integrated vision, dominate rather than merely contribute to the still more complex structure of *Our Mutual Friend*. The book opens sombrely on Gaffer Hexam scavenging a corpse from the murky water of the Thames. His abhorrent activity ranks as a unifying symbolic motif which is reiterated in a multitude of forms throughout the work: parasites, predators, and scavengers abound; it is a very world of vultures. Hexam himself "was a hook-nosed man, and with that and his bright eyes and his ruffled head, bore a certain likeness to a roused bird of prey" (*OMF*, 3). His chief competitor says admiringly, "I a'most think you're like the vulturs, pardner, and scent 'em out" (*OMF*, 4). Veneering and Fascination Fledgeby are political and usurious parasites respectively. The Lammles, each intent on devouring the other's fortune, catch themselves in their own marital trap, both fortuneless. Wegg, Boffin's literary man, is both a bird of prey fluttering over him (*OMF*, 188) and a shark in the Bower waters (*OMF*, 213). The Harmon fortune, which exerts an influence of some sort on most of the principal characters, is itself the profit made from scavenging London garbage. And just as Jerry Cruncher's avocation parodies the resurrection theme in *A Tale of Two Cities*, so Mr Venus's profession parodies the scavenging theme here: lovesick Mr Venus is a taxidermist and articulator of human bones. Hexam's fishing for bodies to plunder is our introduction to the total vision of society as a swamp, with "all manner of crawling, creeping, fluttering, and buzzing creatures, attracted by the gold dust of the Golden Dustman!" and with "Alligators of the Dismal Swamp . . . always lying by to drag the Golden Dustman under" (*OMF*, 213). The technique used here, a more polished version of that we have already seen in *Bleak House* and *A Tale of Two Cities*, is one which effectively integrates the mass of detail and oddity which is characteristic of Dickens's novels.

Let us, however, emerge from the menacing shades of nightmare into the radiance of Dickens's humour. For his savagery, like his melodrama, is chameleonic: tense and serious at one moment, hilariously absurd at another. In a delightful chapter called "Nurse's Stories" in the *Uncommercial Traveller*, Dickens records samples from the repertoire of Mary Weller, to whom, as we noticed earlier, he was "indebted for my first personal experience of a shudder and cold beads on the forehead" (*UT*, 151). Among her stories is a masterly "offshoot of the Bluebeard family", the story of "Captain Murderer", whose "mission was matrimony, and the gratification of a cannibal appetite with tender brides" (*UT*, 150). One of them takes drastic steps to curb this appetite:

> they went to church in a coach and twelve, and were married. And that day month, she rolled the pie-crust, and Captain Murderer cut her head off, and chopped her in

> pieces, and peppered her, and salted her, and put her in the pie, and sent it to the baker's, and ate it all, and picked the bones.
>
> But before she began to roll out the paste she had taken a deadly poison of a most awful character, distilled from toads' eyes and spiders' knees; and Captain Murderer had hardly picked her last bone, when he began to swell, and to turn blue, and to be all over spots, and to scream. And he went on swelling and turning bluer, and being more all over spots and screaming, until he reached from floor to ceiling, and from wall to wall; and then, at one o'clock in the morning, he blew up with a loud explosion. (*UT*, 152)

In a style whose cadence, emphasis, and syntax perfectly mirror the child's awestricken apprehension and Miss Weller's zest for gothic, Dickens here transforms the sort of raw material we found in "The Monster of Scotland" into a luxuriant, *ne plus ultra* vision of horror, colouring the whole with characteristic comic irony.

Dickens employs the same technique and style in the story of Chips in "Nurse's Stories": "There was once a shipwright, and he wrought in a Government Yard, and his name was Chips. And his father's name before him was Chips, and *his* father's name before *him* was Chips, and they were all Chipses" (*UT*, 153). Chips, like his wretched ancestors, makes a compact with the Devil and is thereafter plagued and brought to destruction by malevolent talking rats. Amidst the catalogues of grisly detail and accumulating co-ordinate clauses that express the child's concrete and simple experience, Dickens wryly interposes sophisticated adult reflections: "(I don't know why, but this fact of the Devil's expressing himself in rhyme was peculiarly trying to me)" (*UT* 154), and when Chips's marriage plans are broken up by the intrusions of rats, "(By this time a special cascade of rats was rolling down my back, and the whole of my small listening person was overrun with them. At intervals ever since, I have been morbidly afraid of my own pocket, lest my exploring hand should find a specimen or two of those vermin in it)" (*UT*, 156). Further enriching the blend of innocence and experience, Dickens adds to the horrible narrative and adult commiseration a tough of the nurse's dialect and the psychological bullying of the schoolroom: "The ship was bound for the Indies; and if you don't know where that is, you ought to it, and angels will never love you. (Here I felt myself an outcast from a future state.)" (*UT*, 156).

This stylistic double vision, interspersing the rhythms and syntax of childhood narrative with sophisticated reflections in adult vocabulary (peculiarly trying, morbidly afraid, a specimen or two, outcast from a future state), plain fear combining with retrospective sympathy, is the essence of Dickens's opening for *Great Expectations*, certainly one of the great opening chapters in literature. Young Pip, too, is "a small listening person":

> the small bundle of shivers growing afraid of it all and beginning to cry, was Pip.
>
> "Hold your noise!" cried a terrible voice, as a man started up from among the graves at the side of the church porch. "Keep still, you little devil, or I'll cut your throat!"
>
> A fearful man, all in coarse grey, with a great iron on his leg. A man with no hat, and with broken shoes, and with an old rag tied round his head. A man who had been soaked in water, and smothered in mud, and lamed by stones, and cut by flints, and stung by nettles, and torn by briars; who limped and shivered, and glared and growled; and whose teeth chattered in his head as he seized me by the chin.
>
> "O! Don't cut my throat, sir," I pleaded in terror. "Pray don't do it, sir." (*GE*, 1–2)

Mary Weller recommended "Captain Murderer" to young Dickens "as the only preservative known to science against 'The Black Cat' – a weird and glaring-eyed supernatural Tom, who was reputed to prowl about the world at night, sucking the breath of infancy, and who was endowed with a special thirst (as I was given to understand) for mine" (*UT*, 153). Surely this beast must be the familiar of Magwitch's dreadful young man:

> That young man has a secret way pecooliar to himself, of getting at a boy, and at his heart, and at his liver. It is in wain for a boy to attempt to hide himself from that young man. A boy may lock his door, may be warm in bed, may tuck

> himself up, may draw the clothes over his head, may think himself comfortable and safe, but that young man will softly creep and creep his way to him and tear him open. I am a keeping that young man from harming of you at the present moment, with great difficulty. I find it wery hard to hold that young man from off of your inside. (*GE*, 3–4)

"Captain Murderer", indeed, combines three of the primary elements of Dickens's work as a whole: horror, the child's viewpoint, and fairy tale. The horror in his novels may be presented either directly, as in Nancy's murder, or comically, as in "Captain Murderer", where it is filtered, as much of *Oliver Twist* and the descriptions of Squeers and Dotheboys Hall are filtered, through an ironic style which makes horror tolerable. However presented, it is more than an incidental attraction in his works: it is an integral part of his vision. Dickens amalgamates childhood and ghastliness convincingly: the child's viewpoint, introduced through a host of child heroes and heroines, besides implying an ideal set of moral values, is significantly related to sinister vision in that the child invests his surroundings with mysterious powers and moves at times in a world of menace and dread; but it is also a world in which the dreadful itself may become comic, as do Quilp and Squeers. There, Dickens's world takes on the colour of the unpredictable, often brutal, but never dull world of fairy tale.

NOTES

1. Charles Dickens, "Mr. Barlow", *The Uncommercial Traveller*, XXXIII, *New Oxford Illustrated Dickens* edition (Oxford, 1947–58) p. 338. Subsequent page references to Dickens's works are to this edition. For clarity, the following abbreviations are used: *BH* for *Bleak House, CB Christmas Books, GE Great Expectations, OMF Our Mutual Friend, TTC A Tale of Two Cities, UT The Uncommercial Traveller*.
2. See, however, on Dickens's interest in crime, prisons, and brutality, Edmund Wilson, "Dickens: The Two Scrooges", in *The Wound and the Bow* (Cambridge, Mass., 1941); Humphry House, "The Macabre Dickens", and "An Introduction to *Oliver Twist*", in *All in Due Time* (London, 1955); and George Ford, *Dickens and his Readers* (Princeton, 1955) pp. 249–57.
3. John Forster, *The Life of Charles Dickens*, ed. J. W. T. Ley, BK. I (London, 1928) iii, p. 43 n.

4. George Gissing, *Charles Dickens: A Critical Study* (London, 1898) p. 27.
5. See Edgar Johnson, *Charles Dickens: His Tragedy and Triumph* (New York, 1952) p. 12, based on *Uncommercial Traveller*, xv, "Nurse's Stories".
6. *Terrific Register*, I, 161–3.
7. *Terrific Register*, II, p. 340.
8. Walter Dexter (ed.), *The Letters of Charles Dickens*, Nonesuch edition, vol. II (London, 1938) pp. 446–7, Elliotson, 7/2/53. He thanks Elliotson for a lecture on spontaneous combustion and says he has already investigated some of the cases Elliotson describes.
9. Trans. George Reavey (London, 1957).
10. Thomas De Quincey, *Confessions of an English Opium Eater*, World's Classics edition (London, 1949) pp. 244–5.
11. Much more has been written on spontaneous combustion in Dickens since I wrote this essay. See, for example, *A Cumulative Analytical Index to The Dickensian*, 1905–1974 (Hassocks, 1976) under that heading.
12. Forster, *Life*, I, iii, p. 43 n.
13. George Ford, *Dickens and his Readers*, p. 79.
14. Richard D. Altick, *The English Common Reader* (Chicago, 1957) p. 352 n.
15. *The Times*, 17 October 1861, p. 6.
16. G. W. M. Reynolds, *Mysteries of London* vol. I (London, 1846–50) chs 44 and 108. For a further account of the "resurrection rig" see the anonymous *Real Life in London* vol. I (London, 1821) xi. Lively interest in the subject followed the famous Edinburgh trial of Burke and Hare (see *Annual Register*, 1828, and *All the Year Round*, 16 March 1867).
17. F. G. Kitton, *Dickensiana* (London, 1886) p. 408.
18. House, *All in Due Time*, p. 183.
19. See Johnson, *Charles Dickens: His Tragedy and Triumph*, p. 781.
20. Forster, *Life*, IX, ii, p. 729.

4 Dickens, the Dandy, and the Savage: A Victorian View of the Romantic

Born between the battles of Trafalgar and Waterloo, Charles Dickens grew up during the regency (1811–20) and reign (1820–30) of George IV ("the Magnificent", as a recent biographer labels him[1]), a period that saw the sartorial revolution of Beau Brummell and the flowering of English romanticism. Though Carlyle was to become, as much as anyone could, Dickens's mentor, Carlyle's gloomy but penetrating comments on "The Dandiacal Sect"[2] as a major phenomenon of the times had little effect on Dickens's dress and manner. In an age of masculine elegance, he amused his contemporaries with the extent to which he pursued "coats and trousers, a blaze of velvet and satin waistcoats, golden chains and tie-pins and rings".[3] Like Ainsworth, Disraeli, and Bulwer-Lytton, Dickens was, in Carlyle's definition, "a Clothes-wearing Man"[4] and "dressed à la D'Orsay rather than well".[5] That, however, did not keep him from making the Regency dandy or belle a recurrent symbol in his works of heartless superficiality and unearned social eminence. And where such a figure appears prominently, it usually gets its full significance by ironic allusion either to the romantic poem that seems to have made most impression on Dickens: Wordsworth's Immortality Ode: or more generally, to the Wordsworthian and romantic idea of primitivism and the healing, edifying sanctity of nature.

The dispartities and inconsistencies of moral attitude that Dickens exploits with ever-increasing subtlety are part of the Regency inheritance itself. If, on the one hand, Wordsworth reflects romantic love of pathos, simplicity, gentleness, and humble virtue; on the other, Pierce Egan (one of Dickens's chief predecessors in popular humour) reflects the brutal sense of humour, the superficial, callous world of the Regency buck. Egan's *Life in London* (London, 1821), at once a novel, a guide to the principal dives, ballrooms, and theatres of London, and a dictionary of Flash language, amply illustrates this stream of Regency coarseness. *Pickwick*, as George Ford observes,[6] owed its popularity to its timely blend of Regency high spirits and Victorian moral earnestness. The change of tone can be seen taking place in the novel itself ("It has been observed," Dickens wrote in his Preface, "that there is a decided change in his [Pickwick's] character, as these pages proceed, and that he becomes more good and more sensible"). The difference is between the Pickwick of the second chapter, who praises the "good humour" of a soldier: "The bar-maid had positively refused to draw him any more liquor; in return for which he had (merely in playfulness) drawn his bayonet, and wounded the girl in the shoulder. And yet this fine fellow was the very first to go down to the house next morning, and express his readiness to overlook the matter, and forget what had occurred" (14):[7] and the Pickwick who feels compassion for his old adversaries, Jingle and Job Trotter, when he encounters them in the Fleet.

The idea of nature in Dickens, whether solemn or satirical, offers great scope for investigation. He uses Wordsworth's sense of its sanctity seriously but also treats the idea as a cliché in the mouths of characters like Mrs Skewton (*Dombey and Son*) and Skimpole (*Bleak House*). He uses nature ironically to set up a strain of pastoral satire that emphasises the civilised corruption of society in *Bleak House*, but in *Little Dorrit* an emergent Victorian realism makes him approve of sentiment for a thoroughly industrial object, an iron bridge. It is no longer news that Dickens uses the imagery of wasteland and garden, city and country, symbolically, again and again (as, for example, in *Our Mutual Friend*, where the squalor of the Thames, the giant dustheaps, the "Dismal Swamp" of society, and "Harmon's Jail", the house Boffin inherits, form a wasteland context for "Boffin's Bower", as Mrs Boffin renames the house), but the ingenuity with which Dickens rings changes on these symbols merits more study than it has received. The whole question of what is "natural" or "unnatural" assumes in a work like *Little Dorrit* the kind of moral depth it has in *King*

Lear (which is not a bad analogue for *Little Dorrit* in other ways as well).

The uncomplicated Wordsworthian view of nature as restorer, suggesting a spiritual pre-existence, occurs in *Oliver Twist* when Oliver, wounded in Sikes's attempt to rob the Maylies, is recuperating in their pastoral cottage. Rose Maylie's tears falling on the sleeping Oliver seem to stir "some pleasant dream of a love and affection he had never known. Thus, a strain of gentle music, or the rippling of water in a silent place, or the odour of a flower, or the mention of a familiar word, will sometimes call up sudden dim remembrances of scenes that never were, in this life . . ." (216). And two chapters later, as Oliver's recovery continues, Dickens reflects on Nature's power to move "pain-worn dwellers . . . in crowded pent-up streets . . . to whom custom has indeed been second nature. . . . The memories which peaceful country scenes call up, are not of this world . . . there lingers, in the reflective mind, a vague and half-formed consciousness of having held such feelings long before, in some remote and distant time, which calls up solemn thoughts of distant time to come, and bends down pride and worldliness beneath it" (237). The treatment here is simple and direct. As Arnold Kettle[8] observes, however, much of the book's power derives from its alternating contrast of two worlds: the workhouse and underworld alternating with Brownlow's and the Maylies', the confined darkness of Fagin's den with the airy brightness of the Maylies' rural garden. Since the "shades of the prison house" are doubly real in Oliver's London, the pastoral contrast, though conventional, is effective.

Dombey and Son introduces an intertwining of nature and vigour with artificiality and death that is to be a recurrent motif in Dickens's novels. The Regency theme, with Mrs Skewton as its focus, is an important element in the pattern. A former Regency belle, who in her youth was painted in a languishing pose as Cleopatra, Mrs Skewton retains the pose, the dress, and the Regency manner well into the 1840s. She comprises a grisly mixture of selfish decrepitude and affected romantic jargon:

> "Mr. Dombey is devoted to Nature, I trust?" said Mrs. Skewton, settling her diamond brooch . . . .

> "My friend Dombey, Ma'am," returned the Major, "may be devoted to her in secret, but a man who is paramount in the greatest city in the universe–" (288)

Major Bagstock's reply connects Mrs Skewton with the central irony of the book: Dombey's wasteland world of pride and business eradicating the "heart" that Mrs Skewton pretends so much to want, the "frankness, confidence, less conventionality and freer play of soul" (289). Dombey's dynastic commercialism is as deathly as the ghastly skull and skeleton that Dickens makes us see beneath Mrs Skewton's ornaments. His buying of his wife, Edith; Mrs Skewton's, her mother's, selling her; Edith's consenting to the sale, are all mockeries of Mrs Skewton's Arcadian sentiments. With a mincing sigh, she assures Dombey that "seclusion and contemplation are my what-his-name. . . . Nature intended me for an Arcadian. I am thrown away in society. Cows are my passion. What I have ever sighed for, has been to retreat to a Swiss farm, and live entirely surrounded by cows–and china. . . . In short . . . I want Nature everywhere. It would be so extremely charming", (288–9). Carrying her Regency-coloured senility to greater heights of inconsequence, Dickens resorts again to Wordsworth, as Mrs Skewton reflects on music: " 'Yes. It's very nice,' said Cleopatra, looking at her cards. 'So much heart in it–undeveloped recollections of a previous state of existence–and all that–which is so truly charming. Do you know,' simpered Cleopatra, . . . 'that if anything could tempt me to put a period to my life, it would be curiosity to find out what it's all about, and what it means' " (296). For all her chatter about nature and simplicity, Mrs Skewton is an avaricious old skeleton, decaying bit by bit as the work proceeds. The contrasting of commercial evil with pastoral innocence, a conventional enough device in romantic satire, has been given an ironic twist by having Mrs Skewton affect the reverence for nature Dickens took quite seriously in *Oliver Twist*. In a less sentimental mood than when he was writing *Oliver*, Dickens sees that the Wordsworthian attitude, not false in itself, has become fashionable humbug, like nostalgia for the Middle Ages– "So picturesque!" says Mrs Skewton (384). Her affectation has more point in relation to the whole texture of sea and nature imagery forming a symbolic refrain throughout the book.[9] Using what is to become a customary device of counterpointing a solemn theme with its parody,[10] Dickens parallels young Paul's pathetic death with Mrs Skewton's: "the figure which in grim reality is substituted for the patient boy's on the same theatre, once more to connect it–but how differently!–with decay and death, is stretched there, wakeful and complaining. Ugly and haggard it lies upon its bed of unrest" (583). Then, "with her girlish laugh, . . . the skeleton of the Cleopatra manner rises in her bed" (585), and that is the end of her. As the chapter ends, Edith, standing alone by the sea, "and listening to its waves, has dank weed cast up at her feet, to strew her path in life withal" (587).

The Skewton figure clearly retains its usefulness for Dickens. Just as Mrs Clennam of *Little Dorrit* metamorphoses into Miss Havisham in *Great Expectations*, and Micawber into William Dorrit, so the elements of Mrs Skewton can be seen, seventeen years later, in the briefer portrait of Lady Tippins of *Our Mutual Friend*: "Lady Tippins (relict of the late Sir Thomas Tippins, knighted in mistake for somebody else by His Majesty King George the Third, who, while performing the ceremony, was graciously pleased to observe, 'What, what, what? Who, who, who? Why, why, why?') (118). Though she lacks Mrs Skewton's Wordsworthian echoes, she indulges in poetic fantasies about herself as a nymph pursued by pastoral swains, and, "with an immense obtuse drab oblong face, like a face in a tablespoon, and a dyed Long Walk up the top of her head, as a convenient public approach to the bunch of false hair behind" (10), is forever counting up her "lovers". This "grisly little fiction . . . is enhanced by a certain yellow play in Lady Tippins' throat, like the legs of scratching poultry" (12). Like Carlyle's Dandy, she exists by reason of her clothes: "Whereabout in the bonnet and drapery announced by her name, any fragment of the real woman may be concealed, is perhaps known to her maid; but you may easily buy all you see of her, in Bond Street: or you may scalp her, and peel her, and make two Lady Tippinses out of her, and yet not penetrate to the genuine article. . . . But perennial youth is in her artificial flowers, and her list of lovers is full" (118–19). Much more than Mrs Skewton, who, with her noble Cousin Feenix, considers herself a social success, Lady Tippins is a "voice of Society," but like Mrs Skewton she symbolises its sham. The technique is similar to that in Thackeray's famous sketch of George the Fourth: "I look through all his life, and recognize but a bow and a grin. I try and take him to pieces, and find silk stockings, padding, stays, a coat with frogs and a fur collar, a star and blue ribbon, a pocket handkerchief prodigiously scented, one of Truefitt's best nutty brown wigs reeking with oil, a set of teeth and a huge black stock, under-waistcoats, more under-waistcoats, and then nothing".[11] The combined attraction and repulsion Victorians felt for the Regency dandy

2 "I suppose there were more pictures taken of that personage than of any other human being who ever was born": Thackeray's portraits of George IV, from *The Four Georges*

(see Thackeray's paper on *Life in London* in "De Juventute", *Roundabout Papers*) is perhaps itself a sign, like the new humour of *Pickwick*, of a characteristic Victorian sensibility.

Dickens's fullest exploration of the dandy in connection with the idea of nature comes in *Bleak House* and centres in two characters, Turveydrop and Skimpole. Turveydrop, a completely selfish old parasite, demands and gets admiration because his feelings are "extremely sensitive" and because he is a Master of Deportment. "He had a cane, he had an eye-glass, he had a snuff-box, he had rings, he had wristbands, he had everything but any touch of nature; he was not like youth, he was not like age, he was not like anything in the world but a model of Deportment" (190). He believes "we have made an awfully degenerating business of it since the days of His Royal Highness the Prince Regent" (327); he sits "in imitation of the print of his illustrious model on the sofa"[12] (193); he gives his son the name Prince; and he considers himself to be a gentleman and an aristocrat. His claim to aristocratic status is based on the Prince Regent's inquiring "on my removing my hat as he drove out of the Pavilion at Brighton (that fine building), 'Who is he? Who the Devil is he? Why don't I know him? Why hasn't he thirty thousand a year?' " (193). Having married a dancing-mistress who worked herself to death for him, he now runs a dancing academy, or more precisely his son runs it for him, working twelve hours a day. Turveydrop's posturing carries such effect that those he victimises revere him. His son can only announce his engagement by assuring Turveydrop of unceasing comfort: "The power of his Deportment was such, that they really were as much overcome with thankfulness as if, instead of quartering himself upon them for the rest of his life, he were making some munificent sacrifice in their favour" (329). At the end of the book, Turveydrop, though apoplectic, is still exhibiting his Deportment about town and still believed in.

Outrageous as he is, Turveydrop is a relatively simple figure, one of a series of variations on a theme, the central theme of avaricious exploitation and blind neglect. Mrs Jellyby, in her philanthropic zeal for the natives of Borrioboola-Gha, while her children go uncared for; Chadband, the unctuous preacher whose real concern is for "corn, and wine, and oil–or, what is much the same thing, money" (733), to the point of blackmail; the various lawyers parasitically living on their clients; and the whole Chancery case of Jarndyce and Jarndyce, all develop the same theme. But whereas Turveydrop is a simple caricature, his selfish nature underlined by Dickens's comments, Harold Skimpole is a subtler creation, presented more objectively and with a philosophy to support his actions. In Skimpole's mouth the romantic appeal to nature has a corrupt but persuasive plausibility (at least plausible enough to take in Stephen Leacock, the Canadian humourist, who thought Dickens intended Skimpole to be lovable and failed in his aim[13]). While Turveydrop is a social phenomenon in the form of an art work, Skimpole is an aesthetician whose views have social implications. At first he seems in the romantic tradition, appealing to pastoral innocence and simplicity against the surrounding worldliness of society.[14] "Well," he tells Jarndyce, "you know the world (which in your sense is the universe), and I know nothing of it, so you shall have your way. But if I had mine, . . . there should be no brambles of sordid realities in such a path as that [Ada's]. It should be strewn with roses; it should lie through bowers, where there was no spring, autumn, nor winter, but perpetual summer. Age or change should never wither it. The base word money should never be breathed near it" (72). As "a confiding child" (70), and "very fond of nature, very fond of art" (69), Skimpole uses his professed ignorance of the world to disguise his own avarice and ingratitude. Taking an aesthetic view of morality, he argues that evil, suffering, and muddle enhance the beauty of the world by contrast. Inspired by a blue sky and the fragrance of hay, he deplores the vulgarity of a baker asking for payment: "It showed a want of poetry in the man" (599). His role-playing, like Mrs Jellyby's, is partly revealed by his home environment. Esther and Jarndyce discover him about mid-day "drinking some fragrant coffee from an old china cup . . . and looking at a collection of sunflowers in the balcony" (594) but notice that the windows are dirty and patched with paper and that his daughters have to dress "in a most untidy and negligent way" (598).

Skimpole is more, however, than a satire on the affectation of romantic sensibility or even on aestheticism as a cover for social irresponsibility. In the Preface to *Bleak House*, Dickens concluded: "I have purposely dwelt upon the romantic side of familiar things." The same purpose is a principal burden of the manifesto beginning *Household Words*, and *Hard Times* is an extended attack on social and educational systems that remove wonder, beauty, and imagination from ordinary life. In short, Dickens, like Carlyle in *Sartor Resartus*, is asserting his own vein of romanticism, the need in an age of science and industrialism to see colour and significance in everyday life. He is addressing himself to an artistic problem of special importance not only to himself but to Victorians generally: the problem of how to derive from the drab, utilitarian environment of the industrial city, images and symbols rich enough to replace the traditional images derived from religion and nature. As Humphry House has observed, the Pre-Raphaelite movement furnishes an excellent example of how difficult a problem it was: "There seemed to be an irreparable cleavage between the facts of modern society and the depths it was recognized poetry ought to touch. . . . The medieval world attracted them not only from a mere love of archaic patterns and forms or by nostalgia for more colourful ways of life (though these things entered into it) but because medieval art did not betray any such cleavage between daily visible fact and accepted truth and values."[15] Ruskin, using *Bleak House* and *Père Goriot* as examples, expresses the problem vividly in *Fiction Fair and Foul*. Contrasting the pastoral beauty of Croxted Lane in his youth with its present industrial foulness, he finds a peculiar difficulty of expression; though beauty is difficult to describe, he says, "no existing terms of language known to me are enough to describe the forms of filth, and modes of ruin, that varied themselves along the course of Croxted Lane."[16] He then proceeds, as his best modern critic observes, to define "a new genre, the novel of the city".[17] Appalled by the squalor of London, he writes: "It might have been thought by any other than a sternly tentative philosopher, that the denial of their natural food to human feelings would have provoked a reactionary desire for it; and that the dreariness of the street would have been gilded by dreams of pastoral felicity."[18] Perceptive as Ruskin's criticism is, he is limited by his own Wordsworthian preconceptions and his horror of the sheer ugliness of the populous industrial city.

He is reactionary. Dickens, in Skimpole, shows how sorry a thing romantic pastoralism can be, that however ugly and monstrous the city may be, romantic aestheticism can clothe a ruthlessness as contemptible as that which creates Tom-all-Alone's. For the most part, Dickens's traditional use of pastoral satire is intended to make much the same point as Ruskin's, but to do it ironically–the description of Lincoln's Inn Fields is characteristic: "In these fields of Mr. Tulkinghorn's inhabiting, . . . the shepherds play on Chancery pipes that have no stop, and keep their sheep in the fold by hook and crook, until they have shorn them exceeding close" (663). In his treatment of the Rouncewells, however, especially in the chapter, "Steel and Iron", near the end of the book, he shows a sympathy with the industrialist who creates the "coalpits and ashes, high chimneys and red bricks, blighted verdure, scorching fires, and a heavy never-lightening cloud of smoke" (845) that Ruskin could hardly approve. While he agrees with Ruskin about the social morbidity of the new city (Ruskin's criticism unfortunately attacks Dickens for not doing what he very thoroughly did), Dickens's vision is enriched by a Baudelairian sense of the city's poetry, however sombre. It is part of his feeling for "the romantic side of familiar things". Skimpole's abhorrence for the "brambles of sordid realities" and rejection of the vulgar in favour of pastoral affectation is in its way a topsy-turvy version of the Smallweeds' rejection of all amusements, story-books, fairy tales, fictions, and levities whatever in favour of the sordid god of Compound Interest; both involve a narrowing of reality and distortion of humanity.

In *Little Dorrit*, set in the 1820s, Dickens's poetry of the city and modulation of the ideas of nature and reality achieve an even greater subtlety. Once again he gives us a caricature for a guide. Mrs Merdle, "the Bosom", is a sartorial (or anatomical) abstraction reminiscent of Thackersay's George IV: "Mrs. Merdle's first husband had been a colonel, under whose auspices the bosom had entered into competition with the snows of North America, and had come off at little disadvantage in point of whiteness, and at none in point of coldness" (247). Mr Merdle, the name of the age, financier, banker, speculator, politician (and secretly, fraud and swindler) "had provided that extensive bosom . . . with a nest of crimson and gold some fifteen years before. It was not a bosom to repose upon, but it was a capital bosom to hang jewels upon. Mr Merdle wanted something to hang jewels upon, and he bought it for the purpose"(247). Like Lady Tippins, Mrs Merdle combines an affectation of pastoral primitivism with the arduous role of speaking for Society (the emptiness of her pose underscored by her attendant and unruly parrot):

> "I wish Society was not so arbitrary, I wish it was not so exacting – Bird, be quiet!"
> The parrot had given a most piercing shriek, as if its name were Society, and it had asserted its right to its exactions.
> "But," resumed Mrs Merdle, "we must take it as we find it. We know it is hollow and conventional and worldly and very shocking, but unless we are Savages in the Tropical seas (I should have been charmed to be one myself – most delightful life and perfect climate I am told), we must consult it." (239)

The superior tone here is for Fanny Dorrit's benefit, an actress with designs on Mrs Merdle's son, Edmund Sparkler: "He is very impressible", Mrs Merdle continues. "Perhaps he inherits that misfortune. I am very impressible myself, by nature. The weakest of creatures. My feelings are touched in a moment" (239). Describing herself as "a child of nature if I could but show it" (at which the parrot breaks into a violent fit of laughter), she points out the impossibility of Society's recognising any alliance between Edmund and Fanny, pays her off, and dismisses her with condescending ease:

> "If we could only come to a Millenium, or something of that sort, I for one might have the pleasure of knowing a number of charming and talented persons from whom I am at present excluded. A more primitive state of society would be delicious to me. There used to be a poem when I learnt lessons, something about Lo the poor Indian whose something mind! If a few thousand persons moving in Society could only go and be Indians, I would put my name down directly; but as, moving in Society, we can't be Indians, unfortunately – Good morning!"(242–3).

The contest only appears unequal; Fanny in disowning Edmund has simply manoeuvred adroitly; both women see Society as an arena for ruthless exploitation of advantage, personal or commercial. The point is elaborated later, when Mrs Gowan, the minor aristocrat from Hampton Court Palace, consults Mrs Merdle, lower in the pecking order of rank but unassailable in the order of wealth, on the opinion of Society concerning young Gowan's marriage to a middle-class girl with money: "Mrs Merdle, who really knew her friend Society pretty well, . . . and what Society's matrimonial market was, . . . and what bargaining and huckstering went on"(393), knows it is a good catch, but commiserates with Mrs Gowan according to the prescribed ritual: "And Mrs. Gowan, who of course saw through her own threadbare blind perfectly, and who knew that Mrs Merdle saw through it perfectly, and who knew that Society would see through it perfectly, came out of this form, notwithstanding, as she had gone into it, with immense complacency and gravity" (394). Society is, in fact, as it is to be in *Our Mutual Friend* also, a refined abstraction for displacing the burden of one's own rapacity: "Society has made up its mind on the subject, and there is nothing more to be said. If we were in a more primitive state, if we lived under roofs of leaves, and kept cows and sheep and creatures, instead of banker's accounts (which would be delicious; my dear, I am pastoral to a degree, by nature), well and good. But we don't live under leaves, and keep cows and sheep and creatures" (391). For all her realism and camouflage, Mrs Merdle is no match for Fanny, who bags the somewhat less than brilliant Edmund Sparkler in the end.

The affectation of pastoral simplicity here is much the same as in *Dombey and Son* and *Bleak House*, but its place in the social satire is more complex because of the degree to which Dickens has carried the idea of social abstraction in *Little Dorrit*, the original title of which was "Nobody's Fault", a title intended to emphasise the vacuity and shiftiness of social roles, and remniscent of Roebuck's remark on his inquiry into the Crimean muddle, "I felt corruption round about me, but I could not lay my hand upon it."[19] Merdle is a great hoax; the Circumlocution Office runs on the principle of how not to do it; Mrs Clennam affects piety to seek revenge; Dorrit affects gentility and the grand manner on the basis of an imagined dignity attaching to him as the prisoner who has spent the longest time in the Marshalsea, which becomes a "College". The containing fictions of society proliferate through an endless series of prison images echoing and re-echoing through the novel. Façades, or as Carlyle puts it, clothes, are everywhere, but underneath is nothing, nobody. The continuation and elaboration of satirical technique from *Bleak House* is further evident in the sheer variety of pastoral suggestions. Though Mrs Merdle, the Bosom, the voice of Society, is a satirical butt, Flora Finching is a delightful and essentially warm-hearted bundle of romantic affectations. She plays the role of secret and oppressed lover, "as if there were a secret understanding between herself and Clennam of the most thrilling nature" (155). But her name is significant: "Flora, whom he had left a lily, had become a peony" (150): it relates here to a whole pattern of floral imagery in the tradition of romance.[20] Clennam's love for Pet Meagles, along with his feelings of youth, is resigned as he drops her flowers in the river, and he is recalled from his later despair and illness in the Marshalsea by the fragrance of Little Dorrit's flowers, which remind him of a garden. Another variation, more direct, on pastoral imagery is associated with John Chivery, the turnkey's son who dreams of turning Little Dorrit's prison room into "a very arbour" and gliding with her "down the stream of time, in pastoral domestic happiness" (212). When Amy refuses him, in spite of his attempts at splendour of costume, he relieves himself of his hopeless love by conceiving a series of hypothetical epitaphs and retreating to a very little dull back-yard, where a wash of sheets and table-cloths hides him from the neighbours. "He'll sit there hours. Hours he will. Says he feels as if it was groves!" (257). Like Flora, young John is a sympathetically drawn character, honest and kindhearted. Comic though he is, he attains a degree of pathos and nobility by his continued devotion to Amy in spite of her father's condescension and abuse and in spite of his awareness that she loves Clennam. Pancks, in his investigations concerning Dorrit's fortune, enlists John's willing aid: "In this endeavour he so prospered as to lure that pining shepherd forth from the groves, and tempt him to undertake mysterious missions" (297). John makes such an impression on Rugg, Pancks's lawyer friend, that he declares, "You are a young man that I should like to put in the witness-box, to humanize the minds of the legal profession" (279). While Mrs Merdle's primitivism disguises a ruthless coldness, and Flora's romantic nostalgia and allusion to *Paul and Virginia* are ludicrous, John Chivery's pastoral colouring moves closer to an accommodation with reality. Damp sheets serve him well enough as groves, and he shows a delicacy of emotion that makes us admire him and that shows up Dorrit's empty pretentiousness.

Still another pastoral note is struck with the Plornishes. In the slum of Bleeding Heart Yard, Mrs Plornish poetically heightens her shop parlour by painting on the wall a flowery, thatched cottage in a rural setting and with a brass nameplate lettered T. and M. Plornish.[21] Here is an image with which a Marxist or existentialist critic could have a field-day:

> No Poetry and no Art ever charmed the imagination more than the union of the two in this counterfeit cottage charmed Mrs Plornish. It was nothing to her that Plornish had a habit of leaning against it as he smoked his pipe after work, when his hat blotted out the pigeon-house and all the pigeons, when his back swallowed up the dwelling, when his hands in his pockets uprooted the blooming garden and laid waste the adjacent country. To Mrs Plornish, it was still a most beautiful cottage, a most wonderful deception; and it made no difference that Mr Plornish's eye was some inches above the level of the gable-bedroom in the thatch. To come out into the shop after it was shut, and hear her father sing a song inside this cottage, was a perfect Pastoral to Mrs Plornish, the Golden Age revived. (574)

For Mrs Plornish, fancy is part of reality. It could be argued that the Plornishes live a life of alienation, but that would be to accept the verdict of the official in *Hard Times*, who admonishes McChoakumchild's students: " 'You don't walk upon flowers in fact; you cannot be allowed to walk upon flowers in carpets. You don't find that foreign birds and butterflies come and perch upon your crockery; you cannot be permitted to paint foreign birds and butterflies on your crockery . . . . This is fact. This is taste' " (7). Mrs Merdle, Mrs Clennam and Dorrit erect façades to replace or disguise reality; Mrs Plornish admires the "wonderful deception", but she knows it is deception and values it innocently for its associations. If she were translated to a real thatched cottage, she would no doubt be perfectly at home; imagine Mrs Merdle in the tropical seas, tending cows and sheep and creatures. A dinner at Merdle's is the emotional opposite to an evening at the Plornishes, to which Old Nandy, voluntarily living in a workhouse to prevent burdening his son-in-law, comes from his "grove of little old men" to sing. "He gave us Strephon last night, to that degree that Plornish gets up and makes him this speech across the table. 'John Edward Nandy,' says Plornish to father, 'I never heard you come the warbles as I have heard you come the warbles this night' " (575).

Little Dorrit herself is the one character in the novel who stays content with reality. She brings flowers to Clennam in the prison, but the object most often associated with her, apart from the prison itself, is the Iron Bridge (old Southwark Bridge, renowned for its massive spans of iron). Perhaps put off by the name Little Dorrit, critics tend to react towards her as students react to Arnold's "Sweetness and Light", dreadfully suspicious of something cloying. They see her as simple, sentimental, and exemplary. As one critic puts it, with a flourish of italics: "she is *too good*".[22] Perhaps Amy fails to attract closer attention from critics for the same reason she gets little attention from her family, because she does not resort to romantic hypocrisy, like Mrs Merdle, or even, more pleasantly, to the extravagant popular fancy of Chivery or Mrs Plornish – in short, because as is evident in two outstanding scenes with Dorrit and Fanny, she is a silent reproach to role playing. This, however, does not make her simple; she is perhaps the most Jamesian of Dickens's portraits; her reactions are often subdued or repressed, but the signs are there for a reader willing to see them. What with her accuracy of perception and all the instructive models for her to observe about her, she needs no such personal chastening as Pip in *Great Expectations* needs to bring him back to reality, but the endings of both books are muted, tuned to the acceptance of life as it is, which does not preclude being useful. Clennam and Amy go down the church steps "into a modest life of usefulness and happiness .... They went quietly down into the roaring streets, inseparable and blessed; and as they passed along in sunshine and shade, the noisy and the eager, and the arrogant and the froward and the vain, fretted, and chafed, and made their usual uproar."

Dickens's recurrent use of the dandy and romantic primitivism shows no such erudition as Carlyle commands, though his instinct for the significance of the dandy helps him exploit artistically some of Carlyle's conclusions. The pattern is a small one in Dickens's works, but when placed in the context of his Benthamite hopes for progress and distrust of nostalgia, it has its wider bearings. He dislikes that "conceited, tiresome, bloodthirsty, monotonous humbug",[23] the Noble Savage, for political and social as well as literary reasons. Most interesting in his ironic use of these pastoral and sartorial poses, however, is his exploitation of the texture of everyday reality in the new industrial city. In some ways he outdoes Ruskin, and that is no mean achievement.

NOTES

1. Joanna Richardson, *George the Magnificent* (New York, 1966).
2. Thomas Carlyle, "The Dandiacal Body", in *Sartor Resartus* (1833–4).
3. Edgar Johnson, *Charles Dickens: His Tragedy and Triumph*, vol. I (New York, 1952) p. 360.
4. Carlyle, *Sartor Resartus*, ed. Charles Frederick Harrold (New York, 1937) p. 272.
5. D. A. Wilson, *Thomas Carlyle*, vol. III (London, 1923–34), p. 81 (on seeing Dickens at a dinner in 1840).
6. George Ford, *Dickens and his Readers* (Princeton, 1955) p. 12.
7. Page references are to the *New Oxford Illustrated Dickens* edition (Oxford, 1947–58).
8. Arnold Kettle, *Introduction to the English Novel*, vol. I (London, 1953) p. 142.
9. Kathleen Tillotson, *Novels of the Eighteen-Forties* (London, 1954) p. 189.
10. Jerry Cruncher, the "resurrection man" (grave-robber) of *A Tale of Two Cities*, adds a comic-macabre dimension to the book's central theme of resurrection, just as lovelorn Mr Venus, the articulator of skeletons gathered in bits from hospitals, enlivens the sombre theme of scavenging in *Our Mutual Friend*.
11. William Thackeray, *The Four Georges*, in George Saintsbury (ed.), *The Oxford Thackeray* vol. XIII (London, 1908) p. 783.
12. For the connection between Turveydrop and illustrations of his model see Michael Steig's astute findings in *Dickens and Phiz* (London, 1978) pp. 139–40.
13. Stephen Leacock, *Charles Dickens: His Life and Work* (New York, 1934) p. 164.
14. I am indebted here to an excellent study of the pastoral imagery in *Bleak*

House by Louis Crompton: "Satire and Symbolism in *Bleak House*", *Nineteenth-Century Fiction*, 12 (1958) 284–303.
15. Humphry House, "Pre-Raphaelite Poetry", in *All in Due Time* (London, 1955) p. 155.
16. John Ruskin, *The Genius of John Ruskin*, ed. John D. Rosenberg (New York, 1963) p. 436.
17. *Ibid.*, p. 320.
18. *Ibid.*, p. 440.
19. Asa Briggs, *Victorian People* (London, 1965) p. 84.
20. I have touched on this subject in "*Little Dorrit*: Experience and Design", *Queen's Quarterly*, 67 (1961) 530–8.
21. This decoration seems another reference to Leigh Hunt in Dickens. Imprisoned in Horsemonger Lane gaol for libel against the Prince Regent, Hunt decorated his prison room pastorally: "I papered the walls with a trellis of roses; I had the ceiling coloured with clouds and sky . . ." (*Autobiography*, [London, 1850] ch. 14).
22. Taylor Stoehr, *Dickens, The Dreamer's Stance* (Ithaca, 1965) p. 182.
23. Charles Dickens, "The Noble Savage", in *The Uncommercial Traveller and Reprinted Pieces*, p. 467.

5 *Great Expectations*

"For a mind diseased with vain longings after unattainable advantages," says Doctor Johnson, "no medicine can be prescribed but an impartial enquiry into the real worth of that which is so ardently desired."[1] *Great Expectations* is the narrative of such a search, taking a single consciousness through a series of personal relationships, each of which contributes to its education. Although the book was welcomed as a belated resurgence of Dickens's comic spirit, the simple and cheerful confidence of his earliest novels had long vanished, and he had turned to a series of explorations of twisted and thwarted love in a world figured forth as increasingly labyrinthine: in *Bleak House* a world wrapped in fog and cotton wool, in *Hard Times* a world of muddle mocked by the cold serenity of the stars, in *Little Dorrit* a world of prison within prison, a world of inversion and negation, of frustrated dreams and chastened hope. The comic flashes are surrounded by darkness, despair is relieved by rare and hard-learned charity. In *Great Expectations* these themes and images recur, but with an economy, forthrightness, and ironic humour that make it Dickens's masterpiece. Its irony keeps returning Pip from a world of vain longings to a world of hard experience, contrasting expectation against realisation, forcing the "impartial enquiry into the real worth of that which is so ardently desired".

An orphan, Pip acquires three mothers and three fathers who serve to form his personality and standards of judgment. As an orphan, he is both the typical Dickensian hero and a characteristic figure of modern literature, the alienated man, a product of his civilisation but somehow detached from it, and lonely, wishing to belong, but unable to feel at one with it. On his own confession, Pip is not only an orphan but an injured orphan:

My sister's bringing up had made me sensitive. In the

> little world in which children have their existence, whosoever brings them up, there is nothing so finely perceived and so finely felt as injustice. It may be only small injustice that the child can be exposed to; but the child is small, and its world is small, and its rocking-horse stands as many hands high, according to scale, as a big-boned Irish hunter. Within myself, I had sustained, from my babyhood, a perpetual conflict with injustice. I had known, from the time when I could speak, that my sister, in her capricious and violent coercion, was unjust to me. (57)[2]

From this core of Pip's experience, radiating into his personal and social life, stems Pip's major difficulty in assessing things and people for what they really are: he can find no accord between love and justice. He feels himself more sinned against than sinning, craves love but is too self-centred in his injured sensitivity to see where it really is. Dickens keeps the theme of love versus justice before us, and elaborates its complexity, both in the novel's pervasive atmosphere of crime and in the variations he plays on the child's first figures of tenderness and authority, his mother and father.

Pip's three mothers are psychologically the three aspects any mother presents to her child: queenly protector, lover, and devourer. "Brought up by hand" (6) in more senses than one, Pip sees his sister as, to use Joe's term, "a buster" (pronounced "as if it began with at least twelve capital Bs" [44]). He accepts Miss Havisham as a kind of "fairy godmother" (149), though she too is a devourer; it is as though she were David Copperfield's Aunt Betsey turned sour. Estella, formed to order by Miss Havisham, is simply an attractive extension of her, the queenly lover before whom Pip would abase himself despite her scorn. Chastened by disillusion, Pip returns home to marry Biddy, the mild comforter who replaced his murdered sister. It never occurs to him that she might love someone else; he takes her acceptance of him for granted. Similarly, his three fathers are psychologically familiar aspects of any father: the savage who may make one impotent, the king who astonishes with his power, and the kindly protector. In the key-setting first scene of the novel, Magwitch, in fact, rises like a terrible apparition from among the graves where Pip's dead parents lie, and as he retreats, he seems to Pip "as if he were eluding the hands of the dead people stretching up cautiously out of their graves, to get a twist upon his ankle and pull him in" (4). When Pip's rise in fortune takes him to London he acquires the godlike Jaggers as his guardian, though not without misgivings. Only gradually does Pip learn to respect his affectionate protector, Joe. As Pip's involvement with these characters makes clear, however, the florid provincial prose of his town newspaper is, for all its comedy, quite accurate in calling him "our young Telemachus" (218), Homer's epitome of the boy who, in finding his father, becomes a man.

Inherited from Fielding, from the stage, and from fairy tales, all of them formative influences on Dickens's creative imagination, the technique of splitting one figure into several characters, or developing one idea through compared and contrasted sets of characters, recurs at various levels of sophistication throughout Dickens's works. Pickwick and Sam Weller are paired off against Jingle and Job Trotter, *Martin Chuzzlewit* and *Dombey and Son* are full of characters presenting the various faces of selfishness and pride respectively. As his art progressed and deepened, this device for ordering the abundant variety of his imagination in the wide compass and considerable length of his novels became less mechanical, integrated more thoroughly with theme and texture, articulated with greater psychological subtlety. *David Copperfield* and *Great Expectations*, both autobiographical narratives, refine the technique further by splitting the potential narrator; David's darker feelings being transferred to his sinister friend, Steerforth, and leaving David rather colourless; young Pip's hostilities being transferred to Old Orlick.[3] The irony developed between Pip's childish and adult viewpoints, however, prevents Pip from becoming as simply priggish as David. Seeing Orlick as Pip's "shadow", however, takes us out of the realistic confines of the novel's own world, where Pip is Pip, and Orlick, however enigmatic, is somebody else. Pip's substitute mothers and fathers, on the other hand, not only "stand for" his parents metaphorically but in Pip's own consciousness act as parents and guardians. With this in mind, therefore, there is nothing extra-literary in our seeing in the pattern of

Pip's relationships and his search for real worth what Freud describes as the tasks "laid down for every man": from puberty onwards

> the human individual has to devote himself to the great task of detaching himself from his parents, and not until that task is achieved can he cease to be a child and become a member of the social community. For the son this task consists in detaching his libidinal wishes from his mother and employing them for the choice of a real outside love-object, and in reconciling himself with his father if he has remained in opposition to him, or in freeing himself from his pressure if, as a reaction to his infant rebelliousness, he has become subservient to him.

By dividing and patterning as he has done, Dickens clarifies Pip's ordeal while retaining its full complexity.

Pip starts with a double difficulty: not only are his sister and Joe not his real parents, but their proper roles are reversed, his sister being the tyrant, Joe the comforter. Thus starts a stream of reversals and inverted values in the book. Pip's sense of injustice comes from his sister's example as well as her harshness: "It's bad enough to be a blacksmith's wife (and him a Gargery) without being your mother" (7) Joe, whose understanding Pip partonisingly underrates, knows well enough what motivates her. Ironically she wants what she constantly deplores, building her self-esteem on the injustice of her status: " 'And she ain't over partial to having scholars on the premises,' Joe continued, 'and in partickler would not be over partial to my being a scholar, for fear as I might rise. Like a sort of rebel, don't you see?' " (44). Enjoying her reputed martyrdom, she uses it as a lever to govern: " 'Given to government,' said Joe. 'Which I meantersay the government of you and myself' " (44).

Miss Havisham reveals a similarly upside-down logic. Betrayed by her lover, she seals herself up like a hermit in her decaying house, stops the clocks, and becomes a living symbol of unjustly treated love:

> "Do you know what I touch here?" she said, laying her

> hands, one upon the other, on her left side.
>
> "Yes, ma'am." (It made me think of the young man.)
>
> "What do I touch?"
>
> "Your heart."
>
> "Broken!"
>
> She uttered the word with an eager look, and with strong emphasis, and with a weird smile that had a kind of boast in it. (52)

As with Pip's sister, grievance is reversed into vanity, "the vanity of sorrow which had become a master mania" (378) and as Pip's sister delights in "government", Miss Havisham, pretending to have done with the world, plots to revenge herself on it, not just by forcing it to recognise the evil done her, but vicariously, by fashioning a child into the instrument of her will to wreak vengeance in kind. Intent on making her betrayal the mark of her superiority and the meaning of her life, she tries to prevent the normal dissipating effect of time by stopping it, and thus creates a mask of death: "Without this arrest of everything, this standing still of all the pale decayed objects, not even the withered bridal dress on the collapsed form could have looked so like grave-clothes, or the long veil so like a shroud" (55). Unwilling to accept the temporal condition of humanity, but not really able to reject it, she enters a malignant form of it, the form of decay and corruption expressed in her physical surrounding and furthered in her relationship with Estella. Rebelling against the world as it is, she impiously becomes her own inadequate god to set it right: "in shutting out the light of day, she had shut out infinitely more; . . . in seclusion, she had secluded herself from a thousand natural and healing influences; . . . her mind, brooding solitary, had grown diseased, as all minds do and must and will that reverse the appointed order of their Maker" (377–8). The religious connotations are not fortuitous. Miss Havisham is a reworking of the intensely zealous Mrs Clennam of *Little Dorrit* (1857), also voluntarily imprisoned for years in a decaying house, scrupulously remembering sins committed against her and appointing herself as avenger: "she still abided by her old impiety–still reversed the order of Creation, and breathed her own breath into a clay image of her Creator" (775). In both cases, vanity leads to a withering, ironic reversal. Miss Havisham's idea of love is a telling example:

> She said the word often enough, and there could be no doubt that she meant to say it; but if the often repeated word had been hate instead of love–despair–revenge–dire death–it could not have sounded from her lips more like a curse.
>
> "I'll tell you," said she, in the same hurried passionate whisper, "what real love is. It is blind devotion, unquestioning self-humiliation, utter submission, trust and belief against yourself and against the whole world, giving up your whole heart and soul to the smiter–as I did!" (226–7)

Miss Havisham's definition of love is significant. It reveals the distortion and ambivalence of her own character; her emphasis on annihilation is violence not only against herself but, through Estella, outwards against the world. For her, love has become equated with death. At first glance, moreover, her definition seems to agree with Pip's own experience of love for Estella, and Dickens stresses Pip's confession as essential to a right understanding of the book:

> . . . I did not, even that romantic morning, invest her with any attributes save those she possessed. I mention this in this place, of a fixed purpose, because it is the clue by which I am to be followed into my poor labyrinth. According to my experience, the conventional notion of a lover cannot be always true. The unqualified truth is, that when I loved Estella with the love of a man, I loved her simply because I found her irresistible. Once for all; I knew to my sorrow, often and often, if not always, that I loved her against reason, against promise, against peace, against hope, against happiness, against all discouragement that could be. Once for all; I loved her none the less because I knew it, and it had no more influence in restraining me, than if I had devoutly believed her to be human perfection. (219)

The subtle but significant difference here is between Miss Havisham's gloating emphasis on blindness, and Pip's repeated "I knew". However miserable, however compelled, Pip keeps one part of himself in reserve, observing, judging, seeing clearly – not later, when he can look back in tranquility, but at the very moment of obsession. It is the clue to his maze because here, at his most impassioned, he sees without illusion, and the rest of his story consists of the stripping away of illusion until he is left with a true estimate of himself and of the world. The result is a special tone in the work. With his peculiar knack for seizing the quality of a work in a phrase or two, Chesterton describes it as "a quality of serene irony and even sadness, which puts it quite alone among [Dickens's] other works. At no time could Dickens possibly be called cynical, he had too much vitality; but relatively to the other books this book is cynical; but it has the soft and gentle cynicism of old age, not the hard cynicism of youth."[5]

Biddy, like Joe, receives scant respect or consideration from Pip. Arriving to run his home, she becomes merely a sympathetic ear for his longings and vanity, not to be permitted any personal views or feelings. Chapter 17 plumbs the depths of Pip's egregious asininity with her: "I should have been good enough for *you*; shouldn't I, Biddy? . . . If I could only get myself to fall in love with you . . ." (121–3). When she suggests the uncomfortable idea that Joe might be content to remain in his social station, Pip is startled by the suspicion of a personal reflection on himself and reprimands her loftily for presuming to envy him: "It's a – it's a bad side of human nature" (142). Biddy, in short, is the first aspect of the mother, the unqualified, unquestioning comforter. Pip, therefore, never suspecting that she might refuse him, can postpone coming to terms with her until very late in the book. His attitude to Joe is equally simple. Offering no threat, Joe can be patronized: "I always treated him as a larger species of child, and as no more than my equal" (7). Reconciliation with Joe and Biddy is a matter neither of overcoming antagonism, nor of rising from subservience, but of giving humble respect to what had been taken for granted. Pip manages it after their wedding.

The problems of antagonism and subservience come in very strongly, however, with Magwitch and Jaggers. Just as Miss Havisham and Estella, scorning him as "a common labouring-boy" (55), give a social formula to the inchoate feeling of injustice inspired in Pip by his sister, so Magwitch provides a focus for his feelings of guilt. As a criminal whose name is Abel, Magwitch has an obvious relationship to the theme of love and justice. Pip dates his strange encompassment "by all this taint of prison and crime" (249) from his coerced assistance to Magwitch, but his real complicity was less in aiding than in sympathising with Magwitch: "I thought what terrible good sauce for a dinner my fugitive friend on the marshes was . . . . they were all in lively anticipation of 'the two villains' being taken . . . . the pale afternoon outside almost seemed in my pitying young fancy to have turned pale on their account, poor wretches" (29). The separation in attitude between Pip and his respectable elders, implied in the quotation marks around the phrase "the two villains", is not a matter of Pip's mature reflection; he is describing his pitying *young* fancy, and later Pip "treasonably" whispers to Joe, "I hope, Joe, we shan't find them" (30). Though young Pip is no more easy in his conscience about the virtue of his actions and feelings than is Huck Finn in refusing to betray the escaped slave Jim, he refuses to side with the law and thereby anticipates his own eventual acceptance of the sinner, his answer to Cain's aggrieved cry, "Am I my brother's keeper?"

In the patterning of the novel, Magwitch neatly parallels Miss Havisham, each of them appropriating another human being as a personal extension and means to power. "I'm your second father", says Magwitch. "You're my son–more to me nor any son. . . . If I ain't a gentleman, nor yet ain't got no learning, I'm the owner of such" (304–6). With his record, his fearful appearance, his threat of a deputy with "a secret way pecooliar to himself of getting at a boy, and at his heart, and at his liver" (3–4), and his claim of ownership, Magwitch is a sombre figure. "The abhorrence in which I held the man, the dread I had of him, the repugnance with which I shrank from him, could not have been exceeded if he had been some terrible beast" (304). Pip's moral transformation and freedom from childhood fears and antagonisms, nevertheless, depend on his reconciliation with this terrible father. Dickens, therefore, makes Magwitch a more sympathetic figure, both for Pip and the reader, by allowing him extenuations of his criminality, extenuations that Dickens would hardly have tolerated in real life by the sixties, when he had become rather reactionary in his views on penology, and that he certainly does not allow

Compeyson.[6] In Chapter 42 society is made to share part of the guilt for Magwitch's career: "they measured my head, some on 'em–they had better 'a' measured my stomach" (328). A second way of making Magwitch more tolerable to the reader was to date the story's main action somewhere between thirty and sixty years before the date of the novel's publication, so that while the reader might well have direct knowledge of the horrors of public execution (abolished in 1868) outside Newgate, he would probably be unaware that the sentence of execution was rarely carried out on returned transportees (though Dickens does have the judge emphasise that Magwitch's is an "aggravated case" [434]).

Social and religious themes blend again in Pip's gradual acceptance of Magwitch. Pip's basic desire is to be beyond reproach, in social terms respectable, in religious terms innocent. His concern for respectability, his perennial worry about guilt and injustice, his anxiety about the atmosphere of crime surrounding him, his loathing for the returned criminal, are social attitudes revealing a deeper reluctance to accept the lot of fallen, imperfect humanity. His profound anxiety about personal dignity occasions the great encounter with "that unlimited miscreant", Trabb's boy an episode thematically as well as comically perfect. With uncanny penetration, Trabb's boy cuts to the centre of Pip's vanity:

> Deeming that a serene and unconscious contemplation of him would best beseem me, and would be most likely to quell his evil mind, I advanced with that expression of countenance, and was rather congratulating myself on my success, when suddenly the knees of Trabb's boy smote together, his hair uprose, his cap fell off, he trembled violently in every limb, staggered out into the road, and crying to the populace, "Hold me! I'm so frightened!" feigned to be in a paroxysm of terror and contrition, occasioned by the dignity of my appearance. As I passed him, his teeth loudly chattered in his head, and with every mark of extreme humiliation, he prostrated himself in the dust. (232)

Pip's dignity, of course, is merely vulgar respectability, as he makes clear at once in protesting to Trabb against the employment of a boy "who excited Loathing in every respectable mind" (233). Initially Pip takes responsibility for the inconveniently returned convict for the most bourgeois of motives, indebtedness for money paid down, money to which he had no right, the tainted money of a criminal. He immediately resolves to take no more of Magwitch's compromising wealth, having already felt some queasiness about Wemmick's less complicated views on portable property. As Pip involves himself in Magwitch's affairs, however, what began as burdensome obligation turns into genuine compassion. Nice discriminations of debt and justice cease to be of such great account. The trial, with its shaft of sunlight linking judge and condemned, reminds Pip "how both were passing on, with absolute equality, to the greater Judgment that knoweth all things and cannot err" (434). In some ways the scene reminds one of the trial that turns Camus's character, Tarrou, into an anarchist in *The Plague*. All the young Tarrou can see is the full majesty and zealousness of the legal system bent on the destruction of an owlish-looking little man ("To my mind the social order round me was based on the death-sentence . . . ").[7] Pip, however, cannot condemn the social order as easily, since by now he has already lost his naïve illusion of his own innocence. Some readers have, indeed, disputed the point because of his reaction to Magwitch's death: "I thought of the two men who went up into the temple to pray, and I knew there were no better words that I could say beside his bed than 'O Lord, be merciful to him a sinner!' " (436). Pip's use of the pronoun "him" instead of the biblical "me", it may be argued, shows that Pip, even here, remains the snob and excludes himself from the idea of involvement in sin. Such an interpretation would, however, be uncharitable. "Me" would be logically impossible in the situation; "us" would be a hideous elaboration of the quotation. Magwitch is a sinner, and recognition of the fact, coming after Pip's reflection on the equality of judge and condemned, is simple, direct and unpretentious, not an insinuation that Pip, even in the act of recalling the Pharisee, becomes one. Considered either morally or psychologically, Magwitch's role in Pip's life is to implicate him in humanity, to give him strength in the knowledge of their common weakness.

One of the most ambiguous figures in the puzzle of

relationships with which Pip and the reader must struggle is Pip's third father, Jaggers. He is the one character in the plot of the book who can put all the pieces together; more imposing still, he has a special air of knowing secrets, "a manner expressive of knowing something secret about every one of us that would effectually do for each individual if he chose to disclose it" (128); even Estella believes he is "more in the secrets of every place" than anyone else (255). His second attribute is power. "It's impossible to say what he couldn't get", says Wemmick, "if he gave his mind to it" (194). To say that Jaggers *pleads* a case would hardly be the truth; the very judge is convulsive with awe of him: "The magistrates shivered under a single bite of his finger. Thieves and thief-takers hung in dread rapture on his words, and shrank when a hair of his eyebrows turned in their direction. Which side he was on I couldn't make out," says Pip, "for he seemed to me to be grinding the whole place in a mill" (191). His power is enhanced by remoteness: "He's always so high. His constant height is of a piece with his immense abilities" (249), says Wemmick. Jaggers washes his hands and his face, scours them round with a towel, gargles his throat, scrapes his nails, until his clients are, in the strictest sense, washed off. Even in the street, where his anxious suitors slink about in wait for him, "there was something so conclusive in the halo of scented soap which encircled his presence that they gave it up for that day" (199). Jaggers's ability to manipulate, his power, knowledge and detachment, have suggested to critics that he stands for the artist or even God himself. And it must be noticed that Dickens encourages the reader, even taunts him, to fathom Jaggers. The dinner he gives for Pip and his friends concludes with Jaggers asking Pip, "You know what I am, don't you?" (205). And Pip's visit to Newgate ends with the turnkey shrewdly observing to Wemmick, "Why then, . . . he knows what Mr. Jaggers is" (249). Pip does not know what Jaggers is, but before long the question crops up again, this time in a comic key (an ironic trick Dickens often reserves for his deepest themes) when Pip visits Wemmick's Castle and tries to chat with the Aged: "Curious to know how the old gentleman stood informed concerning the reputation of Mr. Jaggers, I roared that name at him. He threw me into the greatest confusion by laughing heartily and replying in a very sprightly manner, 'No, to be sure; you're right.' And to this hour I have not the faintest notion of what he meant, or what joke he thought I had made" (279). What, then, does one make of Jaggers?[8]

Neither passionate like Magwitch, nor affectionate like Joe, but cold in his secret knowledge of malice, guilt, or stupidity, Jaggers is familiar enough as that aspect of the father the child both admires and resents: the kingly, knowing, rule-maker, seeing through all the petty artifices of the child's world, remote in his cunning and authority. Until the end of the book, Jaggers seems compounded of two of the three main attributes of God: omnipotence and omniscience. Benevolence seems to be lacking. The absence of feeling is particularly distressing to Pip: "that my feelings should be in the same place with him – *that* was the agonising circumstance" (230). Jaggers, indeed, is cynicism raised to a general principle. To Pip's criticism of Orlick, he characteristically replies, "Why, of course he is not the right sort of man, Pip, . . . because the man who fills the post of trust never is the right sort of man" (231). He is exactly the right mentor, however, for the second stage of Pip's expectations, when Pip is learning the rules and conventions of respectable society. For Jaggers, the law, the great codification of social rights and obligations, the grand fabric of justice, is without any aura of sentiment. Law is a game he plays ruthlessly, and his view of it is clear in the episode where he is prepared to use a false witness so long as the rules are observed and no one openly admits the falsity. In short, he demonstrates what Bumble suspected in *Oliver Twist*: "the law is a ass – a idiot". In the description and behaviour of Jaggers and Wemmick, the disparity between love and mortal justice is generalised to grand proportions. Wemmick, who at home is amiability itself, is metamorphosed to a thing as he approaches Little Britain, cold, hard, "with a square wooden face whose expression seemed to have been imperfectly chipped out with a dull-edged chisel" (161). No wonder that the respectable young Pip, the aspirant bourgeois with a deep sense of his rights and dues, his mind diseased with vain longings, should heartily wish for "some other guardian of minor abilities" (249). Like Magwitch, but in a different way, Jaggers teaches an unwilling Pip the ambiguity and imperfection of human nature; with his air of secret knowledge he keeps Pip conscious, when Pip would most like to forget it, that his dignity is not impeccable, that he can claim no perfect justice in the fallen world. How, then, avoid the cynicism Jaggers seems to embody? Just as Pip must gain respect for Joe and compassion for Magwitch in order to grow up and accept the world for what it really is, so he must find an unexpected bond with Jaggers. It turns out to be charity, the one godly attribute that Jaggers notably seems to lack. Dickens prepares the ground by elaborating the deceptive split between Wemmick's private and public faces and finally, when we learn how Jaggers saved the infant Estella, reveals a similar, much better hidden, split in Jaggers. The result is comedy without sentiment, for though charity may compensate for the limitations and cruelty of the world, no more than in *King Lear* does it turn the world into paradise. For a moment, indeed, it threatens to reduce order into chaos between Wemmick and Jaggers: "each of them seemed suspicious, not to say conscious, of having shown himself in a weak and unprofessional light to the other. . . . I had never seen them on such ill terms". Just at this crisis, however, the unfortunate suitor Mike comes tearfully in:

> "What are you about?" demanded Wemmick, with the utmost indignation. "What do you come snivelling here for?"
>
> "I didn't go to do it, Mr. Wemmick."
>
> "You did," said Wemmick. "How dare you? You're not in a fit state to come here, if you can't come here without spluttering like a bad pen. What do you mean by it?"
>
> "A man can't help his feelings, Mr. Wemmick," pleaded Mike.
>
> "His what?" demanded Wemmick, quite savagely. "Say that again!"
>
> "Now look here, my man," said Mr. Jaggers, advancing a step, and pointing to the door. "Get out of this office. I'll have no feelings here. Get out."

With the observance of the rules re-established, Jaggers and Wemmick get down to work again "with an air of refreshment upon them as if they had just had lunch" (393–4).

If the ordinary world of law and business rises fitfully and at moments towards charity, it also at times sinks back to the realm of primordial malice. For the most part, Pip's vain aspirations are the expression of thoughtless inexperience, but behind his thoughtless snobbery, Dickens suggests something darker and more malignant. His sister's dominance, Miss Havisham's and Estella's class distinctions, these give Pip formulations for understanding his longings for distinction and his sense of unjust treatment. Underlying the social formulations, however, is a suspicion of aboriginal evil. And at its centre we find Old Orlick. Like Pip, he suffers a sense of exclusion and injustice, insisting on his rights with Joe, and slinking about "like Cain". He gives young Pip to understand "that he knew the fiend very well" and might give Pip to him for fuel. Orlick's very name, Dolge, is in Pip's view imposed on the village "as an affront to its understanding" (105). His home is on the marshes, and he rises to confront Pip and Biddy "from the ooze (which was quite in his stagnant way)" (124). As Miss Havisham's gate-keeper he looks like "a human dormouse" (220). Everything about Orlick suggests primordial, subhuman malice beyond all psychological or social explanation. And in the end, though Orlick is guilty of two attempted murders, all we hear of him is that he has been arrested for housebreaking. Orlick is the core of a host of consonant images of decay, corruption and envelopment in the book: the marshes, called "meshes", Miss Havisham's sombre room with its smoke and candelabra like the mist and wintry branches of the marsh, and its wedding cake "like a black fungus" (78) with blotchy spiders running about, the ruined garden, the decay of Barnard's Inn, the mud of the Thames in the attempted escape. With the maze of reversed and ambiguous personal relationships through which Pip travels, these images of malignant growth and obfuscation lend the book its peculiar tone and rhythm. The mists especially serve an ironic function, as when Pip first leaves for London: "And the mists had all solemnly risen now, and the world lay spread before me" (152). The suggested clarity of vision is just an illusion, and shortly Pip is wondering whether London is not "rather ugly, crooked, narrow, and dirty" (153). The effect is repeated, mist and clarity counterpointed throughout the novel, until Pip has lost his illusions and, free of both longings and resentment, acquired the most valued possession a Dickens character gains, an educated heart. The story having come full circle, with another young Pip hedged in behind Joe's leg and about to begin his own voyage of discovery, the final line of the first ending, which describes Pip's chance encounter with a remarried Estella but without bestowing on him any "poetic" reward, clinches the theme of the work: "I was very glad afterwards to have had the interview; for in her face, and in her voice, and in her touch, she gave me the assurance that suffering had been stronger than Miss Havisham's teaching, and had given her a heart to understand what my heart used to be" (461).

Dickens's emphasis on the educated heart, and especially on imagination as a means of educating it, finds expression in his approximation of fairy tale,[9] a type of literature that engrossed him all his life. Pip imagines himself as a prince of the *Arabian Nights* and Estella as the princess to be won. The texture of Dickens's world itself, however, brings us closest to fairy tale: objects have a perverse and curious life of their own; people approach the state of inanimate objects; the world shades off into tones of the divine and demonic. A great master of the child's vision, Dickens happily begins this work with his most convincing description of a child's response to the world, and its surrealism never altogether vanishes. In *Pendennis*, though not in the first person, Thackeray also describes the vicissitudes of growing up, drawing on his own experience as Dickens had done in *David Copperfield*, but Thackeray's delight is in depicting the violent convictions and infatuations of adolescence and shading them with the mellow wisdom of the Old Fogy. His world is substantial, realistic, socially articulated to the finest degree of class distinction. In *Great Expectations*, on the other hand, we have little more than the Finches of the Grove to give us an idea of the distinction to which Pip aspires. George Eliot's *Middlemarch*, with its precise sociological and psychological dissection of the relationships and motives of individuals and groups, forms a contrast still more extreme. Even when compared with Dickens's other works, however, *Great Expectations* reveals a rare detachment from specific social issues. Not only is it set back in time (roughly between 1807 and 1826), but it contains virtually no implied or direct criticism of contemporary institutions, such as we find, for example, in *Little*

Dorrit, where the story is also placed somewhat in the past. Compared with *David Copperfield* (1849–50), his earlier attempt at autobiographical form, *Great Expectations* avoids the surface events of Dickens's own career – however true the novel may be to those inner grievances and longings that impelled him with such amazing intensity – just as it avoids the air of self-justification that makes one uneasy about *David Copperfield*.

Combining the vivid surrealism of a child's perception with the mature reflection of adult experience and insight, Dickens has created an intricate masterpiece that engages our imagination on several levels at once to take us through the pattern of exchanging illusion for wisdom. Aptly called a fable for Dickens's times, *Great Expectations* can no doubt be seen to epitomise satisfactorily the selfish aspirations and status-seeking of mid-Victorian society, but its connection with that particular society must remain loose and general at best – for in what period have men been any less possessed by the disease of vain longings? A strange alliance of the grotesque with the universal makes *Great Expectations* a fable not just for its own but for all times.

NOTES

1. Samuel Johnson, *Adventurer*, No. 111.
2. References are to the *New Oxford Illustrated Dickens* edition (Oxford, 1947–58).
3. See Julian Moynahan, "The Hero's Guilt: The Case of *Great Expectations*", *Essays in Criticism*, 10 (1960) 60–79.
4. Sigmund Freud, *The Complete Introductory Lectures on Psychoanalysis*, translated and edited by James Strachey (New York, 1966) p. 337.
5. G. K. Chesterton, *Criticisms and Appreciations of the Works of Charles Dickens* (London, 1911) p. 197.
6. See Philip Collins, *Dickens and Crime* (London, 1962) p. 91–2.
7. Albert Camus, *The Plague*, translated by Stuart Gilbert, Penguin edition (Harmondsworth, 1960) p. 204.
8. Critics in fact make a lot of Jaggers, though they tend not to agree. The Leavises say, "Jaggers is probably Dickens's greatest success in any novel" (F. R. and Q. D. Leavis, *Dickens the Novelist* [London, 1970] p. 311). See also Andrew Gordon, "Jaggers and the Moral Scheme of *Great Expectations*", *Dickensian*, 65 (1969), 3–11; and Anthony Winner, "Character and Knowledge in Dickens: The Enigma of Jaggers", *Dickens Studies Annual*, 3 (1974) 100–21; as well as the dispute between A. L. French and A. F.

Dilnot in *Essays in Criticism*: French, "Beating and Cringing: *Great Expectations*", *EIC* (1974) 147–68: Dilnot, "The Case of Mr. Jaggers", *EIC* (1975) 437–43; French, "Mr. Jaggers", *EIC* (1976) 278–82.

9. Harry Stone in "Fire, Hand and Gate: Dickens' *Great Expectations*", *Kenyon Review*, 24 (1962) 662–91, comments on fairy-tale elements.

6 Thackeray's Things: Time's Local Habitation

As Chesterton said, Thackeray is the novelist of memory.[1] All his sensitive characters, and his narrators too, are occupied in summoning up remembrance of things past. I don't know if Proust read Thackeray, but Thackeray certainly didn't need to read Proust to learn to take up the quest for the recapture of the past. Esmond, George Warrington and Denis Duval write their memoirs at a stage when one expects all passion to be spent, but though they recollect their emotion in tranquillity they find that it is emotion still. Esmond's love for Beatrix ended in that moment when the roses shuddered out of her cheeks and he saw her as merely an intriguing prostitute to a prince; but yet "I invoke that beautiful spirit from the shades and love her still; or rather I should say such a past is always present to a man; such a passion once felt forms a part of his whole being, and cannot be separated from it" (*Esmond*, 383).[2]

Such passages run like a refrain through the novels. Beatrix herself as she reappears in *The Virginians* – an irruption from their grandfather's past into the youth of the Warrington boys – genially recalls her own youth at Castlewood: "I remember in this very room, at this very table – oh, ever so many hundred years ago! – so coaxing my father, and mother, and your grandfather, Harry Warrington: and there were eels for supper, as we have had them to-night, and it was that dish of collared eels which brought the circumstance back to my mind. I had been just as wayward that day, when I was seven years old, as I am to-day, when I am seventy" (*Virginians*, 193). George Warrington, as he recollects the day when his engagement to Theo was broken, finds in the midst of comfortable middle age that he can weep afresh love's long since cancelled woe: "I can hear now the sobs of the good Aunt Lambert, and to this day the noise of fire-irons stirring a fire in a room overhead gives me a tremor. I heard such a noise that day" (*Virginians*, 795).

The sound of fire-irons, the taste of collared eels – these are Proustian *Petites Madeleines* to recall the past. And Thackeray expanded that backward-looking stance of his characters and narrators, who are engaged in *la recherche du temps perdu*, to inform the themes and plots of his novels. George and Harry Warrington, the Virginians, are engaged in a quest to recover their past: George consciously conducts himself after the manner of his grandfather, Henry Esmond; and the novel opens with Harry's arrival at Castlewood, the seat of his ancestors, where he goes through the painful experience of having his nostalgia collide with the unpleasant facts of the present. Arthur Pendennis, whose own youth was recorded in *Pendennis*, writes biographies of his younger brethren at Greyfriars, Clive Newcome and Philip Firmin, by which process he can to some extent renew his own early experience.

Pendennis also reflects another of Thackeray's attitudes in being both novelist and historian. Thackeray wrote both history and fiction, but for him they were not so much different disciplines as different genres – and not very different at that. Not only did he fill his novels with historical figures and events, but he saw orthodox histories as fictions, and vice versa. Esmond believes "that Mr Hogarth and Mr Fielding will give our children a much better idea of the manners of the present age in England, than the *Court Gazette* and the newspapers which we get thence" (*Esmond*, 14); and Pendennis claims that "the speeches attributed to Clive, the colonel, and the rest, are as authentic as the orations in Sallust or Livy" (*Newcomes*, 297). Thackeray laughs in his sleeve at Pitt Crawley for making a distinction in kind between Smollett's "history" and the history of Mr Humphry Clinker. His view of the interrelation of history and fiction is expressed in the formal structure of *The Newcomes*, where Thackeray the novelist transforms himself into Pendennis the biographer. Pen self-consciously works out the process by which a historian must deduce his history:

> As Professor Owen or Professor Agassiz takes a fragment of a bone, and builds an enormous forgotten monster out of it,

> wallowing in primaeval quagmires, tearing down leaves and branches of plants that flourished thousands of years ago, and perhaps may be coal by this time – so the novelist puts this and that together: from the footprint finds the foot; from the foot, the brute who trod on it; from the brute, the plant he browsed on, the marsh in which he swam. (*Newcomes*, 616)

Of Thackeray's six full-length novels, four are written as pseudo-histories, in the form of memoirs or biographies in which the ostensible writers draw on records, letters, "the Warrington papers" and so forth, as well as memory, to reconstruct their accounts.

Nevertheless, though Thackeray had a philosopher's interest in time as process, and a historian's interest in the nation's past, there are reasons why he wrote – primarily – novels, and not philosophy or history. At most he was a very social historian, a very personal philosopher. His instinct was always towards the embodying of the past, the incarnation of the idea. Geoffrey Tillotson has spoken of Thackeray's very concrete imagination.[3] He has the novelist's instinct to visualise rather than conceptualise. In his mind an idea is naturally located in an emblem, and the emblem becomes an object; a proposition expresses itself in an attitude, the attitude takes shape in a person. It is the object and the person we meet in the novels, but they remain informed by the idea and the proposition. And it is on the concrete manifestations of Thackeray's philosophical and historical interest in time that I want to focus my attention: on the pokers and collared eels, and the dinosaur's footprint that are present and palpable extensions of a lost past. In these, time has a local habitation.

Thackeray felt vividly that all we can grasp of the past is remnants, fragments, relics – history for him is resident in cigar-butts, laundry bills, proofsheets, the fossilised footprint. That is why the document, the last will and testament of a dead time, figures so largely in his "veracious histories". Unlike the historian he was at liberty to invent his own documents; but it is characteristic of the way his imagination worked that he should so often feel the need to invent the documents before his people and their histories would come alive for him. He begins *The Virginians* with an account of the correspondence of the Warrington brothers,

> whose voices I almost fancy I hear, as I read the yellow pages written scores of years since, blotted with the boyish tears of disappointed passion, dutifully dispatched after famous balls and ceremonies of the grand Old World, scribbled by camp-fires, or out of prison: nay, there is one that has a bullet through it, and of which a greater portion of the text is blotted out with the blood of the bearer. (*Virginians*, 2)

The seeds of the total action of the novel are here. "Poring over the documents", the narrator explains, he has "endeavoured to revivify the bygone times and people". It is through documents that the past can come to life again.

Thackeray's plots often turn on the finding or losing of a document. The discovery of a lost will or deed or gift by which the hero's fortunes are reversed is the climactic action of *The Newcomes, The Virginians* and *Philip*. And in *Vanity Fair* Thackeray carefully follows the history of George's letter to Becky: delivered in her bouquet at the Richmond ball before Waterloo; surviving the vicissitudes of Becky's career as she carefully preserves it along with other useful mementos; and finally produced to shatter Amelia's idolatrous conception of her dead husband so that she can at last see Dobbin's real worth.

Memorable scenes in the novels are constructed around documents and letters, and characters define themselves according to who does what with which piece of paper. The wily old Beatrix, determined to save Harry from his engagement to the faded Maria, actually robs her niece of his letter of proposal in Church; but Harry annuls her intriguing, and saves his own honour if not his happiness, by staunchly declaring, "written or said – it does not matter which!" (411). The Little Sister in *Philip* plays Judith to Holofernes when she chloroforms her blackmailer and regains the forged bill. Pendennis's progress from generous youth to cautious worldiness is measured by his early reckless written expressions of love for the Fotheringay – his effusions fill drawers – and his later carefully noncommittal letters to Blanche.

Henry Esmond is the character who most courageously

resists the determining power of the document. After the duel, when Mohun has killed Francis, Earl of Castlewood, Henry has in his hand the dying confession that declares he himself is the legitimate heir to the title and the estate. Thackeray makes the moment memorable by his telling use of significant detail:

> Esmond went to the fire, and threw the paper into it. 'Twas a great chimney with glazed Dutch tiles. How we remember such trifles in such awful moments! – the scrap of the book that we have read in a great grief – the taste of that last dish that we have eaten before a duel or some such supreme meeting or parting. On the Dutch tiles at the bagnio was a rude picture representing Jacob in hairy gloves, cheating Isaac of Esau's birthright. The burning paper lighted it up. (*Esmond*, 162)

Esmond is not the only Esau in his family. His grandson, George, also sacrifices his birthright to his mother's favourite, Harry; and that George's grandson, George Warrington in *Pendennis*, again voluntarily surrenders professional distinction and the woman he loves to another man. Esmond's act reverberates down the generations. By contrast, in another novel we are shown Pendennis's empty gesture of throwing the manuscript of his novel into a fire that he knows has gone out. Pendennis is a humbug, but Esmond is made of sterner stuff.

The almost sinister determining force of the written document – that force George Eliot referred to when she called the fifth book of *Middlemarch* "The Dead Hand", in which Casaubon and Featherstone through their wills extend their control over others beyond the grave – is powerfully suggested in Mr Osborne's solemn alteration of the records in his family Bible (the frontispiece represents Abraham's sacrifice of Isaac) when he disinherits George: "Taking a pen, he carefully obliterated George's name from the page; and when the leaf was quite dry, restored the volume to the place from which he had moved it" (284). From that moment George is doomed, and his fall at Waterloo seems predetermined.

Imagery of death is often collected around documents: for

if Thackeray recurrently suggests the past is always present, he as frequently reminds us that it is irrecoverably lost, and that as we outgrow our youthful passions and allegiances, we die by inches. That contradiction is voiced by George Warrington in *The Virginians*:

> You may be ever so old now; but you remember. It may be all dead and buried; but in a moment, up it springs out of its grave, and looks, and smiles, and whispers as of yore when it clung to your arm, and dropped fresh tears on your heart. It is here, and alive, did I say? O far, far away! O lonely hearth and cold ashes! Here is the vase, but the roses are gone. (*Virginians*, 699)

So the Warrington papers may bring George and Harry to life again, as the vase that remains can recall the roses that are dead; but letters, recording the aspirations of people no longer alive, or emotions of your own that you no longer feel, are also dismal *mementos mori*. "What a dreary mourning it is to dwell upon those vehement protests of dead affection! What lying epitaphs they make over the corpse of love!" (*Vanity Fair*, 440) While George is preparing to jilt Amelia (he uses *her* love letters to light his cigars with), Amelia cherishes his past missives and refuses to part with them, "as you have seen a woman nurse a child that is dead". Such melancholy lingering over documents recurs often in the novels. Pendennis disinters the manuscript of his early novel, and smiles at the marks of tears:

> As he mused over certain lines he recollected the place and hour where he wrote them: the ghost of the dead feeling came back as he mused, and he blushed to review the faint image. And what meant those blots on the page? As you come in the desert to a ground where camels' hoofs are marked in the clay, and traces of withered herbage are yet visible, you know that water was there once; so the place in Pen's mind was no longer green, and the *fons lacrymarum* was dried up. (*Pendennis*, 518)

In the same way, Pendennis is to muse over the records of other people's lost feelings when he peruses Clive's and Ethel's youthful letters "in the faded ink, on the yellow paper", and reflects again, "Who has not disinterred mementoes like these – from which the past smiles at you so sadly? ... You open an old letter-box, ... and excavate your heart" (*Newcomes*, 358). I have been multiplying quotations here to convey that tone of Thackeray's melancholy, always so resonant where he finds some present reminder to recall the past.

But written documents are of course only one, and the most obvious, of many physical objects in which the past has its ghostly residence. Pictures – which in their way are documents too – have the same force, and Thackeray's novels are filled with pictures. They are the present image of the past, as Thackeray shows most clearly in the chronicle of Isabel, Lady Castlewood, and her portrait as Diana by Lely. She, like Miss Havisham (whom she foreshadows, as she also echoes Dickens's Mrs Skewton in *Dombey and Son*) refuses to acknowledge the passing of time. She paints her cheeks with the blushes of a girl, and persists in believing herself pregnant long after there is any hope of such a possibility. She keeps the Diana picture by her, and believes it is a mirror rather than the image of lost youth: "As goddesses have youth perpetual, this one believed to the day of her death that she never grew older: and always persisted in supposing the picture was still like her" (*Esmond*, 184). Thackeray uses the same image to measure the difference as well as the similarity between Isabel and her descendant Beatrix, who had *her* youth recorded by Kneller, but who is keenly aware of the difference between image and faded original: "Look at that picture, though I know 'tis but a bad one, and that stupid vapouring Kneller could not paint my eyes, nor my hair, nor my complexion. What a shape I had then – and look at me now, and this wrinkled old neck!" (*Virginians*, 876) Isabel was all vanity and delusion. There is the same vanity about Beatrix, but she has a penetrating knowledge of the truth of advancing age and approaching death. Thackeray uses that picture again to evoke time, vanity and mortality at Beatrix's deathbed, "as the clock ticks without, and strikes the fleeting hours; as the sun falls upon the Kneller picture of Beatrix in her beauty, with the blushing cheeks, the smiling lips, the waving auburn tresses, and the eyes which seem to look towards the dim figure moaning in the bed" (882).

The history of certain pictures, which Thackeray traces carefully through his novels, is an index not only of the original's estimate of himself, as with Isabel, but of his or her place in the estimation and affection of others. Ethel's

3 The picture of Jos Sedley, from the headletter to Chapter 17 of *Vanity Fair*

memorable gesture of sticking the green "sold" ticket from the painting exhibition on her own dress, and calling herself a *tableau vivant*, is a marvellous physical image of the marriage market theme in *The Newcomes*. Thackeray tellingly exposes Amelia's deliberate self-delusion by showing the transfer of her worship for George to his portrait: she has discovered the man was no saint, but after his death manages to enshrine him nevertheless in her picture of him, which she interposes between herself and Dobbin. "You were pure – Oh yes, you were pure, my saint in heaven!" she tells her picture (846).

The other picture with a history in *Vanity Fair* is of course the one of Jos on the elephant, and Jos's value is mercilessly canvassed at the sale of the Sedley effects after the bankruptcy: "The gentleman without the elephant is worth five pound", pleads the auctioneer (202). But poor Jos is knocked down for half a guinea to Mrs Rawdon Crawley. Becky keeps her picture–her "cheap souvenir", as Barbara Hardy aptly describes it[4]–in the same little desk where she hoards her "purse" of banknotes. And finally she produces it to conquer its original and make him her victim: "She had cast such an anchor in Jos now as would require a strong storm to shake. That incident of the picture had finished him" (864). Jos, the fat fish who had escaped the toils laid for him in the early chapter called "The Green Silk Purse", has finally been hooked, and lands in Becky's net after all.

The grisly portrait of Dr Firmin presides over his gloomy dining room, and epitomises his house of death:

> Over the sideboard was the doctor, in a black velvet coat and a fur collar, his hand on a skull, like Hamlet. Skulls of oxen, horned, with wreaths, formed the cheerful ornaments of the cornice. On the side-table glittered a pair of cups, given by grateful patients, looking like receptacles rather for funereal ashes than for festive flowers or wine. Brice, the butler, wore the gravity and costume of an undertaker. (*Philip*, 16)

The skull Dr Firmin holds is an emblem not just for his profession, but for him. In his last completed novel Thackeray is as obsessed with death as Dickens is in *Our Mutual Friend*, and much of the imagery, including that in the illustrations,

4 *Memento mori* headletters from Chapters 3 and 22 of *The Adventures of Philip*

concerns corpses and death's-heads. In figures like Quilp and Rigaud, Dickens dared to introduce the devil incarnate, and in Dr Firmin, or "Dr Fell", Thackeray has suggested not only the devil, but more specifically Death itself. Tufton Hunt, the parson blackmailer, refers to him as "*pallida mors*". He has literal, as well as figurative, skeletons in his cupboards; his house is accommodated with a side door for "*the bodies*"; he wears a watch by which he numbers the heartbeats of his patients; and he himself looks like a death's-head, with a "bald head that glittered like a billiard-ball", deep-set eyes that in certain lighting are shadowy hollows, and "very white false teeth, which perhaps were a little too large for his mouth, and these grinned in the gas-light very fiercely"(7). However, devil and death's-head though he is, the doctor is also a self-dramatising humbug, who manages his own bankruptcy with such prudence and efficiency that he leaves very little in the way of plunder for the scavenging vultures. One thing he does leave behind is that state portrait of himself; and his status as heroic villain is neatly undercut as his image is evaluated and sold: "I am afraid it went for a few shillings only, and in the midst of a roar of Hebrew laughter" (206).

But a fragment that is tenderly rescued from the wreck of Colonel Newcome's ship is the picture of the colonel by his son, undertaken as the first portrait of Clive's career. J. J. Ridley "buys it in" to give back to the family, so the vultures do not get their beaks into the colonel, and his image is the focus of love and compassion as he is himself.

Pictures of course play a leading role in *The Newcomes*, which is the biography of a painter, as manuscripts do in *Pendennis*, the novel about a writer. The stages of Clive's career are reflected in his work: the portrait of his father is his best work, as his filial love is his most enduring quality; his grandiloquent "Battle of Assaye" records his allegiance to British India, his love for Ethel is expressed in "a whole gallery of Ethels"; when she is engaged to Lord Farintosh his subject is "Sir Brian the Templar Carrying off Rebecca"; after the bankruptcy, he paints "The Stranded Boat"; finally, in the ruin and humiliation of his family, he paints his father again, as Belisarius. Unobtrusive touches, these, in the vast accumulation of detail in *The Newcomes*. But Thackeray made paintings express their painters, as well as their subjects.

Thackeray dwells, as creative artists must, on outward and visible manifestations. With a mind that lingers over the past, and memories of roses now withered, his hands caress the vase that once held them, and that is all he has left to grasp of their fragrance. His novels express a faith that what we touch is real–is at any rate the part of reality that we can retain. The opposition of the abstract to the concrete way of thinking is marvellously realised in the love affair between Pen and the Fotheringay in *Pendennis*. He is all passion and poetry; he sees her in a glow of glamour, and art, and vague but noble abstractions concocted out of his own brain. She, however, has her feet firmly on the ground, as Thackeray shows by constantly associating her with down-to-earth ordinary *things*, often edible ones–brown stout, mutton chop, veal-and-ham pie, beef-steak pudding. She rubs white satin shoes with breadcrumb while her father blusters theatrically about vipers and traitors, and when it is decided the engagement must end, she comments "them filberts is beautiful". At the last, "she wrapped up Pen's letters, poems, passions, and fancies, and tied them with a piece of string neatly, as she would a parcel of sugar" (143). Though the fact that her mind is arrested on the concrete is a measure of her mental limitation, Emily Costigan, with her grip on what is solid and palpable, comes best out of that encounter.

The things with which Thackeray crowds his novels – the letters in faded ink on yellow paper, the paintings by painters no longer fashionable, the gifts from people no longer loved or now dead, the swords and pistols that have shed blood and are now ornaments – these things express much about the people they surround, and Barbara Hardy has written marvellously on "The Expressive Things" in Thackeray;[5] but especially and recurrently, in the work of this novelist of memory, they express the past; and their value is as present and palpable extensions of the past.

As a Victorian lecturing to a Victorian audience on the Georgian era, Thackeray chose to summon up a sense of the past by a series of tactual images. This is how he begins *The Four Georges*:

> A very few years since, I knew familiarly a lady, who had been asked in marriage by Horace Walpole, who had been patted on the head by George I. This lady had knocked at Johnson's door; had been intimate with Fox, the beautiful Georgina of Devonshire, and that brilliant Whig society of the reign of George III. . . . I often thought as I took my kind old friend's hand, how with it I held on to the old society of wits and men of the world. (*Four Georges*, 699)

The old symbol of the laying on of hands acquires a new specificity, from the touch of the monarch on the head of the infant and the rapping of the knocker on Johnson's door, to the old lady's hand in Thackeray's own that is to be his and his audience's link with the past.

Hands are always powerful symbols in Thackeray, and they touch many of his central concerns. Hands link, grasp, reject, rejoin, remind, create, perform sleights: so they express his themes of love and lovelessness, acquisitiveness and sacrifice. A study of the handshakes in the novels, in which snobs put their social inferiors in their places by offering three, or two, or one finger to shake instead of the whole hand, is an exploration in social discrimination: Becky resoundingly puts down George by her offer of one finger, and Clive Newcome has all our sympathy in stamping on his cousin's toe when Barnes tries "the finger business" on him. Posturing humbugs like Honeyman and Dr Firmin cultivate gestures for effect: "No man in London understood the ring business, or the pocket-handkerchief business better, or smothered his emotion more beautifully" (*Newcomes*, 104). And hands with rings are reminders, like so much else in Thackeray's novels, of vanity: the Countess Isabel wears as many rings on her gnarled old fingers as the fine lady of Banbury Cross. Thackeray turns heraldic jokes about the red hand that decorates the arms of a baronet: "That blood-red hand of Sir Pitt Crawley's would be in anybody's pocket except his own"(*Vanity Fair*, 102).

But a handclasp can express reconciliation and enduring affection too, like that of the Warringtons that Thackeray used as the cover design for *The Virginians*, where the joined hands symbolise the union of the brothers in spite of their opposed temperaments, nations, and political beliefs. And hand-holding in love-making can express attitudes ranging from the starry-eyed to the worldly-wise. Witness Pen's rapture with the Fotheringay: "He seized her hand madly and kissed it a thousand times. She did not withdraw it" (*Pendennis*, 78)–and measure against it the characteristically disillusioned tone of the narrator in *The Virginians*: "What a part they play, or used to play, in love-making, those hands! How quaintly they are squeezed at that period of life! . . . What good can there be in pulling and pressing a thumb and four fingers?" (*Virginians*, 208).

But predictably a recurring use of hand symbolism involves the recapture of the past. Rachel's hand, which she finally bestows on Esmond, is the link of continuity in a life during which he has regarded her as goddess, guilty widow, mother, and wife. In the first scene of the novel, when she meets him at Castlewood as a boy, she takes his hand and puts her other hand on his head:

> The boy, who had never looked upon so much beauty before, felt as if the touch of a superior being or angel smote him down to the ground, and kissed the fair protecting

> hand as he knelt on one knee. To the very last hour of his life, Esmond remembered the lady as she then spoke and looked, the rings on her fair hands, the very scent of her robe, the beam of her eyes lighting up with surprise and kindness, her lips blooming in a smile, the sun making a golden halo round her hair. (*Esmond*, 17–18)

It is a passage that sets the tone of the novel. As Esmond remembers her first blessing, so he remembers her unjustified cruelty when she sublimates her sense of guilt at her husband's death by blaming him: "Long ago he has forgiven and blest the soft hand that wounded him: but the mark is there, and the wound is cicatrized only–no time, tears, caresses, or repentance, can obliterate the scar" (173). And at the reconciliation, when he understands she has been fighting an adulterous love, "she gave him her hand, her little fair hand: there was only her marriage ring on it. The quarrel was all over" (210). And when, towards the end of the novel, they revisit the old scenes of Castlewood "hand-in-hand", Esmond is moved not only to reflect on the past but to get a rare glimpse of the future, even that which lies beyond the grave.

> We forget nothing. The memory sleeps, but awakens again; I often think how it shall be when, after the last sleep of death, the réveillé shall arouse us for ever, and the past in one flash of self-consciousness rush back, like the soul, revivified. (*Esmond*, 394)

It is characteristic of Thackeray that when his narrator visualises the resurrection, he should envision the resurrection not just of the body but of the past, and suggest that the life everlasting stretches backwards as well as forwards to eternity.

Another woman's hand is focused on in the same way, but this hand links not just one man and woman through their two long lives, but spans generations and identities. It is Ethel's in *The Newcomes*. The great tragedy of Colonel Newcome's life has been the loss of the girl he loved in his youth because she was forced to marry for interest rather than love. When he returns in middle age from India, he finds in the girl Ethel the reincarnation of his lost Léonore:

> He took a little slim white hand and laid it down on his brown palm, where it looked all the whiter: he cleared the grizzled moustache from his mouth, and stooping down he kissed the little white hand with a great deal of grace and dignity. There was no point of resemblance, and yet a something in the girl's look, voice, and movements, which caused his heart to thrill, and an image out of the past to rise up and salute him .... No doubt, as the old soldier held the girl's hand in his, the little talisman led him back to Hades, and he saw Leonora. (*Newcomes*, 200–1)

Léonore and Ethel, the colonel's past and present loves, the love he lost and the love he hopes to win for his son, are more elaborately identified in the course of the novel. Thackeray creates another *tableau vivant* as the old woman and the young kiss in front of the picture of Léonore in her youth; and at the death scene of the colonel, when he makes a backward progress through his army days in India, through his early love, to his boyhood when he has become as a little child and answers "Adsum" to the Master, it is Ethel's hand that he snatches (though Léonore is actually present), as he cries "Toujours, toujours!" Past and present are again made one through the clasp of hands.

But Ethel is different from Léonore, and the conflict in her of her love and worldly allegiance is suggested in her subjection to her other mentor, proud old Lady Kew, who can also find in Ethel her youth, and recall it by the touch of her hand. At her moving appeal to the rebellious Ethel, she pleads, "There – give me the little hand. How hot it is! Mine is as cold as a stone – and shakes, doesn't it? – Eh! it was a pretty hand once!" (505). It is a touch that Saintsbury singled out as one of the great things in Thackeray.[6]

That revivification of the past that is created by Ethel's little hand has its sweetness, but also its pain; for inexorably, and in spite of the colonel's resolution that Clive's life is to be different from his own, and happier, the past repeats itself. Clive cannot win Ethel in the marriage market, and so he marries silly little Rosey on the rebound, and to please his father. That power of the past over the present is captured in the moving scene of reconciliation between Clive and his father, when they recognise and acknowledge their identified destinies: Clive has just met Ethel accidentally at the house of old Sarah Mason, who, bewildered, and mistaking the generations, joins his hand with Ethel's and asks them when they are going to be married–to the accompaniment of bitter laughter from Clive. Haggard and wretched, he comes afterwards to the colonel, telling him how he has seen "the ghost of my youth, father, the ghost of my happiness", and weeps over his father's "trembling old brown hand".

> "And are–are you fond of her still, Clive?"
> "Still! Once means always in these things, father, doesn't it? Once means to-day and yesterday, and for ever and ever!"
> "Nay, my boy, you mustn't talk to me so, or even to yourself so. You have the dearest little wife at home, a dear little wife and child."
> "You had a son, and have been kind to him, God knows. *You* had a wife: but that doesn't prevent other–other thoughts. Do you know you never spoke twice in your life about my mother? You didn't care for her."
> "I–I did my duty by her; I denied her nothing. I scarcely ever had a word with her, and I did my best to make her happy," interposed the colonel.
> "I know, but your heart was with the other. So is mine. It's fatal, it runs in the family, father." (*Newcomes*, 879)

The Newcomes, like the Esmonds, find themselves enmeshed in their family histories, and two slim white hands, Rachel's and Ethel's, have touched and confirmed those destinies.

From the hands that touch to the things they touch. Many novels are visibly shaped by some set of things, solid objects that are the anchors for the points of the web, the "airy citadel", as Keats called it, that the artist spins "from his own inwards". The conceptual weight of *The Nigger of the 'Narcissus'*, as well as the physical load of the corpse of James Wait, is for a long moment sustained by that little nail on the plank that prevents the consignment of the dead to the sea. *Tristram Shandy* is shaped by a green baize bag of obstetrical instruments, a sash window bereft of its lead weight, a hot chestnut; *Great Expectations* by a savoury pork pie, a file, a mouldy wedding cake; *Middlemarch* by an emerald ring and bracelet, a statue of Ariadne, a row of voluminous notebooks towards a Key to All Mythologies. If you moved those things, you would alter or damage the structure and meaning of those novels, as you would a spider's web if you moved the points at which it was achored. Thackeray's things, as I have been showing, express his preoccupation with time. They are there not only to give a physical texture to the world he creates, nor as symbols for its conceptual import, though they do have both those values too. But they have value as they have accumulated associations, as they collect the past. That is why he gives his things histories: they recur, both within a given novel, and, with different import, as motifs, from one novel to another. Ribbons are flaunted, with varying implications, by Beatrix in the Augustan age, by Horrocks the butler's daughter and would-be baronet's lady in the Regency, by Ethel in the mid-Victorian world of *The Newcomes*; and ribbons also decorate the breast of Lord Steyne, that most prestigious and degenerate of noblemen, and of Altamont, the bigamist, army deserter, and fraud. Swords shed the blood of Lord Castlewood in Leicester Fields, dangle as the threat of hereditary madness over the children of the Gaunt family, decorate the walls of the newly established Clavering residence in Grosvenor Place, and hang by the side of the gentle Colonel Newcome. If we look at Thackeray's recurring things, including their associative and emblematic value, we find they take us a long way into the meaning of his novels. So, in my examination of Thackeray's theme of time, I want to extend my discussion from the more obvious records of the past like documents and paintings to a number of things that, like his characters' hands, express relationships changing, time passing, death encroaching.

The meanest flower that blows had moving import for Wordsworth. Thackeray has the same eye for significant detail, the same attention for what is often below other people's notice. Take buttons, for instance: these are Foker's, when he appears in his gear as a "swell": "He had a bulldog between his legs, and in his scarlet shawl neckcloth was a pin representing another bulldog in gold: he wore . . . a green cut-away coat with basket buttons, and a white upper coat ornamented with cheese-plate buttons, on each of which was engraved some stirring incident of the road or the chase" (*Pendennis*, 36–7). No wonder that one can't stop at Thackeray's formally painted portraits. His tale-telling pictures not only hang on the wall, but lurk as frontispieces to family bibles, tiles on stoves, engravings on buttons. Foker is not only a picture in himself, he is all over pictures. And his buttons are little index entries on Foker the man. We have the same loving attention to significant detail in the account of Colonel Newcome's Stultz coat with its "yellow buttons, now wearing a tinge of their native copper". The coat was bought in 1821, and the colonel still considers it a distinguished and fashionable garment twelve years later. And indeed at Mrs Newcome's soirée he is the lion of the evening, for his dress is dated enough to be picturesque, and the company is dazzled by his "flashing buttons". But Thackeray attaches more value yet to this insignificant part of a man's clothing. Remember "a certain trumpery gold sleeve-button of Mr. Esmond's" that he misses in prison immediately after Rachel's cruel and unjust denunciation of him. We meet that button again in the last sentence of the novel, when Esmond tells us, "The only jewel by which my wife sets any store, and from which she hath never parted, is that gold button she took from my arm on the day when she visited me in prison, and which she wore ever after, as she told me, on the tenderest heart in the world" (*Esmond*, 463). That is the final clinching clue that Esmond and the reader need in order to know that Rachel loved him at the very day of her husband's death, and while she was blaming him for it: that she was disguising a guilty and adulterous love; and that the book has been throughout–what careless readers missed–a record of the love story of Rachel and Henry Esmond.

Gold sleeve-buttons figure elsewhere in the novels as the trustworthy tokens of true love. When Rawdon prepares for a duel with Lord Steyne, he gives his comrade and second certain not very coherent instructions about his son: "I say, Mac, if anything goes wrong–if I drop–I should like you to–to go and see him, you know: and say that I was very fond of him, and that. And–dash it–old chap, give him these gold sleeve-buttons: it's all I've got" (*Vanity Fair*, 689). Similarly, in the opening paragraph of *Pendennis*, where the major's period and allegiances are defined by his heroes, Brummell, Wellington, and the Duke of York, we can tell where his heart lies when we learn that he wears on his wristbands "handsome gold buttons given to him by his Royal Highness the Duke of York" (2). (The Duke of York–the same of whom it was slanderously chanted in the nursery rhyme that he marched his men to the top of the hill and marched them down again–was a favourite figure of Thackeray's for placing his characters in time. He appears upside-down on his column in the cover design for *Vanity Fair*; and crusty old Lord Ringwood in *Philip* and Denis Duval were both born in the same year with the Duke, and the period of each novel is fixed by our meeting the one in his old age, the other in his childhood and youth.)

Thackeray generally associates gifts of gold with truth and enduring love. Little Miles Warrington in *The Virginians*, when his parents and all the world turn from George Warrington and Theo in their poverty, brings them his gold moidore, which they carefully preserve for its associative rather than its cash value. Colonel Newcome's gift to his favourite Ethel is a gold watch. On the other hand, diamonds are nearly always associated with vanity and a cold-hearted pursuit of prestige. Dr Firmin's signal is his flashy diamond ring. Blanche Amory jilts Pen for Foker when Foker has come into his father's fortune and gives her "oh, such a magnificent serpentine bracelet, with such a blazing ruby head and diamond tail!" (935). Vanity Fair fairly glitters with diamonds. When Dobbin lends George the money to buy the love-lorn little Amelia a present, George characteristically spends it on a trinket for himself, a diamond shirt-pin. We all remember the tableau of Lady Bareacres in Brussels on the day of Waterloo, sitting in her horseless carriage, with her diamonds sewn into her stays. Those diamonds have a history too, and Becky manages to score off Lady Bareacres again by mentioning them at the dinner at Gaunt House: "... everybody's eyes looked into their neighbours'. The famous diamonds had undergone a famous seizure, it appears, about which Becky, of course, knew nothing" (618). The Bareacres have come down in the world, a fall indicated by the fate of their diamonds, and Becky knows just how to put her finger on the fact.

But Becky herself is a diamond collector. Diamonds in effect are her price. There is a marvellous little scene that calls on all Becky's skill in judicious lying, when she is decked in diamonds for her presentation at court, in the company of her husband and his brother. Now the diamonds have come from two sources, neither of them known to her husband, though one is known to his brother Pitt, who has his panicky little qualms of guilt about his clandestine present to his sister-in-law. So when Rawdon asks, "Where the doose did you get the diamonds, Becky?" Becky has her work cut out to answer to the satisfaction of both brothers.

> Becky looked at her husband, and then at Sir Pitt, with an air of saucy triumph, as much as to say, "Shall I betray you?"
> "Guess!" she said to her husband. "Why, you silly man," she continued, "where do you suppose I got them – all except the little clasp, which a dear friend of mine gave me long ago. I hired them, to be sure. I hired them at Mr. Polonius's in Coventry Street." (*Vanity Fair*, 603)

So Sir Pitt and Rawdon are satisfied – Sir Pitt has not been betrayed, and must be warmed by the appellation of "dear friend"; and neither knows the source of all the other diamonds, which are real enough; "but Lord Steyne", we soon hear, "who was in his place at Court, . . . knew whence the jewels came, and who paid for them".

> As he bowed over her he smiled, and quoted the hackneyed and beautiful lines, from the *Rape of the Lock*, about Belinda's diamonds, "which Jews might kiss and infidels adore."
> "But I hope your lordship is orthodox," said the little lady, with a toss of her head. (*Vanity Fair*, 604)

And so Becky handles her men. But that air of proprietorship with which Steyne bows over her, and his gloating sexual reference, are signals that Becky is sold and the goods are his. The showdown comes soon afterwards, when Becky is again "in a brilliant full toilette, her arms and all her fingers sparkling with bracelets and rings; and the brilliants on her breast which Steyne had given her". When she implores him to tell Rawdon she is innocent, he retorts, "You innocent! Why, every trinket you have on your body is paid for by me" (675). The body has gone along with the trinkets. Rawdon's instinct for justice (like Thackeray's for the final telling detail in his biggest scene) is absolutely accurate when "he tore the diamond ornament out of her breast, and flung it at Lord Steyne. It cut him on his bald forehead. Steyne wore the scar to his dying day" (676). The scene derives a great deal of its power from that specificity about the diamonds, the "serpents, and rings, and baubles", and our knowledge of their history. And it is marvellously enhanced by that last sentence about Steyne's scar that places it in the larger span of time. Thackeray's scene does not begin and end with itself: it is a culmination of what has passed, and it reverberates into the future.

We are not finished with those diamonds yet. Mademoiselle Fifine, the French maid, prudently collects the scattered trinkets, and quietly absconds with them, and with all the other portables she can lay her hands on. "The game, in her opinion, was over in that little domestic establishment" (691). And she is perfectly right. Becky's world, the brilliant and hollow ménage in Curzon Street, has collapsed. Her diamonds have proved to be vanity and emptiness.

Beatrix's diamonds in *Henry Esmond* also have a history. They belong first to old Isabel, locally known to the no-Popery crowds as Jezebel. She always wears them in public, and is rumoured even to wear them in bed. But part with her diamonds at last she must; and she leaves them, no very propitious legacy, along with her other property to Henry Esmond. The rest of her effects he sells, but the diamonds, "having a special use for them", he keeps. He too has his plans to invest in human flesh, though unlike Lord Steyne he doesn't usually speculate in that commodity. But the flesh he has a mind to – Beatrix's – is costly. The diamonds alone can be no more than a scant deposit on so desirable a property, and when Esmond loses Beatrix herself to the Duke of Hamilton, who can afford the whole price, he gives her the diamonds as a wedding-present before the marriage. They give him at least some rights of ownership, and his reflections are like Steyne's, Pope reference and all, though he doesn't actually voice them:

> She gave a cry of delight, for the stones were indeed very handsome, and of great value; and the next minute the necklace was where Belinda's cross is in Mr. Pope's admira-

> ble poem, and glittering on the whitest and most perfectly-shaped neck in all England. (*Esmond*, 366)

Esmond and Lord Steyne, "*noble coeur*" and libertine, are made of the same flesh and blood. The suggestion that the gift of the diamonds confers partial ownership is made clear in the following scene, where the Duke of Hamilton interrupts Beatrix just as she is about to "[pay] her cousin with a price, that he would have liked no doubt to receive from those beautiful rosy lips of hers", and disputes Esmond's right to give diamonds to the future Duchess of Hamilton.

After the Duke's death, Beatrix tries to return the ill-fated wedding-present. But Esmond has meanwhile thought of a way to make up the full price, and he wants her to keep the down payment.

> "If I do something you have at heart; something worthy of me and you; something that shall make me a name with which to endow you; will you take it? . . . If I bring back that you long for, that I have a thousand times heard you pray for, will you have no reward for him who has done you that service? Put away those trinkets, keep them: . . . I swear a day shall come when there shall be a feast in your house, and you shall be proud to wear them." (*Esmond*, 396)

Esmond bargains with and for Beatrix – I bid my diamonds and the restoration of the Stuart dynasty for the hand and body of Beatrix Esmond, he says in effect. Beatrix, who is like Becky part agent and part object in the transaction, chaffers with him, and perhaps resolves like Becky to render as little property for the price as she can manage. When the time comes that Esmond has brought the prince back to England they remind each other of the deal: "Esmond looked at Beatrix, blazing with her jewels on her beautiful neck. 'I have kept my word,' says he: 'And I mine,' says Beatrix, looking down on the diamonds." But as Steyne is wounded by his own diamond brooch, so Esmond's diamonds are ironically the means of his losing her to the prince:

> A light shone out of her eyes; a gleam bright enough to kindle passion in any breast. There were times when this

> creature was so handsome, that she seemed, as it were, like Venus revealing herself a goddess in a flash of brightness. She appeared so now; radiant, and with eyes bright with a wonderful lustre. A pang, as of rage and jealously, shot through Esmond's heart, as he caught the look she gave the prince. (*Esmond*, 414)

Instead of receiving his bride for his bride-price, he finds he has merely decked her for another bridegroom. When you trade in the markets of Vanity Fair, you don't always get the goods you bargained for.

A passage like that I just quoted, incidentally, shows that Thackeray is not offering us the cheap moralising that tells us diamonds are trash. He knows and shows that they are beautiful and desirable, and women like Becky and Beatrix, decked in their jewels, not only look brilliant, but *are* brilliant. The diamonds can indeed confer a magical beauty – they have more than just a cash value on the market. So much the more are they to be feared; so much the greater is the fall when all Becky's splendour is reduced to a heap of baubles that the maid absconds with. Esmond and Rachel can be saved from that fate when "our diamonds are turned into ploughs and axes for our plantations" (463).

Beatrix is also associated with ribbons – ribbons are useful emblems for Thackeray, for they economically link two themes: as decorations both for the beautiful woman and the distinguished man, they represent the two vain quests, for beauty and for wordly success. Beatrix's new scarlet ribbon, which she puts on for Esmond's benefit on his homecoming, sets the tone for that marvellous scene in which he is confronted and mastered by her beauty: "From one of these [doors], a wax candle in her hand, and illuminating her, came Mistress Beatrix – the light falling indeed upon the scarlet ribbon which she wore, and upon the most brilliant white neck in the world" (216). There follows the brilliant description of Beatrix's descent of the stairs, in which everything – the glow and concentration of the light, the angle of vision from the worshipper upwards to the goddess, the manifest consciousness of youth and power before melancholy maturity – visibly presents the kind of relationship that is to exist between these two for some ten years. It is a vivid and memorable moment, but as usual in Thackeray, a moment set in time. The paragraph begins, "Esmond had left a child and found a woman"; and ends "As he thinks of her, he who writes feels young again, and remembers a paragon" (217).

Beatrix's ribbon, her beauty and her pride in it, the bond by which she holds Esmond, is like Becky's green silk purse for Jos. To recall again Thackeray's favourite Pope, they are the "slight lines" by which beauty may draw us "with a single hair". We are not allowed to forget Beatrix and her ribbons. Presently we see her "ordering her ribbons . . . before the glass" – an image that prompts Esmond to moralise, "She never at that time could be brought to think but of the world and her beauty" (337). And when Esmond saves her brother by fighting Mohun himself, and the family presents him in form with a sword "with a blue ribbon for a sword-knot", Beatrix tells him as she playfully dubs him knight, "I give the ribbon" (303). From the red ribbon on the woman's neck, to the blue ribbon on the sword, to the obsession of the nobleman who wastes his life "caballing for a blue ribbon" (338). (Thackeray's Roundabout Paper "On Ribbons" is concerned with awards and decorations, rather than the ornamental ribbons of ladies.) Here Thackeray ties in Beatrix's beauty with that other vain pursuit, the competition for royal recognition. As George Worth points out,[7] Beatrix is connected with all Esmond's false quests – Roman Catholicism, the Stuart cause, advancement by service to faithless princes – and in the culminating scene of the novel we see Esmond withdraw from the secret closet in Castlewood the family documents and titles, the long accumulations of the Esmonds' sacrifices and false expectations from the Stuarts, and burn them before the prince, Beatrix's seducer. They include the marquisate, "that precious title that lies in ashes, and this inestimable yard of blue ribbon. I lay this at your feet and stamp upon it: I draw this sword, and break it and deny you" (458). In stamping on the ribbon Esmond frees himself simultaneously from Beatrix and the false goals that have been involved in his pursuit of her. The history of what Esmond does with diamonds and ribbons is a miniature emblematic history of his own development. By stamping on a ribbon and turning diamonds into ploughshares he redefines himself and his values.

There are other personal adornments that Thackeray uses

recurrently through the novels. Rouge is one of his comic motifs – he delighted in contrasting the blush, the "pretty symbol of youth, and modesty, and beauty", with the externally applied pigment that lays false claim to those qualities. It is the old opposition of innocence and experience. *The Virginians*, set in the heyday of "painting", has constant references to blushing and rouging. Harry never doubts that his elderly Maria's cheeks are naturally rosy, but is understandably disturbed in the jolting carriage when the rest of her face turns "jonquil" while her bright red cheeks "continued to blush as it seemed with a strange metallic bloom". The most memorable rouge-pot in the novels is Becky's, prudently stowed in the bed at the Elephant, along with the brandy-bottle and plate of broken meats – other emblems of the advanced stage of Experience she has reached – before the visit of her innocent victim Jos.

When young Harry Esmond first sees the viscountess Isabel, her "face was daubed with white and red up to the eyes, to which the paint gave an unearthly glare: she had a tower of lace on her head, under which was a bush of black curls – borrowed curls" (34). Old Isabel has in a sense subsumed herself in her possessions and her artificial aids to beauty, and there are certain grisly suggestions sometimes that she is little more than a rag-bag of trinkets, wigs, clothing, stuffing, paint and pomatums. She is not the only figure that Thackeray sees as sacrificing humanity to empty pretension. As we have seen in a previous chapter, George IV was for Thackeray the epitome of the nothing that aspires to be everything:

> But this George, what was he? I look through all this life, and recognize but a bow and a grin. I try and take him to pieces, and find silk stockings, padding, stays, a coat with frogs and a fur collar, a star and blue ribbon, a pocket-handkerchief prodigiously scented, one of Truefitt's best nutty brown wigs reeking with oil, a set of teeth and a huge black stock, under-waistcoats, more under-waistcoats, and then nothing. (*The Four Georges*, 783)

And then nothing. Vanity and emptiness. Thackeray's dwelling on the externals of appearance recurrently suggests that the appearance is all there is, or at least that the appearance has so swelled and spread as to engulf and nullify the little stunted vestiges of the real human being. So we have Jos at his first appearance, "a very stout, puffy man, in buckskins and hessian boots" (the "puffy" suggests not substance, but the lack of it), almost swallowed in his own neckcloths (24); Dr Firmin with his shirt-frill and flashing ring and glittering dentures; and Major Pendennis with his false teeth and his padding, who talks sentimentally about exchanging locks of hair while passing his fingers through his wig. They belong in the world of Blanche Amory, who is simply an encrustation of one sham pasted on another; or of Rosey Newcome, who annihilates herself, preferring "to have her opinions dealt out to her like her frocks, bonnets, handkerchiefs, her shoes and gloves, and the order thereof" (*Newcomes*, 311). A chapter initial in *The Virginians* shows two wigs making love; and the plot of the first volume of that novel turns on Lady Maria's false teeth. The person is lost in his own appurtenances. So it must be in Vanity Fair, where Becky nets a purse in which to catch her fat fish, and a young lady like Agnes Twysden in *Philip* marries not a man, but "a property".

But not all the clothes and decorations in Thackeray's novels signify vanity and emptiness. There are garments, like Colonel Newcome's Stultz coat, or Dobbin's cloak, which "had been new for the campaign of Waterloo, and had covered George and William after the night of Quatre Bras" (*Vanity Fair*, 855), that have gathered through time their associations of love and suffering. And these two gentlest of Thackeray's men are both associated also with shawls – Cashmere ones, usually, such gifts as befit Anglo-Indian veterans. Their banner over those they love is a shawl. The Colonel bestows a Cashmere shawl on nearly every woman in his family. Dobbin's behaviour with Amelia's shawl is an index to the progress of their relationship through the years. During the evening at Vauxhall, the night he falls in love with her, the two couples ignore him and simply make use of him:

> "Honest Dobbin contented himself by giving an arm to the shawls, and by paying at the door for the whole party... Perhaps he felt that he would have liked to have something on his own arm besides a shawl (the people

5 Wigs making love: headletter for Chapter 19 of *The Virginians*

laughed at seeing the gawky young officer carrying this female burden)" (*Vanity Fair*, 63).

To Amelia "old Dobbin" is no more than an ambulatory clothes-horse, a useful piece of furniture. After George's death, Dobbin's status improves, and he is allowed to give the shawls rather than merely to carry them. But Amelia still shamefully abuses him. At their difference over the re-introduction of Becky into the family circle she overrides his objections, and, coming downstairs with her shawl over her arm, she "ordered Dobbin to follow. He went and put her shawl – it was a white Cashmere, consigned to her by the major himself from India – over her shoulders. He saw there was nothing for it but to obey" (838). From clothes-horse, he has become a servant. It is one of the more encouraging signs of the ultimate (though qualified) happiness of their marriage that in their reunion scene it is Amelia who unclasps Dobbin's cloak for him, and that she consigns her shawl to someone else to look after.

And Thackeray had a nostalgic fondness for swords. So far as he offers us romance and heroism in the novels, they are often attached to swords. The aspect of *Henry Esmond* that is historical romance centres on the two swords left by Father Holt in the secret closet at Castlewood, kept there by young Henry as relics of the past, and used again for "satisfaction" from the prince when Esmond has broken his own. The most stirring incident of the military campaigns is that where Webb passes the *Gazette* to Marlborough on the point of his sword. And the conferring of a sword marks Esmond's stature as the "true knight" of his family. Crossed swords are the opening image of *The Virginians*. And Colonel Newcome's two swords, "his old regulation sword" and a presentation sword from his men, are the treasured spars which his friends save for him from the general wreck of his property.

Documents, paintings, buttons, diamonds, ribbons, rouge, wigs, shawls, swords – I seem to be collecting the beginnings of a catalogue of Thackeray's recurring motifs, and I should perhaps have put them in alphabetical order. But instead I shall add to my catalogue another item – catalogues. We hear of Rawdon before his marriage that he sends Becky "shawls, kid gloves, silk stockings, gold French watches, bracelets and perfumery . . . with the profusion of blind love and unbounded credit" (191). And it is with the profusion of a devotion to objects and unbounded imagination that Thackeray packs his novels. But his best kind of catalogue is that which is in effect the summary of a history. There are several of these in *Vanity Fair* alone. On that ominous evening when Mr Osborne locks himself in his study to disinherit George, he opens "a drawer especially devoted to his son's affairs and papers".

> They were all marked and docketed, and tied with red tape. It was – "From Georgy, requesting 5s., April 23, 18–; answered April 25," – or "Georgy about a pony, October 13," – and so forth. . . . Here was a whip he had when a boy, and in a paper a locket containing his hair, which his mother used to wear. (283)

As he muses over "these memorials", "he had the child before his eyes, on a hundred different days when he remembered George". There smiles the ghost of the past again, insubstantially recreated by the little repository of relics. The list of what the maid steals from Becky's house, including the gilt Louis Quatorze candlesticks and a gold enameled snuff-box which had once belonged to Madame du Barri, is a succinct little history of the nature of Becky's Curzon street operation, as the rouge-pot and the brandy-bottle are of her later and more disreputable way of life. Before Waterloo, Rawdon makes a "little catalogue of effects" of the items he can leave to Becky, and what they will fetch if he dies. It includes:

> My double-barril by Manton, say 40 guineas; my driving-cloak, lined with sable fur, 50£; my duelling pistols in rosewood case (same which I shot Captain Marker), 20£ . . . and so forth, over all of which articles he made Rebecca the mistress. (367)

It is a moving document – ill spelling, shaky grammar and all – because through the accumulated emblems of his life Rawdon is bequeathing Becky not just his property but his past – by implication, himself. And there is a touch of humility in that attaching of prices not found in the usual testator: most people contemplating their possible death dwell mentally on the sentimental value of their bequests, and tacitly assume their beneficiaries will keep them as relics. But Rawdon is content that Becky should turn his remains into ready cash.

The sale of effects after a death or a bankruptcy was a favourite scene for Thackeray. When he attended the sale at Lady Blessington's house, well after he had written of the Sedley sale, he wrote in a letter "Ah it was a strange sad picture of Wanaty Fair. My mind is all boiling up with it".[8] It is a scene in which property, prized possessions and the love and allegiances that they represent, the happiness and the suffering and the long experience of years, all come up for auction and are sold for money to the highest bidder. In Vanity Fair everything (and everyone) is for sale. At the Sedley sale Thackeray suggests a disillusioned vision of the total human endeavour: "Down comes the hammer like fate, and we pass to the next lot." And as the people involved in the buying and selling cling to things or sacrifice them, as the speculators finger the merchandise to assess its quality and cash value, or bid for some object because of its past association or its future utility, they demonstrate themselves and their attitude to property, to experience, to life.

I have been talking about Thackeray's favourite objects, his repeating motifs, as they recur through the novels. But of course he adapts them to the issue at hand in a given novel. It would take long to demonstrate this for every novel, but perhaps I can take one novel as a specimen, and examine the orchestration of motifs in *Pendennis*.

Martin Fido and others[9] have pointed out that *Pendennis* is a novel about art and artifice. The hero falls in love first with an actress and next with a flirt who is sham all through; and he himself aspires to be a writer. From the first paragraph on Major Pendennis, when "by a nearer inspection . . . [we see] the factitious nature of his rich brown hair", we are alerted that we are to be on the lookout for the difference between the natural and the artificial, the true and the false. The objects that appear in *Henry Esmond* with a colouring of romance and which even in *Vanity Fair* have a certain sparkle are shown here to be phonies, mere tinsel and stage props. For Becky's and Beatrix's diamonds we have the mountebank's "sham diamond rings covering the first joint of the finger and twiddling in the faces of the pit. . . . The stage has its traditional jewels as the Crown and all great families have" (44).

Jos's treasured hessian boots likewise reappear as part of an actor's costume. Instead of Beatrix's irresistible ribbons and the Castlewoods' hard-won marquisate there are the fake decorations on the breast of the imposter Altamont and the pretentious cook, Mirobolant, so that the patronising Pen comments in amusement, "By Jove, here's some more ribbon!" (321).

The charged motion of hands in the other novels is recalled in the Fotheringay's histrionic talents on the stage:

> It was her hand and arm that this magnificent creature most excelled in, and somehow you could never see her but through them. They surrounded her. When she folded them over her bosom in resignation; when she dropped them in mute agony, or raised them in superb command; when in sportive gaiety her hands fluttered and waved before her, . . . it was with these arms and hands that she beckoned, repelled, entreated, embraced her admirers. (*Pendennis*, 47)

We hear later that this is not even inspired art, for the Fotheringay is little more than an automaton who can mimic exactly and repeat her director's orders. There is the same ironic undercutting of a favourite motif in the talk about Blanche and *her* histrionic manoeuvering with "hand No. 1" and "hand No. 2". The duels that actually happen in *Esmond, The Virginians* and *Denis Duval* and are threatened in *Vanity Fair* and *The Newcomes* are in this novel only unseemly brawls; and Esmond's *botte de Jesuite*, by which he is the master of Lord Mohun, is replaced by Pen's transparent subterfuge of taking fencing lessons from the boozy old Costigan because he wants to be near his daughter. It is almost inevitable that at some point we should encounter, as we do, "double-handed swords and battle-axes made of *carton-pierre*" (471–2).

These swords form part of the décor in the newly-decorated Clavering residence in Grosvenor Square, and Thackeray makes one of his vast lists of the trinkets and *bibelots* in the dining- and drawing-rooms:

> . . . marqueterie-tables covered with marvellous gimcracks, china ornaments of all ages and countries, bronzes, gilt

> daggers, Books of Beauty, yataghans, Turkish papooshes, and boxes of Parisian bonbons. Wherever you sat down there were Dresden shepherds and shepherdesses convenient at your elbow; there were, moreover, light blue poodles and ducks and cocks and hens in porcelain; there were nymphs by Boucher, and shepherdesses by Greuze, very chaste indeed. . . . (472)

It goes on for pages, and it is devastating. This stuff is not only in bad taste, a hodge-podge of borrowed articles from different cultures, a display of opulence; not only useless ("I don't advise you to try one of them gossamer gilt chairs", Lady Clavering amiably warns her guests, "*I* came down on one the night we gave our second dinner-party") – but it's abominably *new*. The décor is pronounced " 'very chaste,' that being the proper phrase". It is both virginal and sterile: a collection of souvenirs that remind no one of anything. This house is the *Pendennis* contrast to Castlewood, which is still partly a ruin from the cannon shots of the Protectorate. With its family portraits, its secret entrances for Jesuits, its secreted swords and incriminating documents – Castlewood is an accumulation of an ugly past, perhaps, but still it *has* one. And a list like this reminds us of the different quality of Rawdon's catalogue of effects or Osborne's drawerful of relics. For Thackeray the value of a place or an object lies in its freight of association. The Clavering interior has no past, and so in a sense it has no present either.

As paintings have a special function in *The Newcomes*, and cards in *The Virginians*, that novel about play and gambling, this novel about a writer features manuscripts and letters in a special role. Pen is naturally disappointed to find that the love-letters he has been keeping next to his heart were not even written by his Emily's hand, but that his actress love employed an amanuensis. Blanche's manuscript book of poems about her thorny past, *Mes Larmes*, does not bear inspection for genuineness, either: "They were not particularly briny, Miss Blanche's tears, that is the truth." We are given a specimen of "the Muse's" talent, à-propos of her little brother: " 'Oh, let me, let me love you! the world will prove to you As false as 'tis to others, but *I* am ever true.' And behold the muse was boxing the darling brother's ears instead of kneeling at his

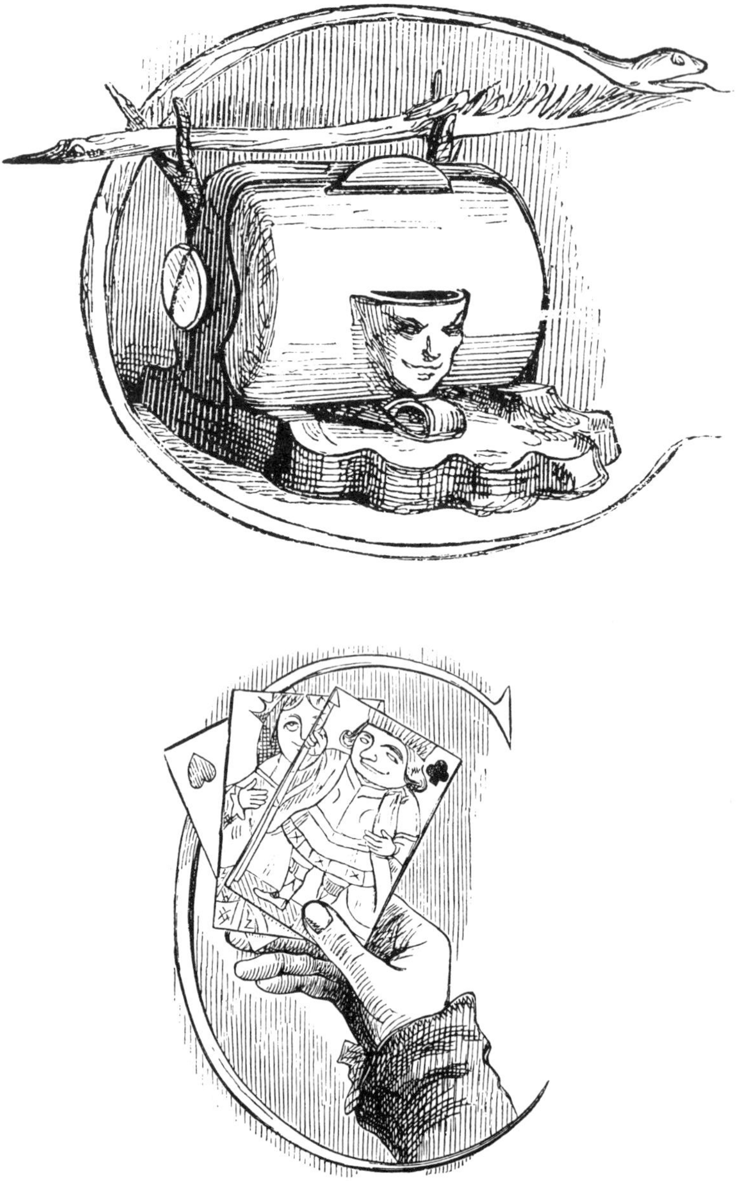

6 Emblematic headletters, from Chapter 35 of *Pendennis* and Chapter 25 of *The Virginians*

feet" (301). Pen's own compositions, for all his striving to be honest, recurrently prove him a humbug, as he adapts poems written in passion to one woman for another, and pretends to throw his manuscript in the fire when he knows the fire is out.

And written works – whether letters, manuscripts, or books – often go through a metamorphosis that changes them from mere sequences of words into things concrete, or consumable, or sometimes almost animate. We see Pen's letters and poems to the Fotheringay tied in a parcel like a pound of sugar; the major's letters at his breakfast table are personified into their writers, and become "so many grand folks who attended his levee"; Bludyer the savage reviewer converts the books he reviews into dinner and a pint of brandy; Pen sends Blanche a box of bonbons with each sugarplum wrapped in a tender verse. If words become things, the metamorphosis works in the other direction too, so that Blanche's actual sighs and tears become *Mes Soupirs* (which runs into two editions) and *Mes Larmes*; and the cook Mirobolant makes his elaborate declaration of love to Blanche in the form of a meal composed of white and pink dishes, in honour of her name and colouring. Like Sterne in *Tristram Shandy*, Thackeray in his novel about a novelist reminds us of the interrelation of the word and the flesh, and makes his things dance in tune with his language.

Thackeray's characters are morally grouped according to their attitude to the past. His familiar rough division of humanity into those who answer to the outer directives of the world and those who answer to the inward directives of love is a rough and ready one, but it works. Becky leads the first group, Amelia the second. Thackeray sees clearly enough the disadvantages of both systems, and his most morally aware characters are those like Pendennis, Ethel and Clive Newcome, and George Warrington of *The Virginians*, who find themselves tested between the two extremes.

It is characteristic of those like Becky who are the denizens of Vanity Fair that their commitment to the past is of the slightest. At its most obvious level this independence of the past takes the form of not honouring one's debts – like Becky and Rawdon, who make a system out of living on nothing a year, or Sir Francis Clavering, who "would sign almost anything for to-morrow, provided to-day could be left unmolested" (*Pendennis*, 552). But those who haunt Vanity Fair take a more elaborate and comprehensive advantage of conveniently short memories. At one point, when the narrator has been brooding over the melancholy satire of old love letters, he lays it down as a maxim: "There ought to be a law in Vanity Fair ordering the destruction of every written document (except receipted tradesmen's bills) after a certain brief and proper interval" (*Vanity Fair*, 230). Becky acts essentially on this law and its implications, and her system is manifested in her treatment of things. She does hoard things – she accumulates that purse for herself in the little desk – but she hoards them not for their associative value, not for their past significance, but for their future usefulness. She intends to turn them to good account hereafter. The billet-doux from George, the picture of Jos, the banknotes from Steyne – these are her valuable versions of "receipted tradesmen's bills". They are fragments she has shored up against her ruin – and very handy they come in too, when the time comes. Of course in the case of the picture of Jos she *pretends* she has kept it for sentimental reasons, and because it reminds her of her lost love. But Becky is quite unashamed about manipulating time: remember her peculiarly heartless ploy of keeping a little half-made shirt for Rawdy that she takes out to sew when she wants to impress people with her maternal feelings – long after Rawdy has outgrown its size.

We are told of Becky after her grief at not being able to accept Sir Pitt, "Rebbecca was a young lady of too much resolution and energy of character to permit herself much useless and unseemly sorrow for the irrevocable past; so, having devoted only the proper portion of regret to it, she wisely turned her whole attention towards the future, which was now vastly more important to her" (186–7). One of her snake-like attributes is her ability to slough off the past like an old skin, or like the empty trunks she leaves behind in Paris to make her landlord believe she will come back and pay his bill. And to this talent she owes much of her vitality and charm. Unlike many characters more moral, she bears no grudges. She swallows the fiery curry, and turns a joke. She downs Lady Southdown's horrible bolus, and then acts out a pantomime of the scene. She knows Dobbin is her adversary, but she likes him and does him a good turn.

Amelia, on the other hand, tends to be morbidly fixated on the past. She can muster nostalgia at the drop of a hat. After only nine days of marriage she goes to her parents in Fulham and mourns over her "dear little white bed" – and this in a house that is not the house of her childhood, but has been her family's rented lodging only since the bankruptcy. "Already to be looking sadly and vaguely back," the narrator comments, "always to be pining for something which, when obtained, brought doubt and sadness rather than pleasure: here was the lot of our poor little creature, and harmless lost wanderer in the great struggling crowds of Vanity Fair" (319). And she continues to live up to this character through years of pointless mourning for a bad past husband, when she could have been giving herself to a good new one. It is a measure of Colonel Newcome's moral superiority to Amelia that he is ready to consign his old Stultz coat to the rag-bag when the time comes: "Get me another coat then", he tells his man; "I'm not above learning."

Thackeray maintains that distinction in attitudes to the past between his worldly and his loving characters in the other novels. The long memory is characteristic of the loving soul, but it has its concomitant disadvantage of making forgiveness almost impossible. Henry Esmond has a long memory, yet even his adoring daughter has to own of him that he would never forgive an offense. His grandson inherits this quality, and one of the central themes of *The Virginians* is that of forgiveness, and what one is to do with that awkward affair called a bygone. When young George is urged to forgive Washington, he replies, "Never, sir, as long as I remember. You can't order remembrance out of a man's mind; and a wrong that was a wrong yesterday must be a wrong tomorrow" (*Virginians*, 98). And years later, though he has reached middle age and a temperate frame of mind, the past is still vivid before him, so that he acknowledges again: "I can't forgive; not until my days of dotage come, and I cease remembering anything" (797). On the other hand, his worldly aunt and cousin, Beatrix and Lady Maria, are not gnawed by the same pangs of lasting resentment. If they can't eliminate the past, they can at least set it aside temporarily, as it were, and for mutual convenience:

> What can there be finer than forgiveness? . . . It was beautiful, for instance, to see our two ladies at Tunbridge Wells forgiving one another, smiling, joking, fondling almost in spite of the hard words of yesterday – yes; and forgetting bygones, though they couldn't help remembering them perfectly well. (*Virginians*, 393)

There is the same opposition between Agnes Twysden and Caroline Brandon, the "Little Sister", in *Philip*. Agnes is ready without regret to "shake hands forever, cancel all her vows" when a more eligible suitor than Philip comes courting: "She will give him up – she will give him up. Good-bye, Philip. Good-bye the past. Be forgotten, be forgotten, fond words!" (191). But the gentle Little Sister has a long memory for a wrong, and she reproaches her father for his past cruelty with some vindictiveness: 'I forgive you; but a hundred thousand billion years can't mend that injury, father, while you broke a poor child's heart with it that day!" (165).

So the otherwise good and loving Henry Esmond, Rachel, Helen Pendennis, Laura, Colonel Newcome, George Warrington and Caroline Brandon are all grudge-bearers, and become at some stage moral tyrants, because it is as impossible for them to forgive as to forget.

Between them and the shallow characters like Clavering and Agnes, there is another breed of hybrids whose creed is the world's but whose memories won't die, but chain them to their other younger and more loving selves. Osborne is one of these, and that is what makes him so great a conception. He fervently believes in the pursuit of wealth as a religion, and so sees no alternative but to disown his son when he chooses "to marry a bankrupt and fly in the face of duty and fortune" (*Vanity Fair*, 284). But he is agonisingly tied to his love and his memories of his son. Even Lord Steyne, the figure in the novels who is closest to being damned, and indeed devilish, has moments of seeming redeemable when his memory connects him with his past:

> "The young one is in a scrape, [he says of Pendennis.] I was myself – when I was in the fifth form at Eton – a market gardener's daughter – and swore I'd marry her. I was mad about her – poor Polly!" Here he made a pause, and

> perhaps the past rose up to Lord Steyne, and George Gaunt was a boy again not altogether lost. (*Pendennis*, 162)

A man's estrangement from his own past is powerfully realised in another of Thackeray's portrait images. The rich and irascible old Lord Ringwood doesn't dare to stay in his own grand house when he comes to town because he is surrounded there by his past, the family portraits:

> ghostly images of dead Ringwoods – his dead son, who had died in his boyhood; his dead brother attired in the uniform of his day . . . ; Lord Ringwood's dead self, finally, as he appeared still a young man, when Lawrence painted him . . . . "Ah, that's the fellow I least like to look at," the old man would say, scowling at the picture. (*Philip*, 303)

Twentieth-century existential literature can scarcely present a sharper image of alienated man. One may be alienated in space, exiled from home or country and at odds with the surrounding society; but one may also be alienated in time like Lord Ringwood, cut off from the past and his own self. And time that gave doth now his gift confound.

For Thackeray, an object becomes a crossroads where the temporal converges with the spatial. His things – his portraits, documents, garments, ornaments – rings and things and buttons and bows – are little local repositories of time past. In the world of his novels, the past is always ready like a genie to spring out and perform its perverse or beneficial magic; and Thackeray's things are so many Aladdin's lamps, with their several genii lurking inside.

NOTES

1. G. K. Chesterton, *The Victorian Age in Literature* (London, 1913) p. 126.
2. As my text for Thackeray's works I use George Saintsbury (ed.), *The Oxford Thackeray,* 17 vols (London, 1908).
3. Geoffrey Tillotson, *Thackeray the Novelist* (Cambridge, 1954) pp. 60, 87ff.
4. Barbara Hardy, *The Exposure of Luxury: Radical Themes in Thackeray* (London, 1972) p. 102.
5. *Ibid.*, ch. 4.
6. See his introduction to *The Newcomes* in *The Oxford Thackeray*, vol. XIV xxvii.

7. George Worth, "The Unity of *Henry Esmond*", *Nineteenth-Century Fiction*, 15 (1961) 345–53.
8. Gordon N. Ray (ed.), *The Letters and Private Papers of William Makepeace Thackeray*, vol. II (London, 1945–6) p. 532.
9. Martin Fido, "*The History of Pendennis*: A Reconsideration", *Essays in Criticism*, 14 (1964) 363–79. See also Edgar Harden, "Theatricality in *Pendennis*", *Ariel*, 4 (1973) 74–94.

7 The Pygmalion Motif in *The Newcomes*

With an indirect kind of narcissism, the mind falling in love with its own creation, Pygmalion produces a statue, the figment of his imagination, worships it, and seeks to bring it to life. This kind of activity, including the worship of statues, is a recurrent pattern in Thackeray's *The Newcomes*. Thackeray is peculiarly interested in the role fictions play in the lives of his characters. Some, like Pygmalion, fall in love with visions they have summoned forth from their own imaginations and try to bring these ideal patterns to life by imposing them on the raw material of other people's lives. Others fashion their own lives according to stylised patterns. Ethel Newcome, for example, at one stage describes herself and other young ladies fashioned for the marriage market as works of art like paintings in a gallery, and the personality she presents to others is made up of various highly artificial projections. Clive Newcome, as a painter, perceives Ethel primarily in terms of statuary and paintings, falling in love with his own imagination of her. The world Thackeray describes is one of perpetual tension between the ordering imagination and the resisting raw material of life. To the individual at the vivid centre of his moment of time, his schemes seem unique and substantial. In a long view, however, he encounters the frustrations that all men encounter in a world of limitations, and there is nothing new under the sun. That is the point of "the farrago of old fables" with which *The Newcomes* begins. And the contrast between the patterns the mind wishes to see fulfilled and the realities of life in the fallen world occasions Thackeray's postscript after he has, like George Bernard Shaw in his play *Pygmalion*, chopped his story short, leaving the reader's romantic longings frustrated.

In familiar moral terms, this idealising drive of the imagination can be seen as the attempt of fallen humanity to rebuild paradise. And if we examine the first number of *The Newcomes* with the kind of care that is now given to the serial parts of Dickens's novels, we find Thackeray carefully setting up these themes and modes of vision both in setting and character. The first number keeps moving back and forth between a paradisal pastoral vision of the world and a more vulgar, commercial, urban view of it. In the first chapter, where the curtain rises, the animals in the introductory fable come to grief with the sudden incursion of reality in the form of butcher, ploughboy, and farmer. Another golden and pastoral world, but containing the threat of its own destruction, immediately follows, the narrator looking far back to a time "when the sun used to shine brighter than it appears to do in this latter half of the nineteenth century" (6).[1] This world, coloured by the narrator's nostalgia and by the green youth of the company he is remembering, centres on a coffee-house called the "Cave of Harmony," a citified Arcadia where "the roses bloom again, and the nightingales sing by the calm Bendemeer" (7), and where the songs are "chiefly of the sentimental class". The innocent swain, who enters with his son, "a fine tall young stripling" with "bright blue eyes", is Colonel Newcome, instant sport of the barely more than adolescent rakes assembled, including Pendennis, who dubs him "Don Ferolo Whiskerandos" (8–9). For a moment the Arcadian note is in danger from the impulse of the wags to "low mimetic", but " '*Maxima debetur pueris*,' says Jones (a fellow of very kind feeling, who has gone into the Church since), and writing on his card to Hoskins hinted to him that a boy was in the room, and a gentleman, who was quite a greenhorn: hence that the songs had better be carefully selected" (9). The Colonel's contribution of "Wapping Old Stairs", sung before an initially embarrassed Clive, is another triumph of finer feeling over fallen nature: "It was like Dr. Primrose preaching his sermon in the prison. There was something touching in the *naïveté* and kindness of the placid and simple gentleman." The moment is achieved, the mood harmonious, "we could see he was thinking about his youth – the golden time – the happy, the bright, the unforgotten".

The moment fails, however, the romance turns ironic, with Captain Costigan's entrance "in his usual condition at this hour of the night" (12). A kind of Irish Silenus, with "a horrid grin, and leering", he launches into a song so outrageous that the scandalised Colonel interrupts him with a moral tirade, amusing, offending, and upsetting the onlookers. Then

> shouldering his stick, and scowling round at the company of scared bacchanalians, the indignant gentleman stalked away, his boy after him.
>
> Clive seemed rather shamefaced; but I fear the rest of the company looked still more foolish.
>
> "Aussique diable venait-il faire dans cette galère?" says King of Corpus to Jones of Trinity; and Jones gave a shrug of his shoulders, which were smarting, perhaps; for that uplifted cane of the Colonel's had somehow fallen on the back of every man in the room. (14)

There is nothing casual about this pastoral embroidery; the next chapter, "Colonel Newcome's Wild Oats", heads unerringly to yet another paradise as we look back upon the elder Thomas Newcome's marriage to a girl with a quarter of a million, a Quaker connection, and a mansion at Clapham "surrounded by lawns and gardens, pineries, graperies, aviaries, luxuries of all kinds". It was, however,

> a serious paradise. As you entered at the gate, gravity fell on you; and decorum wrapped you in a garment of starch. The butcher-boy who galloped his horse and cart madly about the adjoining lanes ... fell into an undertaker's pace.... The rooks in the elms cawed sermons at morning and evening; the peacocks walked demurely on the terraces; the guineafowls looked more quaker-like than those savoury birds usually do.... The head-gardener was a Scotch Calvinist, after the strictest order, only occupying himself with the melons and pines provisionally, and until the end of the world. (21–2)

The chapter ends with young Tom, the Colonel to be, having rebelled against "that stifling garden of Eden" (22) and scandalised his step-mother by wishing to marry a Papist, embarking for India and the army, his father afraid to leave him his fortune "on account of his terror of Sophia Alethea, his wife" (34).

The third chapter, and end of the first number, consists of a series of letters establishing family relationships and bringing the Colonel's son, Clive, on the scene as a child sent home from India. The cycle of generations is ready to begin again, and Thackeray's complex lacing back and forth in time between the Colonel's youth and Clive's is an important element in the "argument" Thackeray will unfold.

With its blending and offsetting of stylised outlooks and environments, its ironic playing with pastoral and cynical conventions, the first number of *The Newcomes* is a skilled and efficient exordium. Its oscillating visions of the world function in two ways: as they are accepted or expressed by the characters themselves, they are examples of life attempting to conform to imaginative pattern and threatened by the unforeseen, the chaos of reality, or else by the impingement of one man's paradise on another's; as they jostle one another for the reader's attention, they implicitly and ironically call into question the very idea of nature as opposed to art. And here one may recall a renowned feature of Thackeray's style that makes him a delight to literate readers. Few novelists, other than Joyce, imbue character and plot with such a range of supplementary fabulation. Not only are we to see the story as a fable with characters as typical as the fable animals, but as fairy tale, with Clive, Ethel, and Lady Kew as Prince, Princess, and Witch, or again as myth, with Clive as Hercules enslaved by Ethel as Omphale, and again as elegant pastoral theatre, in which Ethel plays shepherdess to Clive's swain. In another complex stream of allusion, Ethel repeatedly calls to mind the sculpture of Diana in the Louvre. Head letters often provide pictorial glosses to the narrative, as in Chapter 52, in which Lady Kew, pictured as a witch, casts a spell over a teapot as Macbeth wielding a stick (Barnes) approaches to consult her (681). In another perspective, *The Newcomes* is a moral progress. The head letter of Chapter 2, in which the elder Thomas Newcome, like Dick Whittington, comes to London to make his fortune, "marrying his master's daughter, and becoming sheriff and alderman of the City" (18), shows Hogarth's industrious apprentice.[2] For the marriage market at Baden, Thackeray invokes *Marriage à la Mode*, and later, Lord Highgate hangs about Barnes's wife, Clara, "just in such an attitude as the bride is in Hogarth's 'Marriage à la mode' as the counsellor

7 Lady Kew as a witch: Doyle's headletter for Chapter 52 of *The Newcomes*

talks to her" (720). In John Harvey's view, Thackeray expected his readers to see he was taking his theme from *Marriage à la Mode*, and indeed two reviewers, one of them Edward Burne Jones, did.[3] Behind all these figurative allusions and rephrasings hover the tone and perspective of Ecclesiastes with its themes of recurrence and frustration. My intention, however, is not to labour the obvious point of Thackeray's manifold allusiveness, but to argue that in *The Newcomes* these compounded stories and allusions are essential not only to the decoration but to the principal theme of the work, a theme that has its centre in Colonel Newcome's attempt to mould life according to his imaginary pattern.

The colonel's appearance as a derided but morally triumphant innocent, Don Ferolo Whiskerandos, in the ironic pastoral context of the first number invites us to reconsider a letter Thackeray wrote as the book was just under way:

> "I read Don Quixote nearly through when I was away. What a vitality in those two characters! What gentlemen they both are! I wish Don Quixote was not thrashed so very often. There are sweet pastoralities through the book, and that piping of shepherds and pretty sylvan ballet which dances always round the principal figures is delightfully pleasant to me. . . ."[4]

Thackeray read *Don Quixote* in the summer of 1853 while writing the first four numbers of *The Newcomes*. The connection is evident not only in the ironic pastoralities of the first number, a type of satire Thackeray enjoys in *Vanity Fair* and *Pendennis* as well, but directly in his emphatic conclusion to the second number. Encountering the Colonel's supercilious nephew Barnes, whom he despises as a "dashed little prig", General Sir Thomas de Boots says of the Colonel:

> "I tell you what, young man, if you were more like him it wouldn't hurt you. He's an odd man; they call him Don Quixote in India; I suppose you have read *Don Quixote*."
>
> "Never heard of it, upon my word; and why do you wish I should be more like him? I don't wish to be like him at all, thank you."
>
> "Why, because he is one of the bravest officers that ever lived," roared out the old soldier. "Because he's one of the kindest fellows; because he gives himself no dashed airs, although he has reason to be proud if he chose. That's why, Mr. Newcome."
>
> . . . the indignant general walks away gobbling and red. (85)

This vignette is significant in showing the enmity between Barnes and the Colonel, but the identification of the Colonel with Don Quixote, recurrent throughout the novel, adds another sombre tinge.[5] In Don Quixote we have, *par excellence*, the man who has inherited a conventional vision that fires his imagination and who, trading the world's brass for its gold, insists that it be *the* world, thus creating for himself the tragedy that Sir Philip Sidney attributed to "that first accursed fall of Adam: since our erected wit maketh us know what perfection is, and yet our infected will keepeth us from reaching unto it".[6] As both Cervantes and Thackeray knew, our infected wills can also contribute to the doggedness of our convictions about what virtue and perfection are. As Thackeray wrote, "The wicked are wicked no doubt, and they go astray and they fall, and they come by their deserts: but who can tell the mischief which the very virtuous do?" (246). Any number of characters in *The Newcomes* live encapsulated in thoroughly conventional visions which they nevertheless regard as highly singular and singularly realistic: " 'Know the world, young man!' cries Newcome; 'I should think if I don't know the world at my age, I never shall.' And if he had lived to be as old as Jahaleel a boy could still have cheated him" (327).

Wonderful in its orchestration of time and memory, the Colonel's career is a cycle, starting and ending in childhood, a cycle that under his influence will partly repeat itself in the life of his son. Having lost his first love Léonore in a conflict of class and family interests, the Colonel settles for a pitiful little marriage of second choice from which Clive is born. When the Colonel returns from India as a distinguished officer and meets Clive's cousin Ethel, the past and present merge:

> they fell in love with each other instantaneously. . . . There was no point of resemblance, and yet a something in the girl's look, voice, and movements, which caused his heart to thrill, and an image out of the past to rise up and salute him. . . .It is an old saying, that we forget nothing. . . .No doubt, as the old soldier held the girl's hand in his, the little talisman led him back to Hades, and he saw Leonora. (200–1)

As the chapter ends, the Colonel's work of art takes shape in his imagination and his great enterprise begins. The passage is worth quoting at length:

> The Colonel from his balcony saw the slim figure of the retreating girl, and looked fondly after her; and as the smoke of his cigar floated in the air, he formed a fine castle

> in it, whereof Clive was lord, and that pretty Ethel, lady. . . . "What a fine match might be made between that child and Clive! She reminds me of a pair of eyes I haven't seen these forty years. I would like to have Clive married to her; to see him out of the scrapes and dangers that young fellows encounter, and safe with such a sweet girl as that. If God had so willed it, I might have been happy myself, and could have made a woman happy. But the Fates were against me. I should like to see Clive happy, and then say *Nunc dimittis*." (204)

Seeing a present coloured by his own youthful romance, the Colonel fashions from these materials a dream that will serve both to complete vicariously the pattern of his own frustrated love story and to bring happiness to his son. God did not will his own ideal marriage; now he can be God and arrange things more perfectly. His aspiration is not at first sight arrogant, for the vision arises from the unselfish love of parent for child (and here one might note in passing that readers irritated by the wandering and slow-paced way Thackeray develops the "sentimental question" of Clive's love for Ethel are on the wrong scent – the great and moving love in *The Newcomes* is between Colonel Newcome and his son). The paragraph is nevertheless ominous. Not only do we anticipate what comes of playing God, but that reiterated word, happy, happy, happy – "I might have been happy myself. . . . I should like to see Clive happy" – rings with a frail sound against the burden of Thackeray's moral vision: "Ah! *Vanitas Vanitatum*! Which of us is happy in this world? Which of us has his desire? or, having it, is satisfied?" *(Vanity Fair,* 878).

Boethius explains man's misery as arising from his pursuit of false felicity; we can see the process at work in the Colonel, who, "having fixed his whole heart upon this darling youth, his son, was punished" (260). While the Colonel devotes himself to Clive, Clive devotes himself to art. "Thomas Newcome had now been for three years in the possession of that felicity which his soul longed after. . . . And yet, in spite of his happiness, his honest face grew more melancholy" (258). The impassioned controversies about art between Clive and his youthful friends go over the Colonel's head, and though he longs to share in the camaraderie, "the party would be hushed if he went in to join it – and he would come away sad at heart to think that his presence should be a signal for silence among them; and that his son could not be merry in his company" (259). As he confronts this dilemma, toiling away hour after hour in the National Gallery "before the ancient statues, desperately praying to comprehend them", and asking himself, "why can't I love the things which he loves? . . . why am I blind to the beauties which he admires so much?" (262–5), we come to the central tragedy in Thackeray's world of ardently cherished schemes and patterns. It is the negative side of the book's more cheerful introductory version of Ecclesiastes, that is, "there may be nothing new under and including the sun; but it looks fresh every morning" (5). Now

> a sickening and humiliating sense of the reality came over him: and he sadly contrasted it with the former fond anticipations. Together they were, yet he was alone still. His thoughts were not the boy's: and his affections rewarded but with a part of the young man's heart. Very likely other lovers have suffered equally. Many a man and woman has been incensed and worshipped, and has shown no more feeling than is to be expected from idols. There is yonder statue in St. Peter's, of which the toe is worn away with kisses, and which sits, and will sit eternally, prim and cold. As the young man grew, it seemed to the father, as if each day separated them more and more. He himself became more melancholy and silent. His friend the civilian marked the ennui, and commented on it in his laughing way. Sometimes he announced to the club, that Tom Newcome was in love: then he thought it was not Tom's heart but his liver that was affected, and recommended blue-pill. O thou fond fool! who art thou, to know any man's heart save thine alone? . . . As if Thomas Newcome, by poring over poems or pictures ever so much, could read them with Clive's eyes! – as if, by sitting mum over his wine, but watching till the lad came home with his latchkey (when the Colonel crept back to his own room in his stockings), by prodigal bounties, by stealthy affection, by any schemes or prayers, he could hope to remain first in his son's heart! (265)

Thackeray is both specific and general here. The Colonel's

frustration in his lovingly elaborated scheme for happiness is not singular; his lot is everyone's. However perfect the Colonel's vision of bliss, it is his alone. Instead of Pygmalion's happy result in loving his work of imagination so much that it comes alive, we have here the reverse. The statue sits "eternally prim and cold". The trouble is twofold: not only does the vision disintegrate to a "sickening and humiliating sense of reality", but, even if it did not, it is in its very essence incommunicable.[7] Don Quixote is judged to be mad.

The Colonel's further fantasy of marrying Clive to Ethel founders against Ethel's determination to marry an aristocrat with a fortune, and against the lies, hatred and machinations of her brother Barnes. Frustrated and embittered, the Colonel, as he has done before, falls back on secondary targets, alternative ways of making Clive be happy. The Colonel has become a great bank director, but "this Bundelcund Banking Company, in the Colonel's eyes, was in reality his son Clive" (673). Angered by Barnes's duplicity, the Colonel contests the Newcome election with him: "I have long had the House of Commons in my eye," he says, "but not for me. I wanted my boy to go there" (846). And having failed to win Ethel for Clive, as he had failed to win Léonore for himself, he promotes Clive's marriage to Rosey, the milksop daughter of terrible Mrs Mackenzie, just as he had settled for his own vain and silly Emma. In addition, since Clive is so unenthusiastic, the Colonel "performs all the courtship part of the marriage" (843). In a combination of love for his father, despair of Ethel, and the sheer inertia that also plagues his career as an artist, Clive falls in with the Colonel's plan, bringing misery to them both. He suffers in silence while the Colonel rages at what seems to him his son's perverse unhappiness. "With every outward appliance of happiness, Clive was not happy" (827). "His very silence angered the old man" (835). "His life had been a sacrifice for that boy! What darling schemes had he not formed in his behalf, and how superciliously did Clive meet his projects! The Colonel could not see the harm of which he had himself been the author" (872). The grand vision ends in wreck and, for the Colonel, poverty-stricken, and enfeebled by the bitter shrewishness of Mrs Mackenzie, death. The cycle ends with the pieces from which it started, on the one hand a delirious vision of Léonore, on the other, suggesting a separation he has ever since been trying to overcome, a recollection of his own father beating him for a childish escapade: " 'It wasn't the pain you know: it wasn't the pain, but. . . .' Here tears came into his eyes and he dropped his head on his hand, and the cigar from it fell on to the floor, burnt almost out, and scattering white ashes" (989).

Mrs Mackenzie, surely one of the most dreadful women in all literature, is a savage counterpart to the Colonel in the novel's design, moulding Rosey according to her scenario, as the Colonel with more benign intent arranges life for Clive. With that aim in view, Mrs Mackenzie, the Campaigner, scolds Rosey, angrily beats her, laces her "so tight, as nearly to choke the poor little lass" (282), then simpers downstairs with her, arms entwined, to weep touchingly at sentimental songs before the gentlemen. Like Clive with the Colonel, Rosey "acquiesced gladly enough in her mamma's opinion, that she was in love with the rich and handsome young Clive, and accepted him for better or worse" (928). Unsuspected depths in Rosey appear only at the end, when Ethel comes to visit the harassed and poverty-stricken Clive. Miserable and jealous, Rosey tears her hand away from her posturing mother's proprietary clutch, leaving behind her wedding ring. Symbolically freed from the sour fairy tale her mother has contrived, standing alone, she finds herself confronting utter emptiness. Without the sustaining framework of an imposed pattern, she has no existence. Her illness deepens, and to the accompaniment of Mrs Mackenzie's stamping, raging hysterics, she weakens and dies.

If the Colonel and Mrs Mackenzie show the effects of shaping others' lives according to one's own idea of happiness, Ethel shows the structuring imagination at work within herself. In her career Thackeray compounds two visions of the world, and as she affects one convention or the other she becomes worldly cynic or innocent shepherdess. Like Rosey and Clive, she too is the victim of an imposed vision. Old Lady Kew, "sister of the late lamented Marquis of Steyne" (142), works at shaping Ethel's destiny, but Ethel proves to be a more aggressive and interesting character than Clive. It is customary to see her as clear-sighted in her sense of the family sordidness, especially in view of the famous scene in which she provokes Lady Kew by suggesting that young ladies should wear green tickets with "Sold" on them, like the paintings in a gallery, and then turns up for dinner with a ticket on her frock as "a *tableau vivant*" (362). Ethel, nevertheless, is a complex and sardonic creature, not so easy to classify. Even her insistence on the Newcome sordidness has about it a degree of defiant affectation. She too suits her life to an involved fiction. At one level she is aware, aloof, and direct, repeatedly telling Clive that she is of the world worldly because she chooses to be so. "She chose to be Countess of Kew because she chose to be Countess of Kew. . . . Clive was but a fancy" (363). But in her relationship with Lady Kew, she is governed by a ferocity that intimidates even that tough manager. Her bullying brother Barnes fears her. And her rage appears again in her scornful treatment of the lovers who try to claim her, whether Clive or Kew or Farintosh. Though committed to a mercenary, status-seeking society, she is harshly satirical of it. As a result, there is at times a good deal of ambivalence, self-excuse, and easy fatalism in her, as in her observations to Lady Kew on Clara Pulleyn's marriage to Barnes:

> That poor wretch, that poor girl whom my brother is to marry, why did she not revolt and fly? I would, if I loved a man sufficiently, loved him better than the world, than wealth, than rank, than fine houses and titles – and I feel I love these best – I would give up all to follow him. But what can I be with my name and my parents? I belong to the world like all the rest of my family. It is you who have bred us up; you who are answerable for us. Why are there no convents to which we can fly? . . . you make me what you call happy, and I would rather be at the plough like the women here. (425–6)

Accusation, hasty qualification, fatalism, blame shifting, absurd primitivism – as Lady Kew replies, quite rightly: "No, you wouldn't Ethel. . . . These are the fine speeches of schoolgirls" (426). And there is the crux of Ethel's complicated character: she moves between two fictions of the world, one all hardness for which she is not responsible and one all artless primitivism which she implies is in tune with the real Ethel.

This tension makes for some fine comedy that carries on the pastoral imagery of the novel's first number and reaches its

8 Swain and Shepherdess: Doyle's headletter for Chapter 47 of *The Newcomes*

height in Chapter 47 entitled "Contains Two or Three Acts of a Little Comedy" and introduced by a head-letter sketch of an elegant swain and shepherdess à la Watteau.[8] Further to stress the fact that life is now going to follow the formulas of fiction, Thackeray writes the chapter as play dialogue in three conversations à la Marivaux, setting the scene in the "quaint old garden of the Hôtel de Florac", with a dry fountain, a moss-eaten Triton, and, in a parody of Keats, "a broken-nosed damp Faun, with a marble panpipe, who pipes to the spirit ditties which I believe never had any tune", and a "Cupid, who has been at the point of kissing Psyche this half-century at least, though the delicious event has never come off, through all those blazing summers and dreary winters" (616–17). "After some talk about nuns, Ethel says, 'There were convents in England. She often thinks she would like to retire to one'; and she sighs as if her heart were in that scheme" (617). She now turns to reproaching Clive for worldliness – stage direction: "(*She heaves a sigh and looks down towards a beautiful new dress of many flounces which Madame de Flouncival, the great milliner, has sent her home that very day*.)" (618). Clive enters only a touch ironically into Ethel's fantasy by describing himself as "like the Peri who looks into Paradise and sees angels within it" (618), signifying thereby that he dotes on her London house. And he adds sadly that when he first saw her she was "like that fairy-princes who came out of the crystal box. . . . *Ethel* (*innocently*). Have I ever made any difference between us?" (621).

Conversation II proceeds from a low comedy scene between servants to another contrived meeting between Clive and Ethel, Ethel continuing her vein of world weariness: "Oh, dear me, who is happy in the world? What a pity Lord Highgate's father had not died sooner!" and "O what a life of vanity ours is!" (626–7). In Conversation III, Madame de Florac, the Colonel's Léonore, lost long ago to a marriage of interest, puts an end to these "singular coincidences" of Clive's and Ethel's meetings and reproaches Ethel's schemes of union without love. Moved by the discourse, Ethel admits her ambivalence, her simultaneous love and contempt for jewels, great names, and admiration. Back again in her worldly vision, she once more reproaches Clive for his low social position and his artist's profession, dismissing him with a number of excuses and the dreadful word, "brother".

The whole comedy, of course, is a refinement (in its much more elaborate interweaving of strands) on the superb "Phillis and Corydon" chapter of *Pendennis*, in which Blanche Amory tunes her pastoral emotions stage by stage to the titles of her books of poetry, from *Mes Soupirs* to *Mes Larmes*. Ethel is more intriguing, perhaps, because neither of her visions is altogether false. The pastoral, though it is largely humbug, does show a streak of conscience in Ethel's avowed sordidness, as when she is talking to the Colonel: "Thus the young lady went on talking, defending herself whom nobody attacked, protesting her dislike to gaiety and dissipation – you would have fancied her an artless young country lass, only longing to trip back to her village, milk her cows at sunrise, and sit spinning of winter evenings by the fire" (690). She thoroughly takes in Laura Pendennis, whose Christian discourses sound so ponderously edifying that she has on occasion been regarded as the voice of Thackeray himself setting a moral standard.[9] Rehearsing Ethel's familiar account of being bred to vanity, Laura credits her with fresh insight: "Ethel's simple talk", she says, "made me smile sometimes, do you know, and her *strenuous* way of imparting her discoveries. I thought of the shepherd boy who made a watch, and found on taking it into the town how very many watches there were, and how much better than his .... She told me very artlessly her little history, Arthur; it affected me to hear her simple talk, and – and I blessed God for our mother, my dear, and that my early days had had a better guide" (787). Here is yet another case of self-centred vision – Laura inspired by her own vein of moral enthusiasm and selecting from Ethel's variety of artifices the one she wants to believe is artless.

Just as the Colonel in adoring his son figuratively confronts the prim cold statue that resists his love, so Clive confronts the statue of the virgin huntress, Diana. As a painter, Clive naturally idealises Ethel in works of imagination: "A frequenter of his studio might see a whole gallery of Ethels ... one face and figure repeated on a hundred canvases and papers ..." (569). Before the works of the great masters, "Clive's heart sang hymns, as it were ... and, somewhat as he worshipped these masterpieces of his art he admired the beauty of Ethel" (386). More especially, however, he identifies her with the statue of Diana in the Louvre: the "famous Parisian marble" could not be "more perfect in form than this young lady" (308).[10] Thackeray, nevertheless, suggests the flaw in Clive's imaginary portrait and the latent menace in Ethel even in the midst of Clive's encomiums: " 'By Jove, how handsome she is ... how grand she would look as Herodias's daughter ... with the muscles accented like that glorious Diana at Paris – a savage smile on her face and a ghastly, solemn, gory head on the dish – I see the picture, sir, I see the picture!' and he fell to curling his moustache – just like his brave old father" (314). In the same passage, Clive moves from "a fond eulogium of his sire" to the excited statement "that if his father wanted him to marry, he would marry that instant. And why not Rosey?" The answer to this rhetorical question is evident in his unconsciously ominous comment on how to paint poor Rosey: "You ought to paint her in milk, sir!" (314). Pendennis, as narrator, makes clear the social significance of the Diana image, saying of the most sordid part of Ethel's career, "I was not present when Diana and Diana's grandmother hunted the noble Scottish stag . . . Lord Farintosh" (700). But Thackeray also emphasises "the haughty virginal expression" of the Diana (520), thereby underscoring both the complexities of Ethel's psychology and the poor chances of her worshippers, for her prey once caught is spurned – Lord Kew, Farintosh, and always Clive. Worship as he may, Clive cannot bring this statue alive to suit his artistic vision.

The fault is not simply in Ethel. Clive is a submissive son, an irresolute lover, and a half-hearted artist. Clive's loving compliance combined with the Colonel's loving readiness to pattern lives creates tragedy. If there is a standard in the book against which these pursuers of imaginary designs can be measured, it is probably to be found in Clive's fellow painter, J. J. Ridley, the butler's son whom Clive befriends, patronises, and gradually learns to respect. While Clive plays at art, Ridley works at it. But Ridley is unobtrusive by nature and a background figure in the novel. To the extent that his presence is felt, however, he does distinguish the genuine from the false, the inspired from the shabby, both in his friend Clive and in art. The two concerns come together for a moment at the height of the Colonel's prestige, when, at the annual dinner of the Bundelcund Banking Company, Rosey is presented with

> a superb silver coco-nut-tree, whereof the leaves were dexterously arranged for holding candles and pickles; under the coco-nut was an Indian prince on a camel giving his hand to a cavalry officer on horseback – a howitzer, a plough, a loom, a bale of cotton, on which were the East India Company's arms, a brahmin, Britannia, and Commerce, with a cornucopia were grouped round the principal figures . . . [a] chaste and elegant specimen of British art. (823–4)

Amidst the splendid speeches, Pendennis notices "J. J. eyeing the trophy, and the queer expression of his shrewd face. The health of British Artists was drunk àpropos of this splendid specimen of their skill, and poor J. J. Ridley, Esq., A.R.A., had scarce a word to say in return" (824). J. J. and Clive sit gloomily together, neither satisfied with Clive's condition. The coconut tree in its monstrosity is a miniature version of Clive's home as Rosey and the Colonel have embellished it and where "Clive, in the midst of all these splendours, was gaunt, and sad, and silent" (825).

As a mercenary creature of facts, figures, and malice, Barnes would seem to be far removed from these indulgers in quixotic, artistic, and social fantasies. He hates the Colonel and Clive for the daily beauty of their lives as compared with his own cowardly, simpering snobbery. Warrington sees Barnes as one of "Nature's rogues", far superior to the imaginary villains of novelists – though it may be noted that Warrington has to call on Swift, Pope, and Zoroaster to describe him adequately (716). But Barnes, too, acts out imaginary designs: the impersonal man of business as he maliciously plots against the Colonel, the doughty warrior as he threatens duels with Belsize or the Colonel (but quaking in terror all the time lest they get around his excuses and actually fight him), the banker with a heart of gold as he lectures on The Poetry of Childhood and The Poetry of Womanhood and the Affections (this after rejecting the girl he seduced and beating his wife until she deserts him). If Barnes is the harsh reality of the world against which fairytale schemes and visions are to be measured, what a maze of fantasy that reality encompasses.

Surrounding these major figures, the minor characters of the novel further illustrate the patterns I have suggested, either living within an enclosing conventional fable, or imposing a predetermined pattern on others. While Clara Pulleyn and Jack Belsize on one level show us the frustrations and consequences of the marriage market and are therefore part of Thackeray's renowned and shrewd assessment of society, they are nevertheless presented in terms of thoroughly conventional fantasy and artifice. Lady Clara belongs to the animal fable of the novel's beginning, as her name, Pulleyn, suggests. Her father's estate is Chanticlere, her brother is Viscount Rooster, and Rooster's grandfather once "played two nights and two days at a sitting with Charles Fox" (365). Belsize, threatening general destruction when Clara is sold to Barnes, puts the Vicomte de Florac in mind of Corneille's *Le*

Cid: "Suppose you kill ze Fazér, you kill Kiou, you kill Roostere, your Chimène will have a pretty moon of honey" (382). Lord Kew protests the folly of seeing Belsize and Clara as "Jenny and Jessamy falling in love at first sight, billing and cooing in an arbour, and retiring to a cottage .... Pshaw! what folly is this!" (392). In addition to these containing fictions of Clara and Belsize are the further version drawn from *Marriage à la Mode* and the contrary fictions of the lawyers in Barnes's divorce trial.

The Duchesse d'Ivry, whose jealous plotting sabotages the marriage of Ethel and Lord Kew, is otherwise known as Mary Queen of Scots. She resembles "the master of the theatrical booth" in that "this lady with her platonic lovers went through the complete dramatic course, – tragedies of jealously, pantomimes of rapture, and farces of parting" (444). "She was Phèdre .... She was Medea" (445). When in a pique of jealously she plots to have Lord Kew killed, she hires a poet who is a compound of literary and nationalistic clichés to do the job. The author of *Les Râles d'un Asphyxié*, "he drank great quantities of absinthe of a morning; smoked incessantly: played roulette when he could get a few pieces: contributed to a small journal, and was especially great in his hatred of *l'infâme Angleterre. Delenda est Carthago* was tatooed beneath his shirtsleeve," and he shook his fist at the lion in the Garden of Plants (445). Fantastic but convincing, indeed all too familiar in his bizzare enthusiasm, this poetic patriot may well remind us of Oscar Wilde's comment on the boy burglar inspired by tales of Jack Sheppard: "He is Fact, occupied as Fact usually is, with trying to reproduce Fiction, and what we see in him is repeated on an extended scale throughout the whole of life."[11]

To conclude, then: at close range in *The Newcomes* we see two related patterns of action: on the one hand, attempts to impose the imagination's daydreams and formulas on the lives of others, as with the Colonel; on the other, stylisation of behaviour according to conventional fancies as with Ethel. Standing farther back from Thackeray's canvas, we see life as a series of recurrent formulas, so that, as he says, all stories are old. Everywhere the narrative is saturated with traditional and familiar fictions from art, literature, mythology and social convention that not only adorn reality and displace reality but become reality. A depiction of the world so highly fictive may lead us to reconsider Thackeray's long-standing reputation as a realist, but not because he eschews the accidents of experience for the patterns of imagination – rather, the two are in perennial tension. What seems unique, chaotic, and real is merely segmented from the eternal pattern, and he keeps both before us. Put another way, he is portraying an affliction of the imagination. Man imagines style, order or perfection, but he lives in a world of limitation. As Camus says: "There is not one human being who, above a certain elementary level of consciousness, does not exhaust himself in trying to find formulas or attitudes that will give his existence the unity it lacks. . . . The same impulse . . . also leads to creative literature which derives its serious content from this source."[12] In short, the impulse that shapes both life and art is a reflex from the consciousness that, though imagination and reason would order it otherwise, "the race is not to the swift, nor the battle to the strong, neither yet bread to the wise, nor yet riches to men of understanding, nor yet favour to men of skill; but time and chance happeneth to them all" (Eccles. 9.11).

Traditionally and rightly, readers have considered *The Newcomes* a masterly depiction of a certain social milieu: that of "the most polite, and most intelligent, and best informed, and best dressed, and most selfish people in the world" (320). It is a much richer book than that might suggest, however, and I have been at pains to illustrate one of the several dimensions of that richness. Thackeray himself remarked: "I can't jump further than I did in *The Newcomes*."[13]

NOTES

1. Citations in my text to *The Newcomes* are to George Saintsbury (ed.), *The Oxford Thackeray*, 17 vols (London, 1908).
2. See Thackeray's letter to the editor of *The Times*, 23 November 1853, p. 9, in Gordon N. Ray (ed.), *The Letters and Private Papers of William Makepeace Thackeray*, 4 vols, vol. III (Cambridge, Mass., 1945–6) p.321.
3. John Harvey, *Victorian Novelists and Their Illustrators* (London, 1970) pp. 96–8. The reviews are in *The Examiner*, 1 September 1855, p. 548, and (Burne-Jones's) in *The Oxford and Cambridge Magazine*, January 1856, p. 56.
4. *Letters*, III, p. 304.
5. James H. Wheatley sees a possible attempt at quixotic character in the

Colonel and a theme of "quixotism", or nobility in defeat, in the book but is unhappy "because the subject and resulting book are so unlike that of Cervantes". He concludes that "rarely does his [the Colonel's] quixotism draw on the rich interplay of illusion and reality we associate with Cervantes" (*Patterns in Thackeray's Fiction* [Cambridge, Mass., 1969] pp. 115–19).

6. Sidney, *An Apology for Poetry*, ed. Geoffrey Shepherd (London, 1965) p. 101.
7. The theme is essential in Thackeray and little examined. In *Pendennis*, he wrote: "a distinct universe walks about under your hat and under mine – all things in nature are different to each . . . you and I are but a pair of infinite isolations . . ." (ch. 16). It recurs in one of the finest passages in *The Newcomes*, that in which Clive and Jack Belsize, who are thwarted in love like the Colonel, sit in the dark, visible only by the glow of their cigars, looking out at the flickering lights of Baden: "So every light in every booth yonder has a scheme of its own: every star above shines by itself; and each individual heart of ours goes on brightening with its own hopes, burning with its own desires, and quivering with its own pain" (378). Cf. Juliet McMaster, *Thackeray: The Major Novels* (Toronto, 1971) pp. 167–8.
8. See also the head letter of Chapter 42 (550), very similar in design but with Clive as eighteenth-century courtier and a horrified Lady Kew perched between the lovers instead of Cupid.
9. See Whitwell Elwin's review in *The Quarterly Review*, 97 (1855) 360. Thackeray told Elwin, "Pendennis's uxoriousness and admiration for Laura I take to show that he is a weak character & led by women" (*Letters*, III, p. 469).
10. Presumably the Louvre's *Diane de Gabies*.
11. Oscar Wilde, "The Decay of Lying", in Richard Ellmann (ed.), *The Artist as Critic: Critical Writings of Oscar Wilde*, (New York, 1968) p. 388.
12. Albert Camus, *The Rebel: An Essay on Man in Revolt*, trans. Anthony Bower, (New York, 1956) p. 262.
13. *Letters*, III, p. 619, n. 126.

8 "An Honourable Emulation of the Author of *The Newcomes*": James and Thackeray

But for a few recent works, the modern assessment of Thackeray could be summed up in Thackeray's own rueful anecdote of the St Louis hotel waiter whom he heard exclaim to his comrade: "'Do you know who that is?' 'No,' was the answer. 'That,' said the first 'is the celebrated Thacker!' 'What's *he* done?' 'D——d if I know!' "[1] What everybody does know, because it is repeated so often, is James's query about *The Newcomes*, along with *The Three Musketeers* and *War and Peace*: "but what do such large loose baggy monsters, with their queer elements of the accidental and the arbitrary, artistically *mean*?"[2] Less current is James's wonderful recollection in *Notes of a Son and Brother* of the great Victorian serial novels in general and *The Newcomes* in particular:

> "These various, let alone numerous, deeper-toned strokes of the great Victorian clock were so many steps in the march of our age.... I witnessed, for that matter, with all my senses, young as I was, the never-to-be-equalled degree of difference made, for what may really be called the world-consciousness happily exposed to it, by the prolonged 'coming out' of The Newcomes, yellow number by number, and could take the general civilised participation in the process for a sort of basking in the light of distinction.'[3]

Though occasional reviewers and scholars have from the first noticed affinities between James and Thackeray,[4] comparisons have, on the whole, not gone well. W. D. Howells excited some derision (including an amusing cartoon in *Life* of James standing on Howells's shoulders beside a large statue of Thackeray) for dismissing Thackeray and the great English novelists in favour of "the new school" which "finds its chief exemplar in Mr. James,"[5] but generally James and Thackeray have continued to be set in opposition as in Percy Lubbock's classic confrontation of them in *The Craft of Fiction*. The only one to dwell on their affinities has been Geoffrey Tillotson in his *Thackeray the Novelist*, and there only in part of an appendix. Most significant, of course, is James's own testimony about his regard for Thackeray in comments and allusions, surprisingly frequent and on the whole favourable, scattered throughout his works. "They are always those of an admirer," Tillotson concludes, "and some of the later ones alone make reservations."[6] Robert L. Gale, in his study of figurative language in James, discovered in addition that not Turgenev, not Flaubert, not Eliot, but Thackeray is the author to whom James most frequently alludes: "Judging from the imagery, I should say that Thackeray and Balzac were the two novelists most frequently on James's mind."[7] James is a little inconsistent, indeed, as his immediate concerns may determine. In one place he argues that "the great difference between [George Sand] . . . and the authors (let us say) of *The Newcomes* and of *David Copperfield* is, that whereas the latter writers express in a satisfactory manner certain facts, certain ideas of a peculiar and limited order, Madame Sand expresses with equal felicity and equal grace ideas and facts the most various and the most general."[8] (That Dickens and Thackeray lacked "ideas" was, after all, a canard of the time.)[9] In his article on Balzac, however, James distinguishes between Balzac's almost physical robustness of temperament and the mentality of "the other great novelists", concluding: "When we approach Thackeray and George Eliot, George Sand and Turgenieff, it is into the conscience and the mind that we enter, and we think of them primarily as great consciences and great minds."[10] Thackeray, along with Balzac, also becomes a measure of stature in James's argument with Howells about the necessity of an old civilization for setting a novelist in motion: "I shall feel refuted," says James, "only when we [Americans] have produced . . . a gentleman who strikes me as a novelist – as belonging to the company of Balzac and

A LITERARY COMBINATION.

Mr. H-w-lls: ARE YOU THE TALLEST NOW, MR. J-MES?
Mr. J-mes (ignoring the question): BE SO UNCOMMONLY KIND, H-W-LLS, AS TO LET ME DOWN EASY; IT MAY BE WE HAVE BOTH GOT TO GROW.

Thackeray."[11] Such an estimate of Thackeray was, after all, not exceptional. George Eliot, one of James's more acknowledged mentors, thought Thackeray, "as I suppose the majority of people with any intellect do, on the whole the most powerful of living novelists".[12]

On the level of personal sensibility, James's autobiographies make clear how intimate to him the Thackerayan sense of things became, reinforced no doubt by personal acquaintance. Henry James, Senior, not only welcomed Thackeray to his home but (in the *New-York Daily Tribune*, 13 Nov. 1852, p. 4) to New York, as "the most thoughtful critic of manners and society, the subtlest humorist, and the most effective, because the most genial, satirist the age has known". Young Henry's first meeting with Thackeray contributed in its small way to James's sense of cultural contrasts and oddity when "the celebrated visitor . . . enormously big . . . though he laid on my shoulder the hand of benevolence, bent on my native costume the spectacles of wonder", and "remarked that in England, were I to go there, I should be addressed as 'Buttons.' It had been revealed to me thus in a flash that we were somehow *queer*." In Paris in 1857, James's eight-year-old sister received similar treatment: "the tradition lingered long of his having suddenly laid his hand on her little flounced person and exclaimed with ludicrous horror: 'Crinoline? – I was suspecting it! So young and so depraved!'" As he could well do, Thackeray evidently charmed the young James, as James's touch of regret suggests: "Too few, I may here interject, were to remain my gathered impressions of the great humourist."[13]

The impressions that stayed with James most firmly, assimilated to his own sensibility, were of Thackeray's sense of life, his vision of things as recorded in the novels. When young Henry, twelve years old, arrived with his family in England in 1855, their first stop for refreshment was at the old Gloucester Coffee-House, where Mrs Bute Crawley put up temporarily on her arrival to attend Miss Crawley just as Becky eloped with Rawdon, and where Pendennis's coach dropped him on his arrival in London to study law. London, which the young James explored from Berkeley Square and, later, from St John's Wood, already had a special familiarity: "it offered to my presumptuous vision", says James, "still more [than of Dickens] the reflection of Thackeray – and where is the *detail* of the reflection of Thackeray now? – so that as I trod the vast length of Baker Street, the Thackerayan vista of other days, I throbbed with the pride of a vastly enlarged acquaintance".[14] The family excursion to Boulogne-sur-Mer in the summer of 1857 evoked a similar fusion of sensibility, the *haute ville* achieving "the monumental" from its associations with Colonel Newcome's sufferings:

> The scene bristled, as I look back at it, with images from *Men's Wives*, from the society of Mr. Deuceace and that of fifty other figures of the same creation, with Bareacreses and Rawdon Crawleys and of course with Mrs. Macks, with Rosys of a more or less crumpled freshness and blighted bloom, with battered and bent, though doubtless never quite so fine, Colonel Newcomes not less; with more reminders in short than I can now gather in. . . . it was as good, among them, as just *being* Arthur Pendennis to know so well, or at least to guess so fearfully, who and what they might be.[15]

James's early sense of England, as made up of the texture of Dickens and Thackeray, suffused his consciousness again years later on the "gusty, cloudy, overwhelmingly English morning" in 1869 when James landed at Liverpool to stay.[16]

It would be strange if, with his high esteem for Thackeray, a frequency of allusion which indicates how commonly Thackeray was on his mind, and a sense of the English scene to which he commits himself as particularly Thackeray's – it would be strange in view of all this interest if Thackeray did not leave his mark on the young James's novels. And in fact James's comment on Trollope's early fiction seems perfectly apposite when applied to his own novels, *Roderick Hudson* and *The American*: "It is probably not unfair to say that if Trollope derived half his inspiration from life, he derived the other half from Thackeray; his earlier novels, in especial, suggest an honourable emulation of the author of *The Newcomes*."[17]

Helpful as Cornelia Pulsifer Kelley's *The Early Development of Henry James* is in its diligent sifting of influences on James's early works, it is also an example of how compleat Jamesians neglect Thackeray at their peril. Puzzled by James's weaving of a love story into his account of the artist's collapse in *Roderick Hudson*, for instance, she explores Turgenev, Balzac, George Sand, and the career of the painter Henri Regnault, without satisfaction, when *The Newcomes*, an obvious but disregarded source, could have supplied some interesting answers to her questions.[18]

The principal romantic subject of both *Roderick* and *The Newcomes* is that of an aspiring, talented, but rather feckless artist, frustratingly interested in a spirited, beautiful, but perverse girl whose family is parading her in the European marriage market. Roderick's relationship to Christina Light is affected by her salability just as Clive Newcome's is to Ethel. Prince Casamassima as purchaser is James's equivalent for the Marquis of Farintosh. Christina's intriguingly ambivalent complexity in this situation is precisely Ethel's. Each artist, supported by wealth he has not earned, can take a self-indulgent attitude to art; each is paired with an artist of apparently small stature who, in a hare-and-tortoise way, outstrips him, Sam Singleton playing the same role in *Roderick* as J. J. Ridley in *The Newcomes* and illustrating the same point about talent and tenacity. In subject, character, character relationships, and thematic development, the analogies are clear and, moreover, fascinating. *The Newcomes*, of course, is a much bigger, wider-ranging social novel by a novelist at his peak, whereas *Roderick* is a work of comparatively limited focus by an author engaging, like many another at this stage of his career, in "honourable emulation", adapting what he takes to his own unfolding purposes and talents.

Apparent to a Thackerayan, the analogies are underscored by James himself on occasion by direct reference to Thackeray. Of Roderick's misadventures among the demimonde gamblers of Baden-Baden, James writes, "At this point of his friend's narrative, Rowland was reminded of Madame de Cruchecassée in Thackeray's novel", adding in the New York edition, "but of a Madame de Cruchecassée mature and quasi-maternal, attached as with a horrible sincerity to her prey" (NY, 139).[19] In another addition to the New York text, Madame Grandoni remarks of Mrs Light's attempts to lure a rich, aristocratic husband to her daughter: "She reminds me, like that, of some extravagant old woman in a novel – in something of Hofmann or Balzac, something even of your own Thackeray" (NY, 164). The "even" is manifestly a bit of playful disingenuousness on James's part since the extravagant old woman is unmistakably hard-bitten, witchlike Lady Kew, who browbeats and manages Ethel and who, as we shall see, provides the major inspiration for James's Marquise de Bellegarde in *The American*. A third addition to the New York text is a more general Thackerayan reference, this time to *Vanity Fair*, and again about Mrs Light: "She has opened her booth at the fair; she has her great natural wonder to show, and she beats her big drum outside" (NY, 196). (Though James's loving adaptation of Thackeray is clear from the first text of *Roderick*, the New York revisions are not only, as always, interesting in themselves – I shall mention some in passing – but testify once again to the closeness and constancy of James's interest.)

Ethel is by far the most tantalizing character in *The Newcomes*, bright, proud, fierce, cynical and tender by fits, at one moment frankly admitting her love of fortune and status, at another full of self-reproach, wishing she had been set to the plough, fascinating and perverse, a heart-breaker. Tutored by Lady Kew to seek a wealthy marriage, she assumes the cynical credo, "I believe in elder sons, and a house in town, and a house in the country", but remains flighty.[20] "If the tightest hand were not kept on her", says her brother, Barnes, "there's no knowing what she mightn't do .... Ethel Newcome, by Jove, is capable of running away with the writing-master" (*N*, 433). Christina is similarly trained from the age of five "that her face is her fortune" (124) and is similarly intractable: "The impression remained that she was unsafe; that she was a complex, wilful, passionate, creature who might easily engulf a too confiding spirit in the eddies of her capricious temper" (137), or as the New York edition adds, sounding the siren note from *Vanity Fair*, draw him "into some strange underworld of unworthy sacrifice, not unfurnished with traces of others of the lost" (NY, 186). Ethel affects world-weariness: "How old am I? Twenty – I feel sometimes as if I was a hundred ... so tired, oh, so tired!" (*N*, 626); and of Christina, observers ask, "Where in the world has Miss Light been before she is twenty ... to have left all her illusions behind?" (144), and she protests, "I am tired to death of myself" (150). But, like Ethel, she finds self-contemplation fascinating. Put on exhibition around Europe, Ethel at Baden, Christina at Carlsbad, both girls present a curious mixture of sexual attractiveness and cold aloofness, Christina a figure of "maidenly majesty" (115) extending "greetings with impartial frigidity" to guests at her ball (145), and Ethel recurrently identified with the beautiful cold statue, "the haughty virginal expression" of Diana, the huntress (*N*, 520). "A singular girl indeed!" says Rowland Mallet of Christina (171); "a living riddle", Mrs Light agrees (174). Captain Lord Viscount Rooster more colourfully says of Ethel: " I'd rather dance with her than marry her – by a doosid long score – I don't envy you that part of the business, Kew, my boy" (*N*, 433). James himself was a goner. Captivated by the complex fascination of the Ethel/Christina character, he dwells on it markedly at the end of his Preface: " I knew", he says, "the pity, the real pang of losing sight of her. I desired as in no other such case I can recall to preserve, to recover the vision. . . . Thus one would watch for her . . . . taking her up later on" (NY, xx). He took her up again in *The Princess Casamassima*, just as Thackeray took up *Henry Esmond's* Beatrix, a beauty of similarly sparkling ambiguity, in *The Virginians*.

The treatments of Ethel and Christina are often similar in detail. Ethel is fond of describing herself as a Circassian slave: " 'We are sold,' the young girl went on, 'we are as much sold as Turkish women; the only difference being that our masters may have but one Circassian at a time' " (*N*, 425). And Pendennis reminds the hapless Clive that "Circassian beauties don't sell under so many thousand purses" (*N*, 568). When Mrs Light interrupts Roderick's arrangement of Christina's hair, Rowland considers, "if he had attempted to make a sketch of an old slave-merchant calling attention to the 'points' of a Circassian beauty, he would have depicted such a smile as Mrs Light's", and Christina comments, "She is only afraid that Mr. Hudson might have injured my hair, and that *per consequenza*, I should sell for less" (132). As I noted in my previous chapter, one of the most famous episodes in *The Newcomes* is that in which Ethel, attending a water-colour exhibition, provokes Lady Kew by remarking, "we young ladies in the world, when we are exhibiting, ought to have little green tickets pinned on our backs, with 'Sold' written on them; it would prevent trouble and any future haggling, you know" (*N*, 361). She scandalises the family that evening by appearing "with a bright green ticket pinned in the front of her white muslin frock", and saying, "I am a *tableau-vivant*, papa" (*N*, 362). Mrs Light, on the other hand, performs "a pious duty in bringing up Christina to carry herself, 'marked' very high and in the largest letters, to market" (NY, 249). Accenting their tantalising virginity, the girls even dress alike in white, Ethel in white muslin, her white hand and white shoulders recurrently noticed. James, however, elaborates this imagery much more extensively, dressing Christina "in vaporous white, relieved with half a dozen white roses" so that she seems "to glow with the white light of a splendid pearl" (145–6), and giving her as constant attendant a necromantic "snow-white poodle" (115). The sign that Roderick is involved in Christina's sudden cancellation of her engagement to Prince Casamassima (a counterpart to Ethel's break with Farintosh) is that Rowland discovers the truant Roderick "lying on his divan in a white dressing-gown. . . . smelling a large white rose" (265).

Another detail of execution James emulates from Thackeray, appropriate since both their heroes are artists, is the recurrent association of his heroine with objets d'art. "A frequenter of [Clive's] studio might see a whole gallery of Ethels" (*N*, 569), and her recurrent identification with the statue of Diana in the Louvre suggests not only her perfection of form and virginal haughtiness but her sordid role as huntress. Christina similarly becomes identified with sculpture from the time Roderick, while sketching a mask of Juno at the Villa Ludovisi, first sees her: "The drawing represented the Juno . . . but the eyes, the mouth, the physiognomy were a vivid portrait of the young girl with the poodle" (82). When she turns up later at his studio, he cries, "By Jove! . . . it's that goddess of the Villa Ludovisi!" (115). Eventually, he makes a bust of Christina, "a representation of ideal beauty" (135). Mr Leavenworth, a philistine patron of Roderick's, seeing a marble replica of it, says, "An ideal head I presume, . . . a fanciful representation of one of the pagan goddesses–a Diana, a Flora, a naiad or dryad?" (207). Especially interesting, however, is a revision in the New York edition that more fully recalls Clive's enthusiastic outburst of eros and artistry: "By Jove," says Clive, " . . . how grand she would look as Herodias's daughter . . . a savage smile on her face and a ghastly, solemn, gory head on the dish" (*N*, 314). In the first version of *Roderick*, Gloriani gives his impression of Christina:

> "As soon as I saw her I said to myself, 'By jove, there's my statue in the flesh!'"
>
> "What is your subject?" asked Roderick.

> "Don't take it ill", said Gloriani. "You know I am the very deuce for observation. She would make a magnificent Herodias!" (139)

In the New York edition James both vivifies the passage in a Thackerayan direction and tunes it to his own ironic purpose:

> "Don't take it ill," said Gloriani . . .. "The name of my idea is the name of the young woman–what was *hers*?–who pr-anced up to the king her father with a great bloody head on a great gold tray."
> "Salome, daughter of Herodias?"
> "Exactly, and of Herod, king of the Jews."
> "Do you think Miss Light looks then like a Jewess?"
> "No, he only thinks," Rowland interposed, "that Herodias must much have resembled Miss Light–unless indeed he also sees our young woman with *your* head on her charger."
> "Ah," Gloriani laughed, "it isn't a question of Hudson's 'head'!" (NY, 190)[21]

Although I have so far dwelt on the basic similarity of surface treatment between James's portrait of Christina and Thackeray's of Ethel–part of what James in his Preface included among "the multiplication of touches" that "produced even more life than the subject required" (NY, xx)–no doubt Ethel appealed to James at a deeper level of his sympathy for Thackeray. Whatever their differences on the technique of narration, James and Thackeray share a Victorian interest in the basic ambiguity of facts and in the power of the shaping mind to interpret and arrange facts so as to flesh out its own idiosyncratic view of the world, morally or aesthetically. Both authors, whether in narrative perspective or in the moral outlooks of their characters, are interested in the tension between how the world is and how it is seen through the lenses of the shaping imagination. *The Sacred Fount* is a kaleidoscopic play of shifting personal relationships in the mind of a narrator who, ostensibly seeking the truth, seems more to be seeking symmetry and coherence, "that joy of determining, almost of creating results."[22] And *The Portrait of a Lady* not only suggests composition in its title but follows Isabel's tragic creation of an artificial vision against all sane advice. In *The Newcomes*, as I have argued, Thackeray explores the doubtful boundaries of fact and poetic design deliberately and extensively, writing a novel in which the novelistic impulse is itself a major subject of interest. From the introductory fable, through the lives of the novel's several characters, each seeking dramatic coherence and fulfillment, and on to the suspended ending where the reader is challenged on his own desire for romantic pattern, Thackeray dwells on the vanity of the formal impulse, the tragicomic antipathy between stylisation and lived experience. Colonel Newcome's desire to make his son's career a more successful and poetically satisfactory recapitulation of his own frustrated love is the book's central concern. Within Ethel the tension of fictive design and sordid cynicism, poetic shepherdess and calculating social climber, is another source of her complex appeal. She likes to be incisively tough-minded. And she is ready to profess selfish vanity: "Oh, I like admiration! . . . I love beautiful dresses; I love fine jewels; I love a great name and a fine house . . . I have been heartless and a coquette" (*N*, 639). But she also indulges herself with pretty pastoralisms and a nostalgia for nunneries. And to her affectation of world-weariness she adds the further fashionable affectation of Byronic abandon, posturing about what she *would* do if sufficiently roused to passion.

The same theatrical combination, and in fact the same language, are evident in Christina Light. She too indulges herself with notions of how wickedly worldly she is: "I should like to be a princess . . .. I am fond of luxury, I am fond of a great society, I am fond of being looked at. I am corrupt, corrupting, corruption!" (273). But she too has a soft spot for nunneries: "There was a time when I wanted immensely to be a nun" (193). And Ethel's speech of abandon ("if I loved a man . . . I would give up all to follow him. But what can I be with my name and my parents?" [*N*, 425]) is matched by Christina's declaration:

> "I am silly, I am ignorant, I am affected, I am false. I am the fruit of a horrible education sown on a worthless soil. I am all that, and yet I believe I have one merit! I should know a great character when I saw it . . .. For a man who should really give me a certain feeling–I have never had it, but I

> should know it when it came–I would send Prince Casamassima and his millions to perdition." (182)

A good deal of conventional fiction intermingles with each girl's sense of reality, and what is interesting about both of them is that the reader is never quite sure how much to discount.

Thackeray, perhaps, suggests a deeper level of unresolved conflict in Ethel through these theatrical scenes, but James, in his emulation of Thackeray and while talking about Christina, indirectly provides as sensitive and astute a reading of Ethel as is to be found in Thackeray criticism. It comes partly through Madame Grandoni:

> "I think she [Christina] is an actress, but she believes in her part while she is playing it. She took it into her head the other day to believe that she was very unhappy, and she sat there, where you are sitting, and told me a tale of her miseries which brought tears into my eyes. She cried profusely, and as naturally as possible . . .. I assure you it's well for you susceptible young men that you don't see her when she sobs . . .. She said the life they led was horrible . . .. She was meant for better things; she could be perfectly happy in poverty. It was not money she wanted. . . . sometimes she thought of taking poison!" (143)

James picks up Thackeray's interest in the aesthetic drive taking over and blending with the raw material of life: "she is an actress, but she believes in her part while she is playing it." The point gets reinforced, partly, as in Thackeray, by oblique literary reference, as when Christina, knowing the Prince awaits her at her mother's, asks Madame Grandoni's permission to stay for supper. Her expression of weariness is slightly revised in the New York edition to "I'm weary and dreary; I'm more lonely than ever; I wish I were dead!" (NY, 311), which comes close enough to the refrain of Tennyson's "Mariana" (thus combining histrionics with the irony that Mariana awaits her lover). Similarly Christina asks apropos of her hold on Roderick, "Is there not some novel or some play . . . in which a beautiful wicked woman who has ensnared a young man sees his father come to her and beg her to let him go?" (199–200).

Thus she superimposes the design of *La Dame aux Camélias* on her own situation. More directly, Madame Grandoni sums up her tendency: when Christina's self-estimate grows vague, "she needs to do something to give it a definite impressive form. . . . something of the sort usually termed 'unworldly' " (250), and the New York edition adds just before that, "one hasn't said all when one says, as I have so often done, that she likes drama, likes theatricals – what do you call them? – histrionics" (NY, 368–9).

Thackeray's interest in the subtle merging of life and fiction ("With the very first page of the human story," asks Thackeray, "do not love and lies too begin?" [*N*, 5]) is an interest obviously congenial to James. In an account of Christina, which is another astute summary of Ethel, and inasmuch as Ethel partakes of it, an astute summary of an informing theme of *The Newcomes*, James writes:

> Rowland had already been sensible of something in this young lady's tone which he would have called a want of veracity. . . . But the trait was not disagreeable, for she herself was evidently the foremost dupe of her inventions. She had a fictitious history in which she believed much more fondly than in her real one, and an infinite capacity for extemporized reminiscence adapted to the mood of the hour. She liked to idealize herself, to take interesting and picturesque attitudes to her own imagination; and the vivacity and spontaneity of her character gave her really a starting-point in experience, so that the many-coloured flowers of fiction which blossomed in her talk were not so much perversions as sympathetic exaggerations of fact. And Rowland felt that whatever she said of herself might have been, under the imagined circumstances. (193–4)

As Jones at his club in Chapter 1 of *Vanity Fair* is seen relieving his mind with scribbled marginal notations, I see Thackeray at this point, with his copy of *Roderick* fresh from the heavenly Mudie's, scribbling, "Well done, Buttons!"

As for the young men, the treatment accorded Roderick and Clive in their aspirations is roughly similar. Both are hindered by philistinism and class snobbery. "People in general smiled at the radiant good faith of the handsome young sculptor [Roderick] and asked each other whether he really supposed that beauties of that quality were meant to give themselves to juvenile artists" (144). Major Pendennis, as one might except, makes the point more trenchantly: "Nothing could show a more deplorable ignorance of the world than poor Newcome supposing his son could make such a match as that with his cousin. Is it true that he is going to make his son an artist? I don't know what the dooce the world is coming to. An artist! By gad, in my time a fellow would as soon have thought of making his son a hair-dresser, or a pastry-cook, by gad" (*N*, 302). The philistine shortcomings of Northampton, Massachusetts, pale beside the class distinction operating in *The Newcomes.* Though Ethel defends her "poor painter" against Lady Kew, she writes to Colonel Newcome: "You will order Clive not to sell his pictures, won't you? . . . An artist, an organist, a pianist, all these are very good people, but, you know, not *de notre monde*, and Clive ought to belong to it" (*N*, 358). James, however, instead of this issue of snobbery in the heroine, picks up another thread from *The Newcomes*, the deficiency of the artist's power. Though kind, generous, and open, Clive is an ineffectual artist and a lustreless lover. Roderick, despite fits of genius, also fails in application, and, though a more zealous lover, is a selfish, petulant jackanapes. Ethel, however, can put up with the knowledge that Clive is a second-rate artist – artists are not *de notre monde* anyway – while Christina makes artistic slackness a matter of reproach and, tauntingly, a sign of insufficient ardour in general: "Fancy feeling one's self ground in the mill of a third-rate talent!" (183); "One doesn't want a lover one pities" (274). The theme of class consciousness, though there, is much less evident in *Roderick.* Nevertheless, allowing for variations in outcome (Roderick falling off a mountain, Clive suffering the purgatory of Mrs Mackenzie as a mother-in-law) and some differences of emphasis, the trials of the young men in the marriage market are markedly similar. They are even rejected with the same old saw. "Now do you see, *brother*, why you must speak to me so no more?" asks Ethel (*N*, 637); and Christina echoes, "I wish he were my brother, so that he could never talk to me of marriage" (274).

Another major element of James's novel, clearly inspired by *The Newcomes*, is the relationship of Roderick to the little painter, Sam Singleton, and its significance, a reiteration with variations of Clive's relationship to J. J. Ridley. Singleton ("little" Singleton, as James always labels him) is a bank-cashier's son, J. J. Ridley (a portrait of Thackeray's illustrator, Richard Doyle) a butler's. As Singleton is little, Ridley is slight and round-shouldered. Each enters on a low key. Even J. J.'s mother thinks him "little better than an idiot", a "dull boy at the day-school . . . and always the last in his class there" (*N*, 157–8); Singleton, "the little noiseless laborious artist", paints "worthless daubs" at first (89–90). Each worships his more glamorous friend. "Clive was John James's youthful divinity. . . . his pride, his patron, his paragon" (*N*, 164). "J. J. had no greater delight than to listen to his fresh voice" (*N*, 230). Singleton likewise looks up to Roderick "as if Roderick had been himself a statue on a pedestal" (90), "gazing and listening open-mouthed, as if Phoebus-Apollo had been talking" (93). Both are engagingly modest. But by the end J. J. has become a great artist and an academician, and Singleton has developed into a very good painter, while their heroes prove ineffectual. "You have only to work!" Rowland Mallet tells Roderick on their arrival in Rome (46). But neither Clive nor Roderick is given much to work: Roderick cannot separate "one's will and one's inclinations", and he ignores Gloriani's advice that an artist "must learn to do without the Muse!" (99). Unfailingly condescending to Singleton, he takes "an exclusively facetious view of this humble genius" (189). Suffering a lack of invention, he remarks loftily, "If I had only been a painter – a little, quiet, docile, matter-of-fact painter like our friend Singleton – I should only have to open my Ariosto here to find a subject" (163), while Rowland "sighed to himself and wished that his companion had a trifle more of little Sam Singleton's vulgar steadiness" (165). So, "J. J. worked every day, and all day. Many a time the steady little student remarked his patron's absence . . . but when Clive did come to his work, he executed it with remarkable skill and rapidity; and Ridley was too fond of him to say a word at home regarding the shortcomings of the youthful scapegrace" (*N*, 232).

James builds this moral contrast of Roderick and Singleton to an ironic climax that strikingly recalls a scene of similar point in *The Newcomes*. As Roderick, proclaiming his sterility, lounges at Rowland's expense on a Swiss mountainside, a figure descends, "and in relief against the crimson screen of the western sky it looked gigantic" (320). " 'Who is this mighty man,' cried Roderick at last, 'and what is he coming down upon us for? We are small people here, and we can't undertake to keep company with giants.' . . . and they beheld little Sam Singleton stopping to stare at them" (321–2). The scene is a visual rendering of the moral point. Watching Singleton work later, "Roderick's hilarity, after the first evening, had subsided, and he watched the little painter's serene activity with a gravity that was almost portentous. . . . the modest landscapist's unflagging industry grew to have an oppressive meaning for him" (322). The analogous visual effect in *The Newcomes* comes immediately after J. J. has been regretting Clive's not having had to work for his bread:

> The painter turned as he spoke; and the bright northern light which fell upon the sitter's head was intercepted, and lighted up his own as he addressed us. Out of that bright light looked his pale thoughtful face, and long locks and eager brown eyes. The palette on his arm was a great shield painted of many colours: he carried his maul-stick and a sheaf of brushes along with it, the weapons of his glorious but harmless war. With these he achieves conquests, wherein none are wounded save the envious: with that he shelters him against how much idleness, ambition, temptation! (*N*, 850–1)

To sum up, then: the combined theme of unsuccessful artist and marriage market, the complex personality of Christina, the moral contrast of Roderick and Singleton, have clear sources of inspiration in *The Newcomes*, a book of which James speaks frequently and with great respect and love. The closeness of the detailed execution is striking and the shifts in emphasis and design therefore intriguing. Christina's dramatic, histrionic character allows James to pursue an ambiguous merging of life and artifice that is absorbing to himself and Thackeray alike and that is to form a staple ingredient of his subsequent novels. As the New York revisions show, Thackeray's influence is still vital over thirty-five years later. To make a point in limited space, I have dwelt on specific and similar passages, but more general topics invite commentary;

the relative handling of money and class, for example, or differences in tone, range, and narrative. Nevertheless, James's creative assimilation of Thackeray should now be clear; and, moreover, as his next book shows, it continues to operate significantly.

As she did with *Roderick Hudson*, Cornelia Kelley explores continental novelists for influences on *The American*, concluding that it is "a hybrid of Turgenieff and George Sand".[23] In his review of *The American*, however, George Saintsbury, who knew his Thackeray, considered the old Marquise "a rather perilous likeness to Lady Kew".[24] To a reader of both authors, the likeness is clear. Thackeray's greater success is also clear for reasons James himself proposes in his later Preface.

Once again James turns to the European marriage market for his matrix and explores negotiations between the two humbugs (as Thackeray termed them), wealth and birth. The marriage market is, indeed, a common enough idea – William Hogarth exploited it for *Marriage à la Mode*, and Bulwer saw such marketing as "a notorious characteristic of English society";[25] nevertheless, it is a major Thackerayan theme, and James's assimilation of it in *Roderick* argues, if there were no other evidence, a similar source here. James adopts the idea fairly simply. "I want to possess, in a word," says Newman, "the best article in the market",[26] and he drives the commercial note home in the New York edition with the observation, "some rare creature all one's own is the best kind of property to hold" (NY, 50). "How should you like", asks Tristram, "a fair Circassian, with a dagger in her belt?" (50).[27] Explaining that the Bellegardes "are not rich, and they want to bring money into the family" (101), Mrs Tristram tells Newman that Madame de Cintré "has been sold once; she naturally objects to being sold again" (102). To which Newman innocently responds, "Is it possible . . . that they do that sort of thing over here?" (103). James here, however, admits an error that Thackeray would not have made. In the New York Preface James concedes, "They would positively have jumped then, the Bellegardes, at my rich and easy American. . . . taking with alacrity everything he could give them" (NY, XIX). The Thackerayan accommodation between birth and wealth works both ways. Lady Kew, for example, commands aristocratic Lady Ann to marry the banker Brian Newcome but intends to marry their daughter Ethel to an aristocrat (Clive's money, like Newman's, is of little account at that stage). The social intricacies of *The Newcomes* are much more elaborate and exact than those of *The American*.

For similar reasons, James's Madame de Bellegarde, though very interesting, is less impressive than Lady Kew. What James emulates is the witchlike malevolence of Lady Kew and her complete domination of the family's affairs. The daughter of an English earl, Madame de Bellegarde, an "old feudal countess of a mother rules the family with an iron hand" (52–3); she is "a striking image of the dignity which even in the case of a little time-shrunken old lady – may reside in the habit of unquestioned authority" (210). "She is wicked, she is an old sinner", Newman decides (219). "I wanted to say", says Tristram of her hauteur about commerce, "that I manufactured broomsticks for old witches to ride on" (272). Newman feels, later, that he is "in the presence of something evil" (316). Thackeray's Lady Kew, though also embroidered with motifs and images of witchery, is more interesting in that, in addition to such surface impressions, she is much more articulate and gives verbal expression to a wider and shrewder social sense. "Old Lady Kew's tongue was a dreadful thong which made numbers of people wince. She was not altogether cruel, but she knew the dexterity with which she wielded her lash, and liked to exercise it" (*N*, 140). "Her ladyship, a sister of the late lamented Marquis of Steyne, possessed no small share of the wit and intelligence, and a considerable resemblance to the features of that distinguished nobleman" (*N*, 142). Her sense, realism, shrewdness, wit, and occasional pathos, her toughness but evident inner life make her a brilliant achievement, but perhaps James is here at too early a stage in his career for him to emulate that achievement successfully. He manages the grotesque surface but not the range of Lady Kew.

The determining power of the marriage market and the characterisation of Madame de Bellegarde are the two most notable features of *The American* reflected from *The Newcomes*, but other Thackerayan ingredients are evident. The skeleton in the closet is a device dear to Thackeray's heart, and it shows up melodramatically in *The American* in the "immense secret" of the Bellegardes (349). On the technical level, Thackeray characteristically embellishes his narrative with multiple perspectives, multiple layers of allusion and comparison drawn from fable, drama, poetry, the Bible, fairy tale, and painting. *The Newcomes* exploits fairy tale especially to suggest the dream worlds of its characters as well as to underscore the irony of their actual situations. The Colonel, as we have seen, invents a fairy tale in which Clive and Ethel are Prince and Princess and in which Lady Kew is the witch. Some of that technique appears in *The American* when Newman overhears Madame de Cintré telling a fairy tale about the beautiful Florabella to her niece. Like Florabella, who starves for six months before getting "a plum-cake as big as that ottoman" (197), Newman must wait six months to propose – but the outcome is ominously foreshadowed in Madame de Cintré's comment: "I could never have gone through the sufferings of the beautiful Florabella . . . not even for her prospective rewards" (197). The whole depiction of the gloomy, closed-up, stoutly guarded Bellegarde mansion is in a fairy tale, or as James called it, a romance key. The Duchess d'Outreville, for the sake of bright conversation, fashions a "légende" of Newman's career in which he is in three years "going to be made president of America" (279). "But your real triumph", she adds, " . . . is pleasing the countess; she is as difficult as a princess in a fairy tale" (280). As the Marquis here leads Newman about at his aristocratic reception, James adds, "If the Marquis was going about as a bear-leader, if the fiction of Beauty and the Beast was supposed to have found its companion-piece, the general impression appeared to be that the bear was a very fair imitation of humanity" (281). Such touches in *The American*, however, are little more than ominous embroidery; they do not accumulate to Thackeray's richness of texture nor do they explore the interplay of life and fiction that interested James in *Roderick Hudson* and that is central to Thackeray's vision. The "indifferent statue of an eighteenth-century nymph, simpering, sallow, and cracked" (289) on the Bellegarde stairway and the "fête champêtre" on Madame de Bellegarde's eighteenth-century fan are, indeed, touches of ironic artifice in a Thackerayan vein. And finally, a motif both Thackeray and James treated with amused irony as a flight of fantasy colouring life, the notion of escaping the sordid world by retreating to a nunnery, is in *The American* solemnly acted out as Madame de Cintré buries herself in the harshest nunnery of the lot. On the whole, however, instead of the scintillating texture of artifice and reality intermingled that James developed from Thackeray in *Roderick*, he achieves in *The American* only that uneasy mixture of reality and romance that he complains of in the New York Preface. The Thackerayan touches here are not so fortunate. Nevertheless, in the theme of the marriage market, and in the character of Madame de Bellegarde, James is clearly continuing in *The American* to mine the rich stores of material we see him extracting from *The Newcomes* in *Roderick*.

It is surely time we abandoned the perfunctory habit of playing James and Thackeray off against each other. They obviously differ much in their attitudes to the novel as a form, in their scope of vision, in their formal preferences, in their style and manner. They have genuine points of contention. But they also have interests in common, not only details of subject matter but central concerns such as the impingement of style on life. James plainly held a lifelong admiration for Thackeray, and for *The Newcomes* in particular. In *Roderick Hudson* and *The American*, Thackeray is far more in evidence than are the continental novelists so commonly associated with James. Perhaps in this blinkered vision, we are still affected by the snobbery Edmund Wilson observed in the early twentieth century's scorn for Dickens in favour of his great admirer Dostoevsky.[28] Just as Shaw insisted on his debt to Dickens as much as to Ibsen and Nietzsche, so James, though it would not have suited his general style so much as it suited Shaw's roughing up of contemporaries, could have made a similarly unfashionable acknowledgement of Thackeray. Certainly the early James could. James had no such mandarin aloofness towards Thackeray as people who compare them often manifest; his attitude was very much one of respect, in the early novels the sincere respect of "honourable emulation".

NOTES

1. Gordon N. Ray, *Thackeray: The Age of Wisdom, 1847–1863* (New York, 1958) pp. 262–3.
2. Preface to *The Tragic Muse*, in Henry James, *The Art of the Novel* (New York, 1934) p. 84.

3. Henry James, *Notes of a Son and Brother* (London, 1914) p. 21.
4. A reviewer of *Roderick Hudson* noted, "If the authorship of *Roderick Hudson* were a secret . . . the reading public would be puzzled on whom to fix it . . . the only novelist to whose temper of mind there is the least affinity is Thackeray, and few writers resemble one another less" (*North American Review*, April 1876, 420, rpt. in Roger Gard [ed.], *Henry James: The Critical Heritage* [London, 1968] p. 39). Oscar Cargill ventures suggestions that Rachel and Beatrix Esmond may have inspired the de Vionnets, mother and daughter, and that *The Newcomes* may have contributed the similar name, Newsome, to *The Ambassadors* as well as the relationship of Chad and Strether, which is drawn from that of Clive and Colonel Newcome (*The Novels of Henry James* [New York, 1961] p. 332, n. 30). Geoffrey Tillotson notes a number of similarities in material, authorial presence, and manner of proceeding in *Thackeray the Novelist* (Cambridge, 1954).
5. "Henry James Jr.", *Century Illustrated Monthly Magazine*, NS 3, November 1882, p. 28, rpt. in *Henry James: The Critical Heritage*, p. 133 The cartoon is in *Life*, Feb. 1883, p. 91.
6. Tillotson, p. 296.
7. Robert L. Gale, *The Caught Image: Figurative Language in the Fiction of Henry James* (Chapel Hill, 1954) p. 102.
8. *Nation*, 16 July 1868, p. 52.
9. A canard shared by Henry James, Sr, who told Emerson in 1853: "Thackeray could not see beyond his eyes, and had no ideas, and merely is a sounding-board against which his experiences thump and resound" (Edward Waldo Emerson and Waldo Emerson Forbes [eds], *Journals of Ralph Waldo Emerson*, 10 vols, vol. VIII, [Boston, 1909–14] p. 393).
10. *Galaxy*, Dec. 1875, pp. 823–4.
11. F. O. Matthiessen, *The James Family* (New York, 1947) p. 502.
12. Gordon S. Haight (ed.), *The George Eliot Letters*, 7 vols, vol. II (New Haven, 1954–6) p. 349.
13. Henry James, *A Small Boy and Others* (London, 1913) pp. 93–4.
14. *Ibid.*, p. 316.
15. *Ibid.*, pp. 416, 423–4.
16. Henry James, *The Middle Years* (London, 1917) pp. 4–9.
17. Henry James, "Anthony Trollope", *Partial Portraits* (London, 1888) p. 118.
18. Cornelia Pulsifer Kelley, *The Early Development of Henry James*, rev. ed. (Urbana, 1965) p. 187.
19. Henry James, *Roderick Hudson* (Harmondsworth and Baltimore, 1969) p. 108; reference is to the Penguin Modern Classics edition since it is a generally accessible reprint of the English revised text of 1878 and my concern here is primarily with the early James. Occasional references to the New York Edition (New York, 1907) are indicated by an NY before the page number.
20. *The Newcomes*, vol. XIV of George Saintsbury (ed.), *The Oxford Thackeray*, 17 vols (London, 1908) p. 596. Subsequent references are to this edition and are indicated parenthetically in my text by *N* and the page number.
21. Trollope may be at a similar emulation in that scene of *The Last Chronicle*

of Barset where his artist, Conway Dalrymple, begins his acquaintance with the heiress, Clara Van Siever, with the reflection that "he certainly could make a picture of her . . . but it must be as Judith with the dissevered head, or as Jael using her hammer over the temple of Sisera" (World's Classics edition [London, 1967] p. 254). In the *Newcomes*, Clive thinks Ethel "would do for Judith". Dalrymple's making of the Jael painting forms a subplot of its own.

22. Henry James, *The Sacred Fount* (New York, 1953) p. 214.
23. Kelley, p. 243.
24. *Academy*, July 1877, p. 33, rpt. in *Henry James: The Critical Heritage*, p. 45.
25. Edward Lytton Bulwer, *England and the English* (1833; rpt. Chicago, 1970) p. 85.
26. Henry James, *The American* (Boston, 1877) p. 48.
27. Improved in the New York edition to "How should you like an expensive Circassian with a dagger in her baggy trousers?" (51).
28. Edmund Wilson, "Dickens: The Two Scrooges", *The Wound and the Bow* (New York, 1947) pp. 1–3.

9 *The Portrait of Isabel Archer*

In order to see the ghost of Gardencourt, Ralph Touchett tells his cousin Isabel at the beginning of *The Portrait of a Lady*, "You must have suffered first, have suffered greatly, have gained some miserable knowledge."[1] Isabel, who as "a young, happy, innocent person" evidently does not qualify, nevertheless remains eager to see the ghost; and by the end of the novel, on the night of Ralph's death, "she apparently had fulfilled the necessary condition; for . . . in the cold, faint dawn, she knew that a spirit was standing by her bed" (II, 418).[2] It is as though a quest has been achieved: she has sought her suffering and her miserable knowledge, and found them. Dorothy Van Ghent has seen Isabel's quest as being for happiness,[3] and so it is. But Isabel is deeply ambivalent. On the one hand, like a true American, she is ardently engaged in life, liberty, and the pursuit of happiness; but on the other she is morbidly attracted by their opposites, and devotes herself to death, and immobility, and suffering. She is enamoured of the ghost of Gardencourt. It is this side of Isabel that I want to explore.

Suffering is fatally desirable to Isabel for several reasons. It is for one thing the perverse desire of a mind, otherwise healthy, that is yet preoccupied with its own health. Then, as we know, "the old Protestant tradition had never faded from Isabel's imagination" (II, 349), and the Protestant sanctification of suffering goes hand in hand with its sense of guilt in pleasure and luxury. And again, as the subject matter of great art, and as involving the enlargement of consciousness, suffering appeals to that side of Isabel that reflects the aesthetic movement: she strives, in Pater's phrase, to burn always with a hard, gem-like flame, to make of her life a finely wrought creation. It is this common element in the psychological, moral and aesthetic strands of Isabel's character, as I read the novel, that determines and creates her destiny.

With one part of herself Isabel is strenuously determined to be happy, to hold misery at a distance. She is even rather callously irritable when her suitors inflict their sorrows on her – "You may be unhappy, but you shall not make *me* so. That I can't allow", she tells Lord Warburton (I, 421). (It is one of Osmond's shrewd moves in his courtship that he does not play the melancholy lover, but tells her that his love, whether fulfilled or not, gives him pleasure.) She is even almost ashamed of suffering: "I have mentioned how passionately she needed to feel that her unhappiness should not have come to her through her own fault", James reminds us (II, 281); and she feels half guilty of giving in to it, for "She could never rid herself of the sense that unhappiness was a state of disease – of suffering as opposed to doing" (II, 173). And yet soon after this we hear that for her suffering is not passive but rather passionate: "Suffering, with Isabel, was an active condition; it was not a chill, a stupor, a despair; it was a passion of thought, of speculation, of response to every pressure" (II, 189). It is apparently while suffering that she is most vividly alive and aware, and the part of her that seeks, as Pater directs, "not the fruit of experience, but experience itself",[4] expands and delights in the enlargement of consciousness. And so, for all her energy in the pursuit of happiness, she is simultaneously fascinated by unhappiness, and pursues that too. James suggests this element of perversity in her, I think, in his phrase in the preface, where he speaks of her "affronting" her destiny (I, xii). There is a suggestion there of deliberate insult, of wanton destruction of a potentially fortunate life pattern.[5] In the symbolic setting of the room in her grandmother's house to which Isabel retreats as a child, there is a locked door which leads to an "unseen place on the other side – a place which became to the child's imagination, according to its different moods, a region of delight or of terror" (I, 30). Those are indeed the alternating paths of Isabel's consciousness. At times she is conscious of this fatal tendency in herself: that is why, when she contemplates the placid content of the Misses Molyneux, she almost admires them for being "not morbid, at any rate", – because she has "occasionally suspected it as a tendency of her own" (I, 104). And she is frequently explicit about being afraid of herself.

In the figure of Warburton, it seems to me, James has taken pains to present a man whom we are to take as the right husband for Isabel. He has "a certain fortunate, brilliant exceptional look – the air of a happy temperament fertilised by a high civilisation" (I, 5). He and Isabel should match perfectly, but for her morbid revulsion from those qualities which she herself possesses and admires. James makes a point of his political radicalism to show that even a good child of the republic need have no qualms of conscience in marrying *this* particular English lord. Warburton's love for her would seem just the kind she would thrive on – not tyrannical and demanding like Goodwood's, or egoistic like Osmond's. His declaration makes a moving scene, and Isabel feels its force:

> "I don't go off easily, but when I'm touched, it's for life. It's for life, Miss Archer, it's for life," Lord Warburton repeated in the kindest, tenderest, pleasantest voice Isabel had ever heard, and looking at her with eyes charged with the light of a passion that had sifted itself clear of the baser parts of emotion – the heat, the violence, the unreason – and that burned as steadily as a lamp in a windless place. (I, 147–8)[6]

And yet the more attractive his offer seems, the less is she able to accept it. It is not simply that she does not love him, or that she feels bound to Goodwood, her previous suitor. But she is driven by motives which she does not herself understand, and of which she is in fact afraid. When he proposes, she feels "she would have given her little finger at that moment to feel strongly and simply the impulse to [accept]"; but instead she withdraws, "even as some wild, caught creature in a vast cage". And to Warburton's confession that he is very much afraid of "that remarkable mind of yours", she replies with emphasis, "So am I, my lord!" (I, 152–4). Her refusal is not rational – it surprises and scares her. With her habit of restless self-observation, she tries later to analyse her reaction, and suspects herself of having "ambitions reaching beyond Lord Warburton's beautiful appeal, reaching to something indefinable and possibly not commendable" (I, 161). In her later interview with her suitor she is able to be more explicit about her grounds of refusal, though not more rational. "'That reason that I wouldn't tell you – I'll tell it you after all. It's that I can't escape my fate. . . . I can't escape unhappiness,' said Isabel. 'In marrying you I shall be trying to'" (I, 186). Warburton's comment, "You're bent on being miserable", is a shrewd if oversimplified summary of her sentiments. She is caught between the attraction of happiness, as represented by marriage to Warburton, a finely sensitive and honourable man who offers her a life of warmth and graciousness, and the equal and opposite attraction of unhappiness and suffering.

Later in her life, after her marriage, Isabel reflects, "She had not been simple when she refused [Lord Warburton]; that operation had been as complicated as, later, her acceptance of Osmond had been" (II, 176–7). And in fact the two events have very much the same complex motivation, though Isabel is less conscious of her own perversity in the latter case. It is true that in some ways she is simply mistaken in her view of Osmond – "she had not read him right", as she reflects at one point (II, 192).[7] But it is evident too, I think, that with some part of her mind she recognises that Osmond will cause her the pain and suffering that she perversely desires. And so, just as she rejected Warburton for the happiness he offered, so she accepts Osmond for the misery he promises. After Osmond's declaration she is deeply shaken, and she contemplates the union with fear rather than happiness:

> Her imagination, as I say, now hung back: there was a last vague space it couldn't cross – a dusky, uncertain tract which looked ambiguous and even slightly treacherous, like a moorland seen in the winter twilight. But she was to cross it yet. (II, 22)

And she protects herself from her relatives' disapproval of the match by the reflection, "You could criticise any marriage. . . . How well she herself, should she only give her mind to it, might criticise this union of her own!" (II, 61). She is careful *not* to give her mind to it, however, concentrating rather on defending her choice. "Do you think you're going to be happy?" asks her aunt, thinking to dissuade her from the match. "No one's happy, in such doings, you should know" (II, 54). But such an argument is not likely to put Isabel off, although she staunchly declares she intends to be happy all the same. In fact the opposition of her relatives is another factor in determining Isabel's choice of Osmond. She is so bent on pleasing herself in the matter that opposition makes her the more certain that this is what she is doing. When Ralph ventures bravely to try to make her aware of her fiancé's sinister attributes, she launches into an eloquent defence of him that is a triumph to her, because in justifying her choice to Ralph she has also justified it to herself: "Isabel paused, turning on him a face of elation – absolutely and perversely of gratitude. His opposition had made her own conception of her conduct clearer to her" (II, 75). Isabel is not simply deluded, though she is indeed charmed by Osmond. For all her rationalisation, it seems that somewhere within herself she knows and seeks the misery that marriage to him will entail. Again, we have a shrewd and downright diagnosis, this time from Mrs Touchett: "Such an alliance, on Isabel's part, would have an air of almost morbid perversity" (I, 394).

Yet another reason for her marriage, and one that operates at a quite conscious level, is of course her money.[8] Isabel strikes people as being brilliant and fortunate, and is herself conscious of being so. But her good fortune, and particularly the somewhat grossly material form it takes when Mr Touchett leaves her seventy thousand pounds, is a moral embarrassment to her. The money is not only Osmond's motive for marrying her, it is one of hers of marrying him:

> But for her money, as she saw to-day, she would never have done it. And then her mind wandered off to poor Mr. Touchett, sleeping under English turf, the beneficent author of infinite woe! For this was the fantastic fact. At bottom her money had been a burden, had been on her mind, which was filled with the desire to transfer the weight of it to some other conscience, to some more prepared receptacle. (II, 192–3)

At a conscious level she has sought to enrich the poor by impoverishing herself – her marriage is partly an act of charity, for "there was no charitable institution in which she had been as much interested as in Gilbert Osmond" (II, 193). At a subliminal level she has felt guilty about her good fortune, and actively sought to rid herself of it.

Isabel's subjection to another author of infinite woe – and this one is not so beneficent – is again due to her infatuation with unhappiness. Much of Madame Merle's special appeal for Isabel is made evident in the curious compliment Isabel pays her early in their relation: "'I'm afraid you've suffered much,' she once found occasion to say to her friend .... 'You sometimes say things that I think people who have always been happy wouldn't have found out'" (I, 274). Isabel admires her and longs to be like her. Ironically, of course, she does follow in Madame Merle's footsteps, taking her place as Osmond's mate and as the step-mother of her daughter; and in doing so, reaps all and more of the woe she has found so attractive in her mentor.

As a girl in Albany, and on the night when she has accepted her aunt's invitation to go to Europe, Isabel reflects on her life so far:

> It had been a very happy life and she had been a very fortunate person .... It appeared to Isabel that the unpleasant had been even too absent from her knowledge, for she had gathered from her acquaintance with literature that it was often a source of interest and even of instruction. (I, 42)

And here we come to the aesthetic element in Isabel's attraction to the ghost of Gardencourt. Suffering is the material of tragedy and other great forms of art, and Isabel, as has been pointed out,[9] sees herself as a heroine of drama and romance. There are plenty of incidents and conversations that illustrate this romantic view that the young Isabel takes of herself, since it is frequently under discussion between her and her friends. She tells Mr Touchett that in a revolution she would have been "a high, proud loyalist", not for any political views that she has, but because loyalists have the chance to behave so "picturesquely"; and her uncle humorously condoles with her that she "won't have the pleasure of going gracefully to the guillotine here just now" (I, 100–1). She frivolously comments that her idea of happiness is "a swift carriage, of a dark night, rattling with four horses over roads that one can't see" – to which Henrietta Stackpole retorts sourly, "Like the heroine of an immoral novel" (I, 235). And in fact, we hear, "Sometimes she went so far as to wish that she might find herself some day in a difficult position, so that she should have the pleasure of being as heroic as the occasion demanded" (I, 69).

Isabel's reading is recurrently of import in the action of the novel, or at least in the preparation and atmosphere for it. In his staging of scenes, James repeatedly places her with her eyes on a book, but her mind wandering, before the occurrence of some momentous and decisive event in her life. In her retreat in the house at Albany she is trying to fix her attention on a history of German thought when her aunt arrives to announce her intention of taking her to Europe. She finds she has lost interest in her book in the garden at Gardencourt – "Of late, it was not to be denied, literature had seemed a fading light" (I, 140) – when she receives Goodwood's letter and then Warburton's proposal. It is the same at Pratt's Hotel in London before Goodwood's visit which so shakes her, and again later at the hotel in Rome before Osmond's declaration. Finally, back in Gardencourt at the end of the novel, she finds "she had never been less interested in literature than to-day. . . . She was quite unable to read. . . . Her eyes often wandered from the book in her hand to the open window" (II, 424). The interruption this time is as before – first Lord Warburton, and then Caspar Goodwood arrive to make their final appeals.

These repeated fade-ins from the printed page to the dramatic embodiments of life recurrently suggest Isabel's literary view of experience. Literature becomes a fading light as she invests her own life with its vividness and artistic heightening. This is a more serious and sophisticated version of Catherine Morland's evocations of Gothic horrors in Jane Austen's *Northanger Abbey*, and a more tragic development of Elizabeth Bennet's vivacious self-projection in *Pride and Prejudice*. James himself explores the comic potential of the theme in his other novels, in figures like Mrs Penniman in *Washington Square* and Mrs Wix in *What Maisie Knew*, who all expect life to follow art, and take steps to make it do so. The fact that Isabel tends to be reading histories of German thought rather than Gothic novels attests to her theoretic approach to life, as well as to her greater intellectual sophistication.

All this is perhaps harmless enough, and even engaging in a bright adolescent girl. But Isabel's confusion of literature and life is more serious and lasting than Catherine Morland's or Elizabeth Bennet's, Isabel is consciously and deliberately self-creating. Though no artist herself ("the girl had never attempted to write a book and had no desire for the laurels of authorship. She had no talent for expression and too little of the consciousness of genius" [I, 67]), she undertakes to make her life itself a work of art. She "had a theory . . . that one should be one of the best, should be conscious of a fine organisation . . . . Her life should always be in harmony with the most pleasing impression she should produce; she would be what she appeared, and she would appear what she was" (I, 68–9). She wants appearance and essence to be identical, as they are in art, but not in life. She is simultaneously the artist and the critic of her own nature: "She was always planning out her development, desiring her perfection, observing her progress" (I, 72). Ralph perceives and warns her against this tendency: "Don't try so much to form your character – it's like trying to pull open a tight, tender young rose" (I, 319).

It is Isabel's determination to construct her life like an artifact rather than to let it unfold and bloom naturally that makes her vulnerable to the Europeanised Americans, benevolent and otherwise, who take over her life and make use of her. She is certainly a victim of circumstance and of unscrupulous manipulators, but it lies within herself that she is such easy prey to them. Because she wants to compose her life according to an aesthetic pattern, she complies with the critical requirements of the connoisseurs of life who surround her.

One of the major ironies of the novel, of course, is that Isabel, who has been so fanatic in her quest for freedom, and her determination to create her own destiny, in fact finds that her choices have all along been determined, and her expressive gestures composed, by others. A large part of Isabel's growth in self-knowledge is her final recognition that she has not been as free an agent as she had intended to be, that in fact she has been instrument rather than agent. But she never realises the extent to which, in making a work of art of herself, she has made herself a mere thing for others to use. Like her perverse desire for suffering, this tendency to limit the free and natural expansion of her life operates for the most part at a subliminal level.

The first person to manipulate Isabel's life is Mrs Touchett. Her name is significant, for there is something of the wand-waving fairy godmother about her.[10] She is the one who starts the whole enchantment. Isabel is bewitched by her promise, "You should go to Florence if you like houses in which things have happened – especially deaths" (I, 35): so she does go to Florence with her aunt, and there she meets Gilbert Osmond. Isabel is flattered that Mrs Touchett likes her appearance; and her aunt has her own motives for taking on the business of introducing her to the world: "If you want to know," she tells Ralph, "I thought she would do me credit. I like to be well thought of, and for a woman of my age there's no greater convenience, in some ways, than an attractive niece" (I, 56–7). This, to be sure, does not place Isabel in a very prominent place among the world's artifacts. For Mrs Touchett she is hardly more than a fine piece of lace, some personal appurtenance that enhances the appearance.

Ralph Touchett (who endows Isabel with the further magic gift of wealth) sees her from the first in terms of art, though he values her above the visual arts:

> If his cousin were to be nothing more than an entertainment to him, Ralph was conscious she was an entertainment of a high order. "A character like that," he said to himself – "a real little passionate force to see at play is the finest thing in nature. It's finer than the finest work of art – than a Greek bas-relief, than a great Titian, than a Gothic Cathedral." (I, 86)

Isabel herself, as we have seen, sees her life primarily in literary terms: she intends to compose it as a romance, possibly as a tragedy. But Ralph sees it more specifically as drama, a production to which he has contributed and at which he is to have a front seat. He tells her, early in her career, that he looks forward to "the thrill of seeing what a young lady does who won't marry Lord Warburton . . .. Ah, there will be plenty of spectators!" (I, 212). It is to be his one compensation: otherwise, he asks, "What's the use of being ill and disabled and restricted to mere spectatorship at the game of life if I really can't see the show when I've paid so much for my ticket?" When he speaks thus of the "show" that her life is to be, Isabel "listened to him with quickened attention" (I, 209–10). Because of her own self-creating impulse, she is available for his entertainment.

Ralph is glad of her refusal of Warburton for aesthetic reasons, because he delights in the unexpected in the dramas he watches. When she unexpectedly accepts Osmond, however, real life reasserts itself, and he is dismayed. Nevertheless, he continues to watch the production, and it becomes for him virtually all that keeps him alive: "There was more to come. . . . This was only the first act of the drama, and he was determined to sit out the performance" (II, 146–7). But finally Isabel has had enough of performing, and she sends Ralph away with the other "spectators" of the "comedy" of her married life in Rome. "Do you call it a comedy, Isabel Archer?" asks Henrietta grimly. "The tragedy then if you like. You're all looking at me; it makes me uncomfortable" (II, 303). And Ralph is finally to regret paying the price of his ticket, and his part in encouraging the performance.

It is Gilbert Osmond, of course, who most fully imposes an aesthetic pattern on life, and who most clearly makes of Isabel a work of art. Ralph's air of "thinking that life was a matter of connoisseurship . . . was an anomally, a kind of humorous excrescence, whereas in Mr. Osmond it was the keynote, and everything was in harmony with it" (I, 377). As Ralph says, "He's the incarnation of taste. . . . He judges and measures, approves and condemns, altogether by that" (II, 71). But his taste is not for spectacle and display. The art that he admires is more exclusive and manageable than literature or a dramatic production (his reference to literature about human passion is characteristically contemptuous, when he taunts Madame Merle in her hour of bitterness with the vulgarity of "[talking] of revenge like a third-rate novelist" [II, 335]). The works that he most covets are objects – *bibelots*, pictures, and sculptures, preferably the ones he can possess himself. For him too Isabel must be a work of art, but for his purposes her potential must be limited and curtailed. He does not, like Ralph, want to put wind in her sails, but to make her immobile. She must get rid of her "ideas", he tells her, and she realises later with horror, "He had really meant it – he would have liked her to have nothing of her own but her pretty appearance" (II, 194–5). But it was she, after all, who originally hoped "she would be what she appeared, and she would appear what she was".[11] Here again Isabel has connived at reducing herself and her life to an artistic structure. When Ralph warns her against the "sterile dilettante" who has nothing to recommend him but his taste, she defends him:

> "It's a happy thing then that his taste should be exquisite."
> "It's exquisite, indeed, since it has led him to select you as his bride." . . .
> "I hope it may never be my fortune to fail to gratify my husband's." (II, 71)

Such a reply justifiably disgusts Ralph. But it is not simply a pious comment for the occasion: she is actually proud of meeting Osmond's aesthetic standards. Madame Merle has shrewdly presented him as a challenge to interest, and at their first meeting, as he shows Isabel his collection of *objets d'art*, she consciously presents rather a calculated and composed image of herself than her full nature. Osmond reminds her during their courtship, "Don't you remember my telling you that one ought to make one's life a work of art? You looked rather shocked at first; but then I told you that it was exactly what you seemed to me to be trying to do with your own" (II, 15). And so she voluntarily donates herself "to figure in his collection of choice objects" (II, 9).

Serena Merle, like Osmond, also worships form and surface. As Osmond is "the incarnation of taste", she is "the incarnation of propriety" (II, 370). She has so fashioned her own life that polished manner and cultivated performance are almost all there is of her – or at least all that is visible. Isabel, as she begins to be disenchanted with her friend, finds "it was as if she had remained after all something of a public performer, condemned to emerge only in character and in costume" (II, 39). That is what Osmond does to his women. Madame Merle, Isabel, and Pansy must be reduced to a role, an appearance, a delicate form. The secret passional life as discarded mistress and unacknowledged mother which Madame Merle conceals beneath her serene exterior erupts curiously to assert itself against encroaching formalisation: she tells Rosier that though she finds it necessary to surround herself with "good things", she hates her artistic possessions. "It's good to have something to hate: one works it off!" (II, 91). But if art has encroached on her life, she also imposes it on Isabel's: she is both the artifice and the artificer. She is no great creator, however, rather a skilled craftsman, who makes tools out of people: "I don't pretend to know what people are meant for," she says. "I only know what I can do with them" (I, 345). Even after their friendship has cooled somewhat, Isabel continues to admire Madame Merle:

> That personage was armed at all points; it was a pleasure to see a character so completely equipped for the social battle. She carried her flag discreetly, but her weapons were polished steel, and she used them with a skill which struck Isabel as more and more that of a veteran. (II, 154)

What Isabel does not know at this point is that she herself is one of Madame Merle's weapons, part of her equipment. (The military metaphor recalls the passage, early in their relation, in which Madame Merle tells her, "I want to see what life makes of you", and Isabel "received this assurance as a young soldier, still panting from a slight skirmish, . . . might receive a pat on the shoulder from his colonel" [I, 268]. Again she is eager to live up to the expectations of a manipulator.) The fact that she has been used is one of her major discoveries, when she finally confronts Madame Merle in the light of her knowledge of her relation with Osmond: "She saw . . . the dry staring fact that she had been an applied handled hung-up tool, as senseless and convenient as mere shaped wood and iron" (II, 379). At the end of the novel, and in answer to her aunt's interrogation, Isabel thus defines Madame Merle's great crime against her: "She made a convenience of me" (II, 410). She speaks to Mrs Touchett apparently without irony, though her aunt's motive for whisking her away from America in the first place had been that "for a woman of my age there's no greater convenience . . . than an attractive niece". Mrs Touchett and Madame Merle, fairy godmother and sorceress, have similarly imposed their magic – though Isabel's vulnerability to it has been of her own making – to freeze her life into material for use. Ralph too, whom Henrietta calls "Prospero enough to make her what she has become" (I, 169), has contributed his share of the magic. Isabel, whose determination had been "to choose" for herself, has been like the enchanted princess in the fairytale, acting always under a spell, and with no prince to restore her to life and mobility. One is tempted to see Osmond's name as suggesting finally an ossified world, a world of death and rigidity.

Isabel has seen herself as a goddess in an epic and as a heroine in a romance, and in conforming her life to artistic design she has allowed others to form her and use her too; and they do so with increasing restrictions of her freedom and potential. In her own view her life has the range and variety of narrative fiction; Ralph reduces it to the comparative spatial and temporal confinements of drama; Osmond further contracts her to an *objet d'art*, Madame Merle finally to a mere tool. The hierarchy may reflect James's own preferences among the arts.

Throughout the novel, and starting with the title, the reader has been invited to see Isabel in terms of art. In the gallery at Gardencourt we see her through Ralph's eyes:

> She took a candlestick herself and held it slowly here and there; she lifted it high, and as she did so he found himself pausing in the middle of the place and bending his eyes much less upon the pictures than on her presence. He lost nothing, in truth, by these wandering glances, for she was better worth looking at than most works of art. (I, 61)[12]

Here she is a moving image among static paintings; but after Osmond has had a chance to work on her, her motion begins to be stilled: when Rosier sees her among her guests in Rome, "She had lost something of that quick eagerness to which her husband had privately taken exception – she had more the air of being able to wait. Now, at all events, framed in the gilded doorway, she struck our young man as the picture of a gracious lady" (II, 105). Ralph notices that now she resorts to more artificial adornments to her natural beauty; and, in a passage that connects Isabel's perversity with her readiness to be made into a work of art, he reflects:

> There was an amplitude and a brilliancy in her personal arrangements that gave a touch of insolence to her beauty. [Isabel is indeed "affronting" her destiny.] Poor human-hearted Isabel, what perversity had bitten her? Her light step drew a mass of drapery behind it; her intelligent head sustained a majesty of ornament. The free, keen girl had become quite another person; what he saw was the fine lady who was supposed to represent something. (II, 143)

What James has shown in Isabel, and increasingly as the novel progresses, is life straining towards the condition of art. It is a major theme of Browning's. The Bishop of St Praxed's, as he obsessively talks about the design and structure of the tomb that is to be all that remains of him, and recalls "mistresses with great smooth marbly limbs", imagines himself as his own effigy:

> For as I lie here, hours of the dead night,
> Dying in state and by such slow degrees,
> I fold my arms as if they clasped a crook,
> And stretch my feet forth straight as stone can point,
> And let the bedclothes, for a mortcloth, drop
> Into great laps and folds of sculptor's-work.
> ("The Bishop Orders his Tomb," ll. 85–90)

Even so Isabel:

> She had moments indeed in her journey from Rome which were almost as good as being dead. She sat in her corner, so motionless, so passive, . . . so detached from hope and regret, that she recalled to herself one of those Etruscan figures couched upon the receptacle of their ashes. (II, 391)

Death, or the attainment of a state of immobility that is exempt from the flux and motion of life – a sort of petrification – becomes increasingly attractive to her. Back in the gallery at Gardencourt, she now finds herself envying the pictures and artifacts "which change by no hair's breadth" (II, 403).[13]

There has been considerable critical discussion of the question of why Isabel returns to Osmond, why the book ends as it does. Dorothea Krook finds the problem has been artificially created by modern critics who take too casual a view of separation and divorce – Isabel, she suggests, given her world, her devotion, her fidelity to her promises, and her moral consistency, has no alternative but to return to her husband.[14] But in fact separation is strenuously urged as the best course for Isabel within the novel, by her own friends and countrymen – themselves no mean moralists – Henrietta and Goodwood. ("Nothing is more common in our Western cities", Henrietta argues vigorously [II, 304].) Isabel does indeed think much of her promises, whether made at the altar or elsewhere – it is part of her impulse towards self-determination, her enterprise to live her life according to a preconceived design – but her promises are only part of her motivation. There is a revealing exchange on the subject between her and Henrietta in London at the end of the novel:

> "I don't see why you promised little Miss Osmond to go back" [says Henrietta].
>
> "I'm not sure I myself see now," Isabel replied, "But I did then."
>
> "If you've forgotten your reason perhaps you won't return."
>
> Isabel waited a moment. "Perhaps I shall find another."
>
> "You'll certainly never find a good one."
>
> "In default of a better my having promised will do," Isabel suggested. (II, 397–8)

Isabel is going back to Osmond for reasons that she does not articulate, and of which she is not fully conscious. And they are possibly not all "good" ones either.

There is no doubt that her vigorous moral nature has much to do with it – though hers is a kind of self-conscious morality, based on a proud determination to be "right" (like Strether's at the end of *The Ambassadors*), that is distinct from virtue, though closely related to it.[15] But when Goodwood tries to offer her a moral justification for leaving her husband he unwittingly puts his finger on what I take to be one of her reasons for not doing so. "Why shouldn't we be happy – when it's here before us, when it's so easy? . . . I swear, as I stand here, that a woman deliberately made to suffer is justified in anything in life" (II, 434). Isabel's own Puritan morality unites here with her psychological perversity. She is going to be right, and she is going to reject happiness and return to the man who makes her suffer. She will not lose sight of the ghost of Gardencourt.

Goodwood also asks her, "Why should you go back – why should you go through that ghastly form? . . . It would be an insult to you to assume that you care for the look of the thing" (II, 433–4). But for Isabel the form is not ghastly, but closer to being the "magnificent form" that Osmond takes pride in observing; and as we have seen, she *does* care for the look of the thing, because of her tendency to equate the appearance with the essence. "One must accept one's deeds. I married him before all the world", she had told Henrietta. " . . . One can't change that way" (II, 284). This too is part of her development towards stasis. Her return to Osmond, she says, "won't be the scene of a moment; it will be a scene of the rest of my life" (II, 398). The dramatic moment is to be frozen into a static picture.

What is ultimately to happen to Isabel James leaves partly in doubt, though it is certain that she rejects Goodwood and what he has to offer and returns, at least for the moment, to Osmond. On her weary journey from Rome to England she speculates on her future, and comes to no conclusion: but it is an occasion on which James has clearly shown the opposing forces at work in her.

> Deep in her soul – deeper than any appetite for renunciation – was the sense that life would be her business for a long time to come. And at moments there was something inspiring, almost enlivening, in the conviction. It was a proof of strength – it was a proof she should some day be happy again. It couldn't be she was to live only to suffer; she was still young, after all, and a great many things might happen to her yet. To live only to suffer – only to feel the injury of life repeated and enlarged – it seemed to her she was too valuable, too capable, for that. Then she wondered if it were vain and stupid to think so well of herself. When had it even been a guarantee to be valuable? Wasn't all history full of the destruction of precious things? Wasn't it much more probable that if one were fine one would suffer? It involved then perhaps an admission that one had a certain grossness; but Isabel recognised, as it passed before her eyes, the quick vague shadow of a long future. She should never escape; she should last to the end. Then the middle years wrapped her about again and the grey curtain of her indifference closed her in. (II, 392–3)

It is as though with the rhythm of the train the various qualities of her mind were tossed to the surface and again submerged. There we see her appetite for life and her conscious determination to be happy, which is nevertheless inevitably accompanied by her preoccupation with suffering. And there too is her appetite for renunciation, her vigorous and sometimes perverse morality, which she recognises and takes into account. She is aware also of her own good opinion of herself, but not fully conscious of her automatic association of fineness with suffering, nor of her tendency to see human value in terms of "precious things".

If the conscious and healthy side of Isabel is to dominate, then "life is to be her business for a long time to come", and presumably she will be liberated from Osmond and again experience change and variety and growth. But if the other side dominates, the side I have been discussing, which is ruled by her morbid desire for suffering, her self-castigating morality, and her paralysing aestheticism, then indeed she will never escape, she will last to the end. She will return to Osmond so that he may hereafter, strolling through the collection that his wife's fortune has so enhanced, deliver to his guests his own version of "That's my last duchess painted on the wall."

NOTES

1. Henry James, *The Portrait of a Lady*, 2 vols, vol. I, (New York, 1908) p. 64. Subsequent references to this novel will appear in the text.
2. In an article on the theme of perversity in one of Trollope's novels, I mentioned Isabel's story as an analogy to Lily Dale's, and it was the reaction to this suggestion, by some of my readers, that prompted the present study. See " 'The Unfortunate Moth': Unifying Theme in *The Small House at Allington*", *Nineteenth-Century Fiction*, 26 (1971) 127–44.
3. Dorothy Van Ghent, *The English Novel, Form and Function* (New York, 1953) p. 214.
4. From the Conclusion to Walter Pater, *The Renaissance*, 1st ed. (1873).
5. The phrase has always seemed to me loaded with implications, and Richard Chase makes the same point in his excellent study of the novel in *The American Novel and its Tradition* (New York, 1957) p. 128.
6. It seems to me that Warburton's claim that his love for Isabel is "for life" is to be believed, even in the light of later events. His decision, following close upon his half-hearted courtship of Pansy, to marry "a member of the aristocracy; Lady Flora, Lady Felicia – something of that sort" (II, 408) has been taken as a sign of lightmindedness and emotional superficiality; but it is sufficiently clear in his final interview with Isabel that though he is engaged so far as Pansy is concerned, he still holds himself at *her* disposal.

7. Dorothea Krook, in her balanced and revealing study of *The Portrait*, finds Isabel's reasons for marrying Osmond " 'good' or 'creditable' ". She points out Osmond's virtues and attractions, and claims "above everything, he has personal distinction of a kind and in a degree overwhelming to her" (*The Ordeal of Consciousness in Henry James* [Cambridge, 1962] p. 39). But that personal distinction exists only for Isabel – for Ralph he is "small", and to Mrs Touchett "There's nothing *of* him" (II, 70, 54). I find Professor Krook neglects the suggestions that Isabel deliberately deludes herself about him.
8. F. R. Leavis finds it a reason for *The Portrait*'s inferiority to *Daniel Deronda* that Isabel is exempted from the financial pressure to which Gwendolen Harleth is subjected (*The Great Tradition* [London, 1948] p. 112). But Isabel's decision to marry is influenced just as much by her large fortune as is Gwendolen's by her lack of one.
9. Particularly deserving of mention, among the critics who have examined this trait in Isabel, are Richard Chase; Richard Poirier, *The Comic Sense of Henry James* (London, 1967) Ch. 5; Manfred Mackenzie, "Ironic Melodrama in *The Portrait of a Lady*", *Modern Fiction Studies*, 12 (1966) 7–23; and Dorothea Krook, pp. 58–9.
10. Maxwell Geismar notes the association with sorcery and enchantment in Madame Merle's name, but does not make the connection with Mrs Touchett's. *Henry James and the Jacobites* (Boston, 1962) p. 42. Isabel's "crazy Aunt Lydia", who returns to the family after a long period of huffy estrangement as a "little thin-lipped, bright-eyed, foreign-looking woman, who retrieved an insignificant appearance by a distinguished manner and, sitting there in a well-worn waterproof, talked with striking familiarity of the courts of Europe" (I, 36), is strongly reminiscent of other memorable fairy godmother figures with whom James would have been familiar: Thackeray's Fairy Blackstick, and Dickens's Betsy Trotwood and Fairy Grandmarina. Like the last of these, she exhorts her interlocutor to "be good".
11. As Tony Tanner points out, "It is hard to resist the conclusion that a part of her – the theorizing, idealizing part – is quite prepared to be placed in Osmond's collection. The lady herself is half willing to be turned into a portrait." "The Fearful Self: Henry James's *The Portrait of a Lady*", *Critical Quarterly*, 7 (1965) p. 208. This is precisely the conclusion I have not resisted.
12. Ralph and Rosier are distinguished from Osmond as connoisseurs of life by the fact that they both see their loved women as *superior* to the art forms to which they compare them. "I care more for Miss Osmond than for all the *bibelots* in Europe!" declares Rosier (II, 92); and he proves it by selling his collection in the hope of winning her. There is no comparable speech or gesture from Osmond.
13. When Madame Merle unexpectedly appears in the convent, Isabel finds that it "was like suddenly, and rather awfully, seeing a painted picture move" (II, 375). It is a simile that James uses twice towards the end of the novel, to remind us of the essentially static nature of painting for Isabel.
14. Dorothea Krook, pp. 357ff.

15. Marion Montgomery has discussed Isabel's "morbid sense of duty", and suggests that her return to Osmond is "the self-inflicted punishment she insists upon". "The Flaw in the Portrait", *University of Kansas City Review*, 26 (March, 1959) 218.

10 *The Turn of the Screw*

One cannot but be apologetic in giving yet another turn to *The Turn of the Screw*, on which there already exist various casebooks and collections in which critics have ranged themselves in the two major camps, according to whether they read the tale as a straight ghost story or as psychological novel. But, my apology being given, I shall proceed regardless, being unable to resist the temptation to get my say in. My excuse, such as it is, is that I hope to some extent to reconcile the two readings with one another.

In one of the most powerful and memorable passages of the novel, the governess relates how, after she has been terrified by seeing the ghost of Peter Quint looking in at her through the dining-room window at Bly, she goes outside to find him, and is then moved by a curious impulse:

> It was confusedly present to me that I ought to place myself where he had stood. I did so; I applied my face to the pane and looked, as he had looked, into the room. As if, at this moment, to show me exactly what his range had been, Mrs. Grose, as I had done for himself just before, came in from the hall. With this I had the full image of a repetition of what already occurred. She saw me as I had seen my own visitant. (185)[1]

She watches the effect of her appearance on Mrs Grose, giving her, indeed, "something of the shock that I had received".

Oscar Cargill has called attention to this scene as an instance of James's "marvelous symbolic irony, perhaps the best example in his fiction";[2] and the incident certainly seems to have an impact that goes beyond its immediate import in the narrative. However, what appears to have been overlooked is the significance of the fact that this is not the only instance in *The Turn of the Screw* of an ironic reversal of locations; that in fact

James consistently replaces the ghosts with the governess to recreate the "full image" of her own perception. She herself feels compelled to act out the image in her mind.

The first time she encounters Peter Quint, as Freudians will recall,[3] is while she is wandering in the garden and daydreaming about the master, and she sees him at the top of the tower. On this occasion she does not, as when she next meets him, immediately go to where she saw him; however, on the night when she wakes to see Flora gazing intently out of the window, communicating, as the governess supposes, with Miss Jessel, she determines herself to look out of a different window that faces the same way: "There were empty rooms enough at Bly, and it was only a question of choosing the right one. The right one suddenly presented itself to me as the lower one – though high above the gardens – in the solid corner of the house that I have spoken of as the old tower" (229). From this room high upon the tower, by again applying her face to the pane, she sees Miles looking up. She herself is sure that he is looking higher still, at Peter Quint *on* the tower, but by Miles's own assertion it was she he was looking at. Again, she is appearing to someone else as the ghost had appeared to her.

Sometimes it is only herself that she horrifies by this identification with the ghosts. On one of her nocturnal ramblings, "I once recognised the presence of a woman seated on one of the lower steps with her back presented to me, her body half-bowed and her head, in an attitude of woe, in her hands" (226–7). Later she adopts the same attitude in the same place: she has just returned alone from her disturbing interview with Miles outside the church: "Tormented, in the hall, with difficulties and obstacles, I remember sinking down at the foot of the staircase – suddenly collapsing there on the lowest step and then, with a revulsion, recalling that it was exactly where, more than a month before, in the darkness of night and just so bowed with evil things, I had seen the spectre of the most horrible of women" (256). She goes up to the schoolroom, only to find her "vile predecessor" usurping her place at the table, and to have "the extraordinary chill of a feeling that it was I who was the intruder" (257).

Miss Jessel's first and definitive appearance, of course, is at the far side of the lake in the grounds of Bly. And it is almost predictable that is should be there that the governess later confronts Flora. The little girl has escaped her vigilance, has taken the boat and rowed herself across the lake.[4] There the governess finds her and now openly accuses her of being aware of Miss Jessel's presence. But as the governess had once seen Miss Jessel there, a horrifying and evil presence, so now Flora sees *her*:

> "I see nobody. I see nothing. I never *have*. I think you're cruel. I don't like you" [and she pleads to Mrs Grose:] "Take me away, take me away – oh take me away from *her*!"
> "From *me*?" I panted.
> "From you – from you!" she cried. (281)

In the same way, in her agonising and fatal confrontation with Miles, the governess calls his attention to Peter Quint, looking through the dining room window as she had once looked through at Mrs Grose; but the only "devil" he can see is the governess herself.

Lear's image for the essential identity of the justice and the thief could be appropriately adapted for *The Turn of the Screw*: "Change places, and handy-dandy, which is the governess, which is the ghost?"

My point should be sufficiently clear. The occasion on which the governess runs round to look in through the window and terrify Mrs Grose as the ghost had just looked in and terrified her – this is only the most obvious instance of a consistently maintained pattern in the action, in which the governess takes the place of the ghost. Part of James's purpose in this systematic exchange of locations is no doubt to give us another facet of the governess' complex psychology. She herself is conscious of some appropriateness in her taking the ghosts' places, and it is evidently part of her longing to be "justified" in her perceptions that moves her to endow her mental images with some measure of spatial reality: she becomes the embodiment of her own mental projections.

But there is a further significance in this image. What we have in effect is the symmetrical reversal of an object and its image in a glass (and if there is no actual glass there is usually the possibility of some other kind of projected image – a reflection in water, a shadow, or a trick effect of distance or half-light). And the question that James deliberately raises is whether that glass is a transparent pane, through which Peter Quint can clearly be seen, or whether it is, as it may become at dusk, opaque like a mirror, simply giving back to the governess a reflection of herself. The apparition and the perceiver may be distinct, each with a separate existence, or the one may be only the reflection of the other.

The image of the reflection is a dominant one in the novel. It is not only glass that can receive and reflect an image, but the human mind; and the recurrence of this word *reflection* becomes significant in the governess' communication as well as in her perceptions. Her mental projections are effected not only spatially, but psychologically, and by this means she makes Mrs Grose 'a receptacle of lurid things' (231). When she tells her of Miss Jessel's appearance, "I was conscious as I spoke that I looked prodigious things, for I got the slow reflexion of them in my companion's face" (203). The reflection is sometimes a two-way affair between these two, we find. It is noticeable that we hear about the major encounters with the ghosts not as they appear to the governess but as she relates the matter to Mrs Grose afterwards. The total creation of the apparition is not immediate, nor singly in her own mind; it is a product partly of Mrs Grose's mind, too, as the two catch and reflect back and forth the gleams of suspicion and awareness. Harold Goddard pointed out that it is from Mrs Grose herself that the governess first gets a hint of some evil male presence at Bly.[5] And now, as she is describing the apparition, she could be enlarging on that hint.

At first, looking for confirmation, she suggests that Mrs Grose has "guessed" the identity of the male apparition. " 'Ah I haven't guessed!' she said very simply. 'How can I if *you* don't imagine?' "(188). For the moment the governess is halted and cannot describe him: " 'What is he? He's a horror. . . . He's – God help me if I know *what* he is!' " (189). But after a few blind alleys, a few gleams of communication, their minds are working in concert, and it is now that, "seeing in her face that she already, in this, with a deeper dismay found a touch of picture, I quickly added stroke to stroke" (190). As in running round to look in through the window she has created a general impression in Mrs Grose's mind, so through her urgent and intimate communication with her afterwards she fills out the full image of Peter Quint.

The children's minds, on the other hand, are more opaque than Mrs Grose's, and like untarnished mirrors give back to the governess only the image of her own distraught face. In talking to Miles, she recalls, " . . . to gain time, I tried to laugh, and I seemed to see in the beautiful face with which he watched me how ugly and queer I looked" (249–50). Similarly, when she has bundled off Mrs Grose and Flora in the coach, and set the stage for her harrowing solo encounter with Miles, she communicates her own almost hysterical apprehension to the whole household: "I could see in the aspect of others a confused reflexion of the crisis" (293).

Douglas, too, testifies to her power of communicating her experience with an image that is close to that of the reflection: when asked if he took down her narrative, he replies, " 'Nothing but the impression. I took that *here*' – he tapped his heart. 'I've never lost it' " (149).

That pane of glass between the human being and the apparition becomes a focus for the total and deliberate ambiguity in the tale. We may take our own choice as to which side of the pane we want to be: with the governess, looking outwards at the baleful stalking ghosts, or on the other side, looking inwards at her and the working of a diseased imagination. Or alternatively, in another operation of the image, we may think of the glass either as a transparent medium through which real ghosts can be seen, or as a mirror in which the governess sees, essentially, only her own reflection.

The choice is with us from the first, in the account of how Douglas prepares his audience for the governess' narrative. Leon Edel, in his careful analysis of the point of view in *The Turn of the Screw*,[6] draws no conclusions as to the significance of this rather elaborate introduction. It seems to me, however, that James has in this passage, the first of the twelve instalments, quite carefully defined two kinds of readers for his story. There are two distinct elements in Douglas' audience. One is a group of sensation-hungry women, who want a few chills and terrors to enliven their long winter evenings in the country house, and so will hear Douglas' reading of the manuscript as another ghost story. For them dreadfulness is in itself "delicious", and the more turns of the screw the better. Subtlety is not their concern: one of them laments that the story is not told "in any literal vulgar way", because "that's the only way I ever understand" (151).

On the other hand Douglas is more particularly addressing the original narrator of the story, whom for convenience we may call [James]. It is for this kind of hearer, for [James] and, one might add, Goddard, Edmund Wilson and their followers, that the fact of the governess' love for her master becomes particularly relevant:

> He continued to fix me. "You'll easily judge," he repeated: "*you* will."
>
> I fixed him too. "I see. She was in love."
>
> He laughed for the first time. "You *are* acute. Yes, she was in love. That is she *had* been. That came out – she couldn't tell her story without its coming out." (150)

For this kind of listener the impact of the tale is not so simple as "sheer terror"; and the distinction is carefully made:

> "Nobody but me, till now, has ever heard. It's quite too horrible." This was naturally declared by several voices to give the thing the utmost price, and our friend, with quiet art, prepared his triumph by turning his eyes over the rest of us and going on: "It's beyond everything. Nothing at all that I know touches it."
>
> "For sheer terror?" I remember asking.
>
> He seemed to say it wasn't so simple as that; to be really at a loss how to qualify it. He passed his hand over his eyes, made a little wincing grimace. "For dreadful – dreadfulness!
>
> "Oh how delicious!" cried one of the women.
>
> He took no notice of her; he looked at me, but as if, instead of me, he saw what he spoke of. "For general uncanny ugliness and horror and pain." (148)

There we see Douglas' two kinds of hearer. For the general entertainment, he presents another ghost story; for [James], for "me in particular", he presents something more subtle, that demands deeper psychological perception. Douglas' look through [James] at the illusion he is about to present is like the governess' look through the window at the visions she communicates. [James] the narrator and listener, like James the author, is our transparent medium of perception.

According to my contention, there isn't a right way and a wrong way to interpret the tale, but rather *two* ways, which the same reader may enjoy alternately, if he wishes; and James has carefully established this, both through the imagery of the glass and its reversal of locations, and in the narrative set-up of the story. Just as we may choose to look through the glass *with* the governess or *at* her, so we may choose to listen with the ladies, and hear a ghost story, or with [James], and hear a psychological novel. We have "the full image of a repetition", as in a mirror, and we may decide for ourselves what to take for substance and what for shadow.

NOTES

1. Page references are to Vol. 12 of the New York Edition of *The Novels and Tales of Henry James* (New York, 1908).
2. "Henry James as Freudian Pioneer", *Chicago Review* (1956). This is reprinted in Gerald Willen (ed.), *A Casebook on Henry James's "The Turn of the Screw"*, (New York, 1960), a useful collection of critiques and interpretations.
3. See Edmund Wilson's seminal essay "The Ambiguity of Henry James", *The Triple Thinkers* (London, 1948).
4. T. M. Cranfill and R. L. Clark, Jr, in *An Anatomy of The Turn of the Screw* (Austin, 1965), suggest that Flora's abduction of the boat is another of the governess's delusions; however, there is no doubt about the location of the confrontation: at the far side of lake, where the governess had first seen Miss Jessel.
5. In his essay of "about 1920 or before", published posthumously as "A Pre-Freudian Reading of *The Turn of the Screw*", in *Nineteenth-Century Fiction*, 12 (1957) p. 136, Goddard draws attention to the scene in which the governess has her suspicions raised by Mrs Grose's reference to a "he" who is apparently not the master.
6. *The Psychological Novel, 1900–1950* (London, 1961) pp. 39–46.

11 The Curse of Words in *He Knew He Was Right*

Uneasiness about relationships between fact, language and truth pervades Victorian literature. For Browning's Pope in *The Ring and the Book*, language itself is a sign of the fall:

> barren words
> Which, more than any deed, characterize
> Man as made subject to a curse.
>
> (x, 348–50)

Trollope seems to share his opinion. What he says about an attempt by Grey and Palliser to reach agreement in *Can You Forgive Her?* could equally well apply to the "lawyer-pleadings" of Browning's poem: "We all know that neither of them would put the matter altogether in a true light. Men never can do so in words, let the light within themselves be ever so clear."[1] In *He Knew He Was Right* Trollope conducts his most sombre exploration of mismatching between language and truth. A. O. J. Cockshut has observed that "the book raises the whole question of the value of truth and the importance of words" and has examined how, for the principal characters, Trevelyan and his wife, Emily, "words have a power of their own which the protagonists constantly undervalue".[2] But the subject invites further examination. The intractability of words not only affects the Trevelyans' marital harmony but links several of the novel's multiple plots and builds up a general impression, largely tragic, about the ability of people either to define themselves or communicate with others in words. Linguistic interpretation is a major activity for nearly everyone in the book. Silence itself speaks amiss. And, as elsewhere in Trollope, when people take particular pains to hold fast and pin down the Proteus of language – writing

10 Marcus Stone's headletter for "Hard Words", Chapter 73 of *He Knew He Was Right*

letters, for example, where they can study their language right down to the punctuation points – they fare no better. The novel is awash with letters, but the calculated, sculptured expression they contain still manages to elude intention and become itself the subject for manifold further interpretation. In one instance, victory over such stylisation, such compulsion to make words reflect one's sense of oneself, can only be achieved by leaving out of the carefully premeditated letter the essential thing to be communicated. In the forefront of the novel the mismatch between words and the mind selecting them moves gradually towards obsession and derangement. And in an altogether different key, the amorous Reverend Mr Gibson becomes a comic victim of the words he chooses, or, as he might more sombrely put it, of the words which perversely choose him as a means to express themselves. The rift between language and reality is everywhere in the novel, and, as *Can You Forgive Her*? shows, is a subject of more than passing interest to Trollope. As J. Hillis Miller observes: "His fiction concentrates with admirable consistency on the question of what constitutes authentic selfhood",[3] and the reflection of self in language is a vital aspect of that question.

Dr Johnson argued that "All power of fancy over reason is a degree of insanity. . . . fictions begin to operate as realities, false opinions fasten upon the mind, and life passes in dreams of rapture or of anguish."[4] So it is with the Trevelyans. With his usual lively interest in perversity, Trollope observes how the elements of fiction and game-playing in the Trevelyans' discourse displace reality, ruin their marriage, and lead to obsession and madness. Both are stiff-necked, both acutely sensitive about what they take to be their due. Louis is the Trollopian husband as lord and master pushed to an extreme degree, "one to whose nature the giving of any apology was repulsive" (8).[5] Becoming jealous of Colonel Osborne, whose personal game is to promote in society the notion of his dangerous attractiveness to married women, Louis demands that Emily refuse Osborne's visits and letters, though Osborne, as Emily insists, is an old friend of her father's. Louis fantasises about the infinite tenderness he will have for her when she yields. He is always torn between the determination to be master and the less effectual desire that "he should make his mastery palatable" (44). For her part, Emily is "as stiff as a man in armour" (99), every bit as unable to be forbearing to him as he is unable to be forbearing to her. She obeys his commands but "so cunningly that the husband received none of the gratification which he had expected in her surrender" (47). Each exacerbates the other's sense of injury.

Trevelyan's words assume the fiction that Emily is errant, disobedient, faithless. Emily's assume that Louis is unreasonable, tyrannical, mad – her fiction is that of the injured saint.

Waging campaigns of overstatement, speaking for victory, they drastically underestimate the power of words, however at odds with reality, to displace reality. Their words are like monsters that, once summoned into being, take on a fatal, determining power over their lives. "Mr. Trevelyan had become very angry, and had spoken those words which he could not recall. . . . he almost felt that he ought to beg his wife's pardon. He knew his wife well enough to be sure that she would not forgive him unless he did so. He would do so, he thought, but not exactly now" (8–9). The relentlessness of the uttered word reverberates through the novel in hopeless attempts to let bygones be bygones. "I cannot forget that I have been – cautioned", says Emily (53). And when her sister Nora, pleading forbearance, asks her, "Could you not say to him simply this? – 'Let us be together, wherever it may be; and let bygones be bygones' ", Emily answers, "not unless I went to him as one who was known to be mad", that is as one whose words can be dismissed as fantastic, unresponsible (564). When the position later reverses and Emily in her turn entreats, "let it all be forgotten. . . . I will tell you of nothing that is past", Louis is every bit as implacable, provoked by a manoeuvre he detects in her choice of words: "Could she have condescended to ask him not to tell her of the past; – had it occurred to her so to word her request, – she might perhaps have prevailed" (633–4). Beneath this verbal battle lies fierce sexual anxiety. Louis, to assert his masculine ego, clings to words he knows to be false: "Should he yield to her now . . . might not the result be that he would be . . . robbed of what he loved better than his liberty, – his power as a man?" (742). Emily, to assert her feminine ego, makes an issue of them, carrying off scenes and symbolic gestures in a high style.

Given the importance language assumes in *He Knew He Was Right*, it ends on an appropriately bleak verbal ambiguity. Emily, on the assurance that Louis is mad, condescends to ask forgiveness. But as Cockshut points out, conventional evasiveness in the language people use about sexual infidelity allows Trevelyan to seem to interpret her request, and Emily to suspect that he so interprets it, as a specific confession of adultery. The language has two registers. "When he says, 'You must repent,' he means repent of her disobedience, but for her the word resounds in a narrower yet vaguer sense, suggesting, no doubt, Magdalens and houses of correction. But reticence even prevents her from revealing her horror of the implied charge. This verbal misunderstanding tends to effect her with a share of his monomania."[6] Then, as time grows short with Louis's death looming, the doctor unhappily undermines Emily's assurance of Louis's madness, doubting whether Louis was ever "so mad as to make it necessary that the law should interfere to take care of him. . . . A man, – so argued the doctor, – need not be mad because he is jealous, even though his jealousy be ever so absurd" (900). The doctor takes large views: " 'In one sense all misconduct is proof of insanity,' said the doctor" (923–4). That airy opinion (not one the narrator is ready to countenance: "he was mad; – mad though every doctor in England had called him sane" [925]) revives Emily's "trick of obstinacy" (13). She agrees with him: "She could not think that he was mad" (920), and returns vehemently to protesting her innocence as obsessively as Louis questions it. As he dies she beseeches him for the word of release:

> 'Can you say one word for your wife, dear, dear, dearest husband?'
>
> 'What word?'
>
> 'I have not been a harlot to you; – have I?'
>
> 'What name is that?'
>
> 'But what a thing, Louis! Kiss my hand, Louis, if you believe me.' . . . at length the lips moved, and with struggling ear she could hear the sound of the tongue within, and the verdict of the dying man had been given in her favour. He never spoke a word more either to annul it or to enforce it. (927)

Emily finally believes what she wants to believe: " 'He declared to me at last that he trusted me,' she said, – almost believing that real words had come from his lips to that effect" (928).

Though fictions created by verbal posturing bring the Trevelyans to grief, Trollope indicates in several ways that the Trevelyans are not peculiar in their tendency to fictional heightening. To Lady Milborough, Osborne is "a snake in the grass" (26), to Dorothy Stanbury, he is "Lucifer himself" and "a horrible roaring lion" (203), to Aunt Stanbury, he is "the

Evil One . . . come among us in person because of our sins" (146), and to the Reverend Mr Outhouse, he is both "an iniquitous roaring lion" and "Apollyon" (385). It is part of the novel's ironic point that such constructs are creations *ex nihilo*: Kincaid notes that "Colonel Osborne, who starts all the trouble by pursuing Emily, is himself a symbol of pure nothingness: 'it was generally thought of him that he might have been something considerable, had it not better suited him to be nothing at all' " (11).[7] Osborne is not the only object of linguistic embellishment. To Osborne, "Trevelyan was a cruel Bluebeard; Emily . . . a dear injured saint" (187). The rhetoric of melodrama is busy everywhere substituting itself for reality. Sir Marmaduke thunders about his daughter Nora's determination to marry Hugh Stanbury: "Do you mean that you'll go out and marry him like a beggar, with nothing but what you stand up in, with no friend to be with you, an outcast, thrown off by your mother, – with your father's – curse?" (658). The melodrama of Emily's revery about Louis's threat to take away her child is heightened by exclamatory extravagance in the third person: "Divide these two! No; nobody should do that. Sooner than that, she, the mother, would consent to be no more than a servant in her husband's house. Was not her baby all the world to her?" (104). Louis tends increasingly towards the stylisation of drama, his words absorbing his life. Explaining his woes to Outhouse, "Before he left the parsonage he was brought even to tears by his own narration of his own misery" (275). In his madness he takes to quoting *Othello*, with a sly sense of how Emily's sister, Nora, will get the point: " 'The pity of it, Iago; oh, the pity of it,' he said once. The allusion to her was so terrible that she almost burst out in anger" (898). Kincaid, too, notes the "self-conscious staginess" of Trevelyan's manner, the grand style being denied him, but a certain pathos arising from his very failure to reach it: "he dashed his hand upon the table, and looked up with an air that would have been comic with its assumed magnificence had it not been for the true tragedy of the occasion" (650).[8] A displacement of reality in the direction of oratory rather than melodrama is seen in the Yankee rhetorical flourishes of Wallachia Petri, the Republican Browning.

Trollope presents us, then, with the results of a general

linguistic malaise, extreme in the Trevelyans but evident in many other characters. The language in which they indulge sets up fictions which gain a dreadful substantiality from being spoken – people feeling a peculiar compulsion to live out the stylisations they have verbally created unless they can contrive somehow to short-circuit or subvert their own words. The sense of a character's being victimised by his own words is clearest, perhaps, in Mr Gibson, "the amorous Vicar of St. Peter's-cum-Pumpkin" (781). Sought by both Misses French for themselves and by Aunt Stanbury for her niece, Dorothy, Mr Gibson manages to lie to the French girls about his proposal to Dorothy, propose out of cowardice and vacillation to marry the younger French daughter, Camilla, although he was previously supposed to be attached to the elder, Arabella, and then reverse himself once again and marry Arabella after all. The strain of this complicated life understandably drives him to curacao in the morning and to wishing he had never been born. In an interview in Arabella's bedroom (after he has proposed to Camilla), he philosophises dolefully on the position his own words have put him in:

> 'And I have meant to be so true. I fancy sometimes that some mysterious agency interferes with the affairs of a man and drives him on, – and on, – and on, – almost, – till he doesn't know where it drives him.' As he said this in a voice that was quite sepulchral in its tone, he felt some consolation in the conviction that this mysterious agency could not affect a man without imbuing him with a certain amount of grandeur. . . . (621)

Leaving the sympathetic Arabella, he kisses Camilla, thinking as he does so "of the mysterious agency which afflicted him. 'Tell me that you love me, Thomas,' she said. 'Of course I love you' " (622). Walking home he reflects hopelessly: "There was no moment . . . in which he had not endeavoured to do right" (623). This mysterious agency that weaves verbal cobwebs about Gibson is, in effect, a comic crystallisation of the malign power words exert throughout the book. Mr Gibson merely becomes peculiarly conscious of it. In fact he becomes downright jumpy, as when Bella, no doubt with good enough reason, asks him, "You do love me?" and Trollope comments, "it would have been better perhaps if she had held her tongue. Had she spoken to him about his house, or his income, or the servants, or the duties of his parish church, it would have been easier for him to make a comfortable reply" (781). Though in a comic key, Gibson nevertheless shares with Louis Trevelyan the sense of a peculiar fate. Trevelyan too says, "There is a curse upon me" (789).

As Gibson demonstrates, there is a certain vanity in seeing oneself as a victim of destiny. With his keen interest in perversity, Trollope shows not only Trevelyan but other characters as well actually teaching themselves to displace what is authentic in them with what is fictional, artificial, stylised, assumed. "They", he says, "who do not understand that a man may be brought to hope that which of all things is the most grievous to him, have not observed with sufficient closeness the perversity of the human mind" (364). Trevelyan, for example, "had taught himself to believe that she had disgraced him; and, though this feeling of disgrace made him so wretched that he wished that he were dead, he would allow himself to make no attempt at questioning the correctness of his conviction" (252–3). The Colonel, after his scandalous visit to Emily in the country, "had by this time quite taught himself to believe that the church porch at Cockchaffington had been the motive cause of his journey into Devonshire" (611). Of Mr Gibson, under cross-examination about his proposals, the narrator comments that "the gentleman usually teaches himself to think that a little falsehood is permissible. A gentleman can hardly tell a lady that he has become tired of her, and has changed his mind . . . . in such a strait as this he does allow himself some latitude" (338). Dorothy, on the other hand, though harassed by her aunt to marry him, "tried hard to teach herself to think that she might learn to love him . . . . but she did not think that she loved him as yet" (281–2). In short, except for the unusually simple and direct person like Dorothy, the characters not only speak at a level of para-reality at odds with their authentic beliefs and feelings but perversely attune themselves to it. Some peculiar fascination with stylisation or fiction compulsively draws them away from the truth about themselves and others and towards a chaos of fictional structures. A cleavage occurs between language and what is genuine, so that what should be a means of communicating truth becomes instead a texture of only dimly-perceived conventional structurings seen by the reader most clearly in cliché, melodrama, rhetorical posturing, labelling. "Sir Marmaduke", for example, "in speaking of Stanbury after this, would constantly call him a penny-a-liner, thinking that the contamination of the penny communicated itself to all transactions of the Daily Record" (660).

This readiness to strike and cultivate postures may, perhaps, contribute to the sense many readers have of game-playing in *He Knew He Was Right*.[9] One might describe it as a general compulsion to play rhetorical games of "as if". Trevelyan, for example, chooses to speak as if Emily were unfaithful to him, though he believes she is not. Aunt Stanbury, though less extremely, also plays the game with intensity: "No one had ever been more devoted to peculiar opinions or more strong in the use of language for their expression; and she was so far true to herself, that she would never seem to retreat from the position she had taken" (839). When her mind has changed, she must still speak as if it had not. Games involve arbitrary rules on the whole, and in a recognised game we accept them. Outside a recognised game the arbitrary ranges from harmless eccentricity to downright madness. Trollope suggests that the boundaries are none too clear, that the language games of *He Knew He Was Right* are not too comfortably far removed from obsession, disintegration, and madness.

In the latter part of the novel, where he so movingly portrays Louis Trevelyan's solitary derangement, Trollope covers the spectrum from madness as a mere figure of speech, to homicidal jealousy and bitterness, to manifest madness, all in the space of two monthly numbers. Number 26 begins with Louis's desolate existence at Casalunga and ends with the diplomatic society at Florence, where, in Chapter 80, the notion of madness flickers from character to character as a mere form of words. The British Minister's wife considers it "not surprising that poor Lady Rowley should be nearly out of her mind" about the Trevelyans, and Lady Rowley, confronted with Nora's indifference to Lord Glascock, "would throw up her hands in despair and protest that her daughter was insane" (747). Thinking Glascock means to marry Wallachia Petrie, she swears that "he must be insane" (754), and she confesses, when her error is revealed, "I thought that you were all demented. I did indeed" (755). From this series of conventional exaggerations, however, we move in Number 27 to Mr Gibson's acknowledgement to himself "that he had been very foolish, mad, – quite demented at the moment, – when he allowed himself to think it possible that he should marry Camilla French" (773). We are ready to be amused by Mr Gibson's predicament as no great matter when Trollope jolts us with the discovery in Camilla's room, "hidden among some linen", of "a carving knife! such a knife as is used for the cutting up of fowls" (775). There is nothing trivial or comic in the "look about her that made them all doubt whether she was not, in truth, losing her mind" (778). She has to be packed off in a wild state to recover. Trollope is very effective in the way he merges extremes with the ordinary, prosaic texture of everyday life, preserving both their plausibility and their power to surprise and shock. For all that his world is a generally comfortable one, madness and kidnapping occur in the novel, adultery and murder hover in the air, and despite Trevelyan's loathing for his private detective, Bozzle, Bozzle's world of "things dark and dishonest, fights fought and races run that they might be lost, plants and crosses, women false to their husbands, sons false to their fathers, daughters to their mothers, servants to their masters, affairs always secret, dark, foul, and fraudulent" (268) is the world that Trevelyan's obsession feeds on. Conventional fictions and exaggerations shade off into the bizarre and desolate.

Chaucer's Manciple, having, like Chaucer himself, asserted that "The word moot nede accorde with the dede", ends up advising over and over again: "Kepe wel thy tonge." If language breeds chaos, what of silence? Much of the discord in the novel comes of the inability to speak. Louis, while saying the wrong things, avoids the right ones through fear: "It was almost on his tongue to beg her pardon .... If she would only have met him with gentleness .... But she was hard, dignified, obedient, and resentful." He "was almost afraid to say anything that would again bring forth from her expressions of scorn" (53). Trollope makes silence the focus, however, of two finely wrought episodes. In an outing to Niddon Park, the arrangement of couples falls out accidentally, Hugh Stanbury with Emily, Priscilla Stanbury with Nora. This is awkward since Hugh intends to talk love to Nora, and Nora, though she intends to reject his love, is peculiarly vexed at not receiving it. Telling herself, "he did not care for her in the least", Nora drops into "speaking now and again as though she were giving words and not thoughts" (229–30). She babbles about the scenery and the weather so as to cause Priscilla to accuse her of not having her mind on the Park. "Then there came a faint sound as of an hysterical sob, and then a gurgle in the throat, and then a pretence at laughter" (230). And when she refuses to descend to the river with Hugh, he surmises that she is angry with him, resenting "the absence of his attention" (230), so that now, when they return, this time properly paired, Hugh is unable to come to the point: "They had walked half a mile together and he had spoken of nothing but the scenery" (231). Finally, thinking of his poverty and her being accustomed to affluence, Hugh makes an unhappy comment to the effect that "they who have once been dainty . . . never like to divest themselves of their daintiness" (232). She interprets this as an accusation; she bridles: " 'If I have ever been dainty, dainty I hope I may remain. I will never, at any rate, give it up of my own accord.' Why she said this, she could never explain to herself. She had certainly not intended to rebuff him when she had been saying it. But he spoke not a word to her further as they walked home . . ." (232). As in Henry James's "silences of even deeper import",[10] what is not spoken here is as important as what is said. The complex mixture of silence, constraint and indirection produces a lively effort of interpretation that simply fails disastrously. Inspired by love, the couple winds up angry and depressed. And the issue, moreover, rankles. Philosophising about men later, Nora tells Priscilla: "they never seem to listen to women. Don't you think that, after all, they despise women? They look on them as dainty, foolish things" (240–1).

The second instance of unhappily interpreted silence involves Caroline Spalding's marriage to Lord Glascock. Made anxious by Wallachia Petrie that Lord Glascock's friends will resent his marrying an American, Caroline sensibly decides to ask Nora Rowley's opinion. Nora's very scruple to be precise causes misapprehension:

> Nora on being thus consulted, was very careful that her tongue should utter nothing that was not her true opinion

> as best she knew how to express it. . . . She would have been delighted to have been able to declare that these doubts were utterly groundless, and this hesitation needless. But she conceived that she owed it as a duty from one woman to another to speak the truth as she conceived it on so momentous an occasion . . .. What she did not remember was this, – that her very hesitation was in fact an answer, and such an answer as she was most unwilling to give. 'I see that it would be so,' said Caroline Spalding. (750–1)

Now, of course, even Nora's contradiction and reassurance bear for Caroline an opposite signification: "Even what you say to me makes me think it" (752). At this impasse, still determined "to do her best to counteract any evil which she might have done", Nora resorts to the written word. Having failed in the first place, now she can take even greater pains to be precise. But Caroline, receiving the letter, "declared to herself that the girl's unpremeditated expression of opinion was worth more than her studied words" (757). At this point Wallachia returns to the attack and ironically is "specially indignant at finding that her own words had no effect. But, unfortunately, her words had had much effect; and Caroline, though she had contested her points, had done so only with the intention of producing her Mentor's admonitions" (760). If these ironic disjunctions of communication are Jamesian, the effect is worthy of Hardy. There is no need for a malign destiny to hide letters under a rug as in *Tess* – in *He Knew He Was Right* the most studied expression doesn't achieve its end. Fortunately, when Caroline tells Glascock her conclusion that she will disgrace him, demanding in the face of his calm, "Do you suppose that I do not mean it?" he replies with ironic good-humour: "You have taken an extra dose this morning of Wallachia Petrie, and of course you mean it." And he then corrects "her far-fetched ideas respecting English society" (763).

The multitude of letters in *He Knew He Was Right* provides ample illustration of the ironies of studied language – studied, weighed, scrutinised, dissected, worried and triumphed over. Often to no avail if not to downright harm. In the give and take of conversation, language is always subject to a degree of chance, likely to be ill-chosen or magnetically attracted towards colourful analogies ("You yourself, – you would be a Griselda, I suppose?" [93]). But letters, however impassioned the composer, become by the very act of composition, more deliberate. Even the writer's heat finds expression in more strategically deployed, more vehemently crushing words. And the writer who remains cool can give himself more thoroughly to the enjoyment of artful selection and arrangement. There, of course, is the trouble – while the conversationalist is subject to unconscious and haphazard patterns of implication, the writer of a letter is seduced by stylisation, and depending on his capacity as a lover of design, surrenders himself more or less fully to the allures of shape, point, polish, complete linguistic fulfilment. Once again the gap between reality and para-reality widens. Louis Trevelyan, as one might suppose by now, "was inclined to believe of himself that he was good at writing long, affectionate, argumentative, and exhaustive letters" (175), so much so that he defers speaking in favour of writing to his wife. And he then defers writing lest her suffering be too short to be salutary. In what he considers to be one of his more accomplished letters, he tells her that she is spied upon, that she has disgraced herself, him, and Mrs Stanbury's house by seeing Osborne and must move, that he will take her child from her if she continues so to misconduct herself, and that he will reduce her allowance to a bare sustenance and divorce her. "When he had finished this he read it twice, and believed that he had written, if not an affectionate, at any rate a considerate letter" (257). Lady Milborough, asked to approve its good sense, asks, "Don't you think that what you say is a little, – just a little prone to make, – to make the breach perhaps wider?" (259). Crossly disagreeing, he nevertheless spends the rest of the day pondering "the weight of every phrase that he had used. . . . In the evening he went all alone to an eating-house for his dinner, and then, sitting with a miserable glass of sherry before him, he again read and re-read the epistle which he had written. Every harsh word that it contained was, in some sort, pleasant to his ear. . . . So he went out and posted the letter" (260–1). It falls "like a thunderbolt among them at Nuncombe Putney" and inspires Emily to a characteristically hard, correct, frigidly submissive response (261).

Emily's correspondence with Colonel Osborne is itself an important issue in the novel and is conducted less for communication than to insist on the point that, since she knows herself to be innocent, there can be nothing wrong in it: "I will not submit", she says, "to acknowledge that there can be any danger in Colonel Osborne" (193). Indifferent in itself, the correspondence provides a ground for suspicion, gesture and obstinacy. Mr Bozzle, the detective, keeps his eye on it as part of his general commission to live up to "Othello's demand of Iago" and produce the ocular proof (419). "Facts", he says, "is open, Mr. Trewillian, if you knows where to look for them" (592), but facts are too much for even the industrious Bozzle, and he incorrectly reports a letter from Emily to Osborne on the basis of mere presupposition. "Men whose business it is to detect hidden and secret things", says Trollope, "are very apt to detect things which have never been done" (267–8). Even for the professional, reality and supposition will not stick together in this novel.

Two neatly constructed episodes point up the disparity between the designed verbal world of letters and the way things are. In the first, Aunt Stanbury, full of righteous wrath about the ineptitude and presumption of her sister-in-law and her prickly niece, Priscilla, in agreeing to house the banished Emily, hears through the local grapevine that Colonel Osborne, the "roaring lion", has been allowed to visit Emily at Nuncombe Putney. She zealously writes a crisp letter to Mrs Stanbury, concluding:

> It is intolerable that the widow of my brother, – a clergyman, – should harbour a lady who is separated from her husband and who receives visits from a gentleman who is reputed to be her lover. I wonder much that your eldest daughter should countenance such a proceeding.
>
> Yours truly,
> JEMIMA STANBURY (168)

Priscilla, of course, appreciates the finer points of such combat: " 'She had such pleasure in writing it,' said Priscilla, 'that one ought hardly to begrude it her.' " Aunt Stanbury, unfortunately, has been misinformed about the visitor. Her facts are quite wrong. "It was now a triumph to her [Priscilla] that her aunt had fallen into so terrible a quagmire, and she was by no means disposed to let the sinning old woman easily out of it" (169). No blunderer, Priscilla gauges her reply to a nicety, "mild enough in words . . . and very short" (170) – the correction of Aunt Stanbury's error even goes in a post-script. But she knows her target: "When Miss Stanbury had read and re-read the very short reply which her niece had written, she became at first pale with dismay, and then red with renewed vigour and obstinacy" (171). Upon reflection, however, she swallows her pride and humbly begs, not Priscilla's, but Mrs Stanbury's pardon. Now comes the irresistible step: Priscilla cannot forgo "an attempt at the last word" (173). She caps the occasion with a reply full of hauteur, injured innocence, and advice to her aunt not to write "unless you are quite sure of your ground". " 'Impudent vixen!' said Miss Stanbury . . . when she had read the letter. . . . 'There. I was wrong. . . . There, – there!' " Triumph for Priscilla. But in the chapter's final sentence Colonel Osborne is at that very moment "eating his breakfast at Mrs. Crocket's inn, in Nuncombe Putney!" (173). Emily receives Osborne and it is Priscilla's turn to eat humble pie, writing to acknowledge the visit before Aunt Stanbury gets wind of it. Deeply impressed by what such confession means to Priscilla, Aunt Stanbury honestly writes to express her respect and affection for Priscilla – mentally reserving a certain balance of credit with Priscilla's sister, Dorothy, who, "though Dorothy knew nothing about it, ought in her gratitude to listen patiently to anything that she might now choose to say against Priscilla" (209). Both Priscilla and Aunt Stanbury attempt in their letters to give life the polish of art – both are humbled by experience. Life resists style.

The second episode built around this tension involves Aunt Stanbury and Dorothy, whom Aunt Stanbury has generously taken in to live with her. Dorothy endures her aunt's combination of tyranny and generosity with remarkable sweetness of temper. They fall out over Dorothy's affection for Brooke Burgess, Aunt Stanbury's chosen heir, and Dorothy goes home, leaving her aunt increasingly desolate in spirit – but "as Miss Stanbury would not give up her opinion, she could not ask her niece to return to her" (624). How to get Dorothy back and still maintain the high style? The answer amusingly reveals how much Trollope's characters are prisoners of the elaborate system of words they weave, unless, somehow, they can contrive to short-circuit it. Aunt Stanbury addresses this problem with care and three modes of expression. The first is "a nice fore-quarter of lamb" to be specially selected and delivered by Martha, the maid (625). The second is Martha herself, who fully appreciates the problem's complexity:

> 'May I tell Miss Dolly straight out that you want her to come back, and that I've been sent to say so?'
> 'No, Martha.'
> 'Then how am I to do it, ma'am?'
> 'Do it out of your own head, just as it comes up at the moment.' (626)

Martha, in effect, is to subvert the third, and ostensibly principal mode of communication, a letter, the tone and content of which Aunt Stanbury labours at, suggesting her own loneliness but going no further in the direction of reconciliation than saying that Dorothy's room will be ready should she ever pay a visit. Reflecting "that it was too solemn in its tone to suggest to Dorothy that which she wished to suggest", she adds a postscript: "P.S.—If Martha should say anything to you, you may feel sure that she knows my mind" (628). Martha knows her mind, she knows her own mind, but she cannot bring herself to close the gap between her style and her mind. Closing it would be a kind of linguistic cannibalism. The postscript involves "a certain blow to her pride in the writing of it! She did tell herself that in thus referring her niece to Martha for an expression of her own mind, . . . she was in truth eating her own words. But the postscript was written, and though she took the letter up with her to her own room in order that she might alter the words if she repented of them in the night, the letter was sent as it was written, – postscript and all" (628–9). Through Martha, then, Aunt Stanbury outmanoeuvres the tyrannical power of words. The chapter ends amusingly with Aunt Stanbury castigating Camilla French and Mr Gibson as "poor feckless things, who didn't know their own minds", and thinking of "the sweet pink colour which used to come and go in Dorothy's cheeks, – which she had been wont to observe so frequently, not knowing that she had observed it and loved it" (629). How finely Trollope discriminates the disconnected layers of experience, realisation, and articulation. The episode works almost as a neat little paradigm of the novel. As Trollope has said earlier of Priscilla and Aunt Stanbury, implicitly linking them with Trevelyan and the title:

> Each could say most cruel things, most unjust things, when actuated by a mistaken consciousness of perfect right on her own side. But neither of them could lie. . . . in all [the Stanburys] was to be found the same belief in self, – which amounted almost to conceit, – the same warmth of affection, and the same love of justice. (204)

In Trevelyan, as Trollope tried to make clear but felt that he had failed to make clear, these feelings also combine, but in different measure; and most fatally, Trevelyan, unlike Aunt Stanbury, finds no way to defeat his own verbal extension of himself.

Trollope is concerned about the authentic, but the problem is how to get at it or express it. Schooling and verbal articulation involve selection, order, stylisation – and stylisation, seductive in its form and unity, its definition and fulfilment, its rectification of the real world, departs from reality and the authentic self. Trollope's true lovers, appropriately, are expert in a different, non-verbal language. Florence, in *Mr. Scarborough's Family*, observing Harry Annesley's behaviour before he speaks a word, "was so quick a linguist that she had understood down to the last letter what all these tokens had meant. . . . [She] had read every word in Harry's language, not knowing, indeed, that she had read anything, but still never having missed a single letter."[11] When Emily and Trevelyan resort to their tongues and pens, they are done for.

It is the sense of this cleavage between self and language that makes the gloom of the Trevelyans' relentlessly destructive intractability pervasive. As Kincaid says of the feminist issue in the novel, "we are led to believe that the dilemma is far too deeply rooted and basic every to be touched by the feminists' solutions: they are too easy, too optimistic in that they are solutions at all".[12] I suggested in passing, that Aunt

Stanbury's feeling of "eating her words" was a kind of cannibalism in that she is devouring and doing away with the idea of herself that she has created in her hard, brittle style of discourse. It is, therefore, interesting to note that when she has carried that subversion to its end in her generosity to Dorothy she comes "to think of herself as though all the reality of her life had passed away from her" (915). What has passed away is, of course, not the reality but the projection. The reality, the authentic self, lay in that part of her that had lovingly observed the colour of Dorothy's cheeks "not knowing that she had observed it and loved it" (629).

The "deeply rooted and basic" dilemma Kincaid observes suggests to us a ground of being for the most part radically at odds with the articulation that rises from it. And the final vision is unsettling. Though the novel contains its measure of reassuring romance, the dominant impression its preoccupation with language conveys is of discord, chaos, the threat of madness – its world not the world of the divine logos, the Word that was with God and the Word that *was* God, but Browning's fallen world of barren words which characterise man as made subject to a curse.

NOTES

1. Anthony Trollope, *Can You Forgive Her?* World's Classics edition, vol. II (Oxford, 1938) p. 463. Juliet McMaster has examined how language itself, "words, and what is said, or written, are all very much part of the subject matter" of *Can You Forgive Her?* (*Trollope's Palliser Novels: Theme and Pattern* [London, 1978] p. 26).
2. A. O. J. Cockshut, *Anthony Trollope* (London, 1955) p. 174.
3. J. Hillis Miller, *The Form of Victorian Fiction* (Notre Dame, 1968) p. 123.
4. Samuel Johnson, *Rasselas*, Ch. XLIV.
5. Page references for *He Knew He Was Right* are to the World's Classics edition (Oxford, 1948).
6. Cockshut, p. 176.
7. James R. Kincaid, *The Novels of Anthony Trollope* (Oxford, 1977) p. 151.
8. *Ibid.*, p. 150.
9. See, for example, Cockshut on Osborne's game, p. 173, and Kincaid on risk-taking, pp. 151–3.
10. The quotation is from the first paragraph of James's "The Beast in the Jungle".
11. Anthony Trollope, *Mr. Scarborough's Family*, World's Classics edition (Oxford, 1946) pp. 21–3.
12. Kincaid, p. 154.

Index

Page numbers in italics indicate a sustained discussion.